Instant GENIUS

FAST FOOD for THOUGHT

BITE-SIZE MORSELS OF ESSENTIAL
(AND NOT-SO-ESSENTIAL) KNOWLEDGE

by the Knowledge Commons

Ashland, Oregon

Instant Genius:
Fast Food for Thought

For information, write:
Portable Press
P.O. Box 1117, Ashland, OR 97520
www.portablepress.com • 888-488-4642

Cover design by Michael Brunsfeld, San Rafael, CA
(Brunsfeldo@comcast.net)

ISBN-13: 978-1-59223-915-3 / ISBN-10: 1-59223-915-3

Library of Congress Cataloging-in-Publication Data

Instant genius : fast food for thought.
      p. cm.
ISBN-13: 978-1-59223-915-3 (hard cover)
1. Handbooks, vade-mecums, etc. 2. Curiosities and
      wonders.
AG105.I57 2008
031.02—dc22

                                    2008018101

Printed in Canada
First Printing
1 2 3 4 5 6 7 8 9 12 11 10 09 08

ACKNOWLEDGMENTS

The editors would like to thank the people whose
advice and assistance made this book possible.

Gordon Javna · Thom Little · Jay Newman · Brian Boone
John Dollison · Amy Miller · Kait Fairchild · Melinda Allman
Julia Papps · Michael Brunsfeld · Eric Warren · Bruce Bayard
Jeff Altemus · Lorraine Bodger · Jeff Cheek · Jef Fretwell
Judy Plapinger · Christine DeGueron · Angela Kern · Claire Breen
Claudia Bauer · Dan Mansfield · Sydney Stanley · JoAnn Padgett
Lisa Meyers · Amy Ly · Ginger Winters · Monica Maestas
Mary S. · Gary Bundzak · Duncan McCallum · Ralph Hamm
(Mr.) Mustard Press · Scarab Media · Publishers Group West
Steven Style Group · Raincoast Books · Porter the Wonder Dog

INTRODUCTION

Welcome to *Instant Genius: Fast Food for Thought*. We've spent the last 16 months digging through magazines, journals, newspapers, encyclopedias, pamphlets, novels, almanacs, comic books, dictionaries, liner notes, baseball programs, racing forms, and even the Internet to find the most extraordinary, the most interesting, the most useful, the most entertaining, and the most mind-boggling information we could possibly gather for this publication.

We love information. We love facts. We love to know things—things about people, animals, science, history, how things work, what things do, who said what...we could go on forever, but here are a few samples:

✦ There are monkeys in Mexico that apply natural, plant-based perfumes to their bodies.

✦ All the planets in our solar system were once part of a single, spinning, disk-shaped mass of molten pre-planetary goo.

✦ There is a theory that Venus flytraps are extraterrestrial life forms brought here by meteors.

✦ Albert Einstein's brain was kept in two Mason jars in a small office in Wichita, Kansas, for more than 20 years.

Not only that, we've come up with the answers to questions that have haunted us for years, such as:

✦ Where does outer space begin?

✦ What's the difference between "e.g." and "i.e."?

✦ What's in an atom?

✦ How do they make tofu? Or paper? Or electricity? Or whiskey?

Why *Instant Genius*? Because we've taken all those bits of information—some of them quite large and quite deep—and distilled them into easy-to-absorb nuggets that make for an entertaining, thought-provoking reading experience. Then we set up the book in a sort of scroll format, so you can go from one topic to the next, just like you would in real life: You learn something from a great segment on a television show, read something fascinating in a newspaper, hear an amazing story from a friend, encounter an unusual fact from a magazine in the doctor's waiting room, and so on. That's what this book is like—24 chapters of random wonders that will leave you wanting more.

With that we invite you to dive into *Instant Genius: Fast Food for Thought*. Start at the beginning or just open it anywhere, and see what you find. Have fun and get smarter…it'll only take an instant.

—The Editors at the Knowledge Commons

CHAPTER 1

GENIUS: THE WORD

Etymologists believe that the word "genius" has its roots in the hypothetical progenitor of all Western languages, Proto-Indo-European. Spoken by an unknown people some 5,000 years ago, the language had an oft-used word root: *gen* (or *gn*), which meant both "to beget" and "to know." The "beget" meaning led to words such as "pregnant," "genesis," "generation," "genitals," and "gender." The "know" meaning led to words like "knowledge," "cognition," "prognosis," "diagnosis," and even "genie" (as in "genie in a bottle").

✦ The word "genius" appears to have come from both meanings: It goes back between 2,000 and 3,000 years to a Latin word of the same spelling that referred to a guardian deity, a spirit that watches over each person from the moment of their birth (every man had a *genius*, every woman a *juno*). The meaning evolved over the centuries and came to refer to a person who seemed to have an innately (from birth) superior intellect. It made its way from Latin to English circa 1500 with basically the meaning it has today.

✦ The plural: "geniuses" is preferred; "genii" is accepted.

✦ Genius can be pronounced with two or three syllables: *JEEN-yus*, or *JEE-nee-us*.

THEY CALL IT WATERMELON SNOW

If you've ever been high up in a snowy mountain range and come across an expanse of bright, pink snow—you weren't seeing things. It's the result of tiny organisms called *Chlamydomonas nivalis*. They're actually a species of green algae, not unlike the algae on a pond's surface—except this kind is cold-loving algae (*nivalis* refers to "snow" in Latin). These tiny, single-celled organisms go dormant in snow through the winter, then during the spring they germinate (meaning they awake from this dormant period). Once germinated, they use their whiplike tails to propel themselves to the surface, where they feed on leaves and other organic matter. *C. nivalis* protects itself from the harsh light in snowy conditions by secreting and covering itself with a gelatinous substance; sunlight causes that coating to turn a pinkish color (similar to the color of watermelon), causing the snow to turn that color, too. Want to eat the watermelon snow? It's not advised: Many alpine hikers claim it causes diarrhea (and doesn't taste at all like watermelon).

LITTLE LEAGUE BASEBALL'S DIVISIONS

As defined by Little League International:

✦ **Little League Tee Ball:** ages 5–6 (in some places also 7–8)

✦ **Minor League Baseball:** ages 7–12 (may be divided into machine-pitch, coach-pitch, and player-pitch subdivisions)

- **Little League Baseball** (also called the Major Division of Little League): ages 9–12 (some regions start it at 10)
- **Junior League Baseball:** ages 13–14 (the first level to use a major league-sized infield)
- **Senior League Baseball:** ages 14–16
- **Big League Baseball:** ages 16–18

MY FURRY PIG

The Hungarian *Mangalitsa* is a rare and ancient breed of "woolly" pig—their coats can grow so thick and curly that if you saw one, you might think it was a sheep...until you saw its snout. Once prized all over Europe for their bacon (and still commonly raised for food), Mangalitsas are gaining popularity as pets—they're docile and friendly, hardy, and fun to pet. The pigs come in three colors: swallow-bellied (black with a white underbelly), blonde (whitish-gray to yellow), and red (these are larger and have thick red coats). Some people have even sheared the pigs' thick winter coat and made sweaters out of their wool. (And the curly hairs that grow behind the ears are said to make great flies for fly-fishing.)

TWO INDENTATIONS

- What's a *calyx basin*? The indentation at the bottom of an apple.
- What's a *natal cleft*? The scientific name for your butt crack.

INCAN HIGHWAYS

At the height of the Incan Empire in western South America in the 1500s, before the arrival of Europeans, a well-developed road system covering some 24,000 miles connected all parts of the empire over an immense tract of territory. It stretched from what is now Ecuador in the north to more than 2,000 miles southward into what is now Chile. The wheel was unknown in the Americas before Europeans came, so people traveled the roads on foot, often accompanied by pack-carrying llamas. From the long coastline to altitudes of more than 16,000 feet in the Andes, the roads were dotted with thousands of inns, called *tambos*, offering travelers (and their llamas) food and shelter. They were also famously used by the *chasqui*, specially trained runners who carried messages for Incan royalty and military commanders in relay fashion from tambo to tambo. The system was very efficient, allowing messages to be carried more than 150 miles per day, and was a big reason that the Incas were able to control such a large territory. Many of these Incan roads still exist today and are popular hiking destinations.

USEFUL TIP FOR BAR OWNERS

Police in Bristol, England, have been advising pub owners to spray WD-40 on flat surfaces in their bathrooms (the sink, hand dryer, toilet seats, etc.) since 2005—that's the year a local constable discovered that it causes cocaine to congeal and become unusable.

WHY IS THE SKY BLUE?

Simple answer: The sky actually only *appears* blue when viewed through the atmosphere, and only during daylight hours on clear days. The reason for this is that when sunlight strikes the Earth's atmosphere, most of the light passes straight through it, unaffected. But certain wavelengths of light are reflected and scattered in every direction; different wavelengths are perceived as different colors. The wavelength most affected by our atmosphere produces the color blue. The effect is that when we look up, we see blue light coming from all directions in the sky. So the sky appears blue.

More detail: This effect is known as *Rayleigh scattering*, named after English physicist John William Strutt, 3rd Baron Rayleigh. In 1871 he discovered that when sunlight comes into contact with miniscule particles, the short-wavelength light rays are thrown off their paths and "scattered" much more profusely than longer-wavelength light rays. In short: 1) Earth's atmosphere is made up of tiny particles; 2) tiny particles disrupt short-wavelength light rays; 3) shorter-wavelength light is at the blue end of the spectrum; and 4) that's why the sky is blue.

One more thing: At sunrise and sunset, the sky appears red or orange near the horizon. That's because sunlight seen from such an angle has passed through more of the atmosphere than sunlight viewed from directly overhead. This results in the blue-wavelength light being "used up" before it gets to you, and the reds and oranges, which weren't scattered, can now be seen. So remember that when you're enjoying a blazing red sunset, there is someone far to the west, where the sun is still high overhead, who is seeing all that scattering blue light that didn't make it to you—and made that beautiful sunset possible.

THE SUBPRIME MARKET

The *subprime market* is the name given to the practice of *subprime lending,* a general term that refers to the practice of making loans to borrowers who, usually because of poor credit history, would not normally qualify for such loans. The term "subprime" refers to the status of the borrower and the interest rate they will be charged: Those with good credit histories are deemed to be in the "prime" market and are charged lower rates; those with poor credit histories are charged higher rates to compensate the lender for taking the additional risk. The subprime market covers many lending forms, including home mortgages, car loans, and credit cards. They are also known as *B-, C-,* and *D-Paper* (as opposed to better *A-paper* loans given to people with the highest credit scores), *near-prime,* or *second chance* loans.

MASHA AND DASHA

Daria Kriwoshlyapowa was born somewhere in the Soviet Union on January 3, 1950. Shortly after, she was taken from her mother, who was told some days later that her baby had died of pneumonia. That wasn't true. Daria had lived, and "she" was actually "she and she": twin girls joined at the waist, leaning away from each other at about a 180° angle. They had two heads, four arms, and three legs.

Dasha and Masha, as they became known to those who bothered to address them by name, were taken to Moscow's Pediatric Institute. Film taken over the first six years of their lives shows the girls being subjected to medical experiments, often involving inflicting pain on one of the girls and registering how it affected the other. They were never taught to walk, feed themselves, or go to the bathroom, and spent most of the time naked in a bed.

For the next seven years they lived in a hospital for disabled children, where they learned to walk and were allowed some schooling. At age 13, Masha and Dasha were accepted into a school for disabled children in the town of Novocherkassk in the south of Russia, and at age 20 they were put into a home for the elderly in Moscow. There they stayed for the next 20 years, mostly secluded in their rooms.

In 1989, with Communism nearly eliminated in the USSR, Masha and Dasha were allowed to leave the facility and were given a spacious home in Moscow. They even became celebrities of a sort when they appeared on a popular Russian television show. A British doctor offered to separate them; they refused. In 1990 they met their mother for the first time since they were only days old. "The past 40 years haven't been so good," said Dasha, "but things are looking up for the next 40." On April 17, 2003, Masha died from complications due to alcoholism. Dasha, who didn't drink, *still* refused to be separated, and died 17 hours later. At 53 they were, at the time, the oldest conjoined twins in the world.

WORD SEARCH: *SARCASM*

The ancient Greek word *sarkazein* was used to describe dogs tearing the flesh off of animals. By the time the word entered medieval Greek as *sarkasmos*, it had evolved from a dog's toothy sneer when its food was threatened, into the politician's toothy sneer when he spoke in front of crowds. The word changed to *sarcasmos* when it entered Late Latin, but by then the dog aspect was completely gone—the word was reserved for describing the politician's duplicitous nature of "smiling through his teeth." By the time "sarcasm" finally entered the English language in 1579, it had taken on its modern meaning of any "biting remark."

GNOMONS

What is a *gnomon*? The part of a sundial that casts a shadow.

HOUSEHOLD GENIUS

Three uses for old coffee grounds:

1. Food deodorizer. Spread coffee grounds on a cookie sheet to dry, then put them in a bowl in the refrigerator or freezer to absorb food odors. You can also rub them on your hands to get rid of food preparation smells.

2. Dust inhibitor. Toss wet coffee grounds over the ashes in your fireplace to tamp down the dust before cleaning it out.

3. Fabric dye. Steep old coffee grounds in a basin of hot water to make brown dye for fabric, paper, or even Easter eggs. (Old tea bags work, too.)

AIR AMERICA: CIA FRONT COMPANY

"Front companies" are companies or other organizations set up with the express intention of keeping the true ownership and purpose of the company unknown. They're commonly used by government intelligence agencies around the world to provide cover for those agencies' employees, making it appear that they have legitimate and seemingly innocuous jobs and incomes. The CIA has allegedly owned many such companies during its existence.

Air America was founded by American aviation hero and head of World War II's "Flying Tigers," Claire Chennault. After the war, in 1946, Chennault went to China, bought surplus aircraft, and established a public air transport company. Its actual purpose, however, was to help Chiang Kai-Shek defeat the Communists in the Chinese Civil War. When Chiang was defeated in 1950, the CIA secretly offered to buy the company from Chennault and use it to fight the spread of Communism in Southeast Asia. Chennault agreed, and the CIA owned Air America for the next 26 years, covertly participating in hundreds of espionage and combat missions during the Korean War, the First Indochina War (between the French and Vietnamese), and the Vietnam War.

FOOD FOR THOUGHT. Two CIA agents, Richard G. Fecteau and John T. Downey, were captured by the Chinese in 1952 after the crash of a covert Air America flight over Manchuria. They were imprisoned there for two decades. Fecteau was released in 1971, Downey in 1973.

A MATTER OF FACT

According to the *Oxford English Dictionary,* a "fact" is "something that has really occurred or is actually the case; hence a particular truth known by actual observation or authentic testimony, as opposed to what is merely inferred." And that's a fact.

"WE ARE THE WORLD"

After the 1985 American Music Awards, nearly 40 major pop singers gathered in a recording studio to record "We Are the

World," a song to raise relief money for the Ethiopian famine. It was a landmark cultural event of the 1980s and raised millions for famine relief. All of the stars sang backup, but a few soloists each sang a line or two (Michael Jackson, who cowrote the song, got to sing more). The soloists were, in order:

1. Lionel Richie
2. Stevie Wonder
3. Paul Simon
4. Kenny Rogers
5. James Ingram
6. Tina Turner
7. Billy Joel
8. Michael Jackson
9. Diana Ross
10. Dionne Warwick
11. Willie Nelson
12. Al Jarreau
13. Bruce Springsteen
14. Kenny Loggins
15. Steve Perry
16. Daryl Hall
17. Huey Lewis
18. Cyndi Lauper
19. Kim Carnes
20. Bob Dylan
21. Ray Charles

Singers who didn't get solos: Dan Aykroyd (as part of the Blues Brothers, he's technically a musician), Harry Belafonte, Lindsey Buckingham, Sheila E., Bob Geldof, John Oates, Smokey Robinson, Bette Midler, Jeffrey Osborne, the Pointer Sisters, and Jackie, Marlon, Randy, Tito, and LaToya Jackson.

KNOW YOUR BRITISH ISLES

The British Isles is the geographical name for the large group of islands—more than 6,000—off the northwest European coast, the two largest being Great Britain and Ireland.

✦ **Great Britain** is the name of the largest of the British Isles. It is home to most of the territory of England, Wales, and Scotland. (All three own additional territory on surrounding islands.)

✦ **Ireland** is the name of the second-largest of the British Isles. It is home to the independent nation known as the Republic of Ireland, as well as Northern Ireland, which is part of the United Kingdom.

✦ **The Republic of Ireland**, known there as Eire, takes up roughly 80% of the island. Northern Ireland, located in the far north, takes up the remainder.

✦ **The United Kingdom of Great Britain and Northern Ireland** is the official name of the nation that consists of four regions with differing amounts of autonomy: England, Wales, Scotland, and Northern Ireland. (It is commonly shortened to "United Kingdom.")

✦ **The Isle of Man** is located in the Irish Sea. It is known as a "Crown dependency," along with the Bailiwick of Guernsey and the Bailiwick of Jersey (both located in the English Channel off the French coast of Normandy). All three are possessions of—but not officially a part of—the United Kingdom, even though the people who live there are considered U.K. citizens.

✦ **The British Islands** is the legal term used to describe all the lands comprising the British Isles—the United Kingdom of Great Britain and Northern Ireland, the Isle of Man, the Bailiwick of Guernsey, and the Bailiwick of Jersey—*minus* the Republic of Ireland.

THE GREAT PACIFIC GARBAGE PATCH

The North Pacific Subtropical Gyre is a slow, clockwise-spinning ocean current that stretches from the west coast of North America to Japan. The gyre is home to two gigantic, slowly swirling masses of garbage, collectively called the Great Pacific Garbage Patch. The Eastern Garbage Patch is located between Hawaii and California; the Western Garbage Patch between Japan and Hawaii. Together they contain more than 100 million tons of garbage, about 90% of it plastic.

In the ocean, plastic doesn't *biodegrade*, or break down via living microbes. Instead, it *photodegrades*, or breaks down via the photons in sunlight. That happens much more quickly than biodegradation, which can take as long as 1,000 years. You'd think that would be a good thing…but it's not. Over the course of a few decades, the plastic in the gyre photodegrades into smaller and smaller pieces, right down to individual molecules of plastic that have the ability to soak up and concentrate toxins that would normally be diffused in seawater. That's bad for two reasons: *Filter feeders*—animals such as clams, krill, sponges, some sharks, and baleen whales—feed by passing water through their bodies, and therefore absorb those tiny, toxin-soaked plastic molecules. Other animals, including many fish, simply mistake the plastic bits for food; still others eat the filter feeders. Either way, the toxic effect is spread through the entire food chain—including to you, if you eat seafood. On top of all this, the Great Pacific Garbage Patch is just one of several swirling, continent-sized "plastic soups" located in all of the world's oceans.

"CANADIAN" GEESE?

Although the term is commonly used, there is no such animal as a "Canadian goose." The scientific name of this large North American waterfowl species is *Branta canadensis*, and the proper common name is "Canada goose" for the singular and "Canada geese" for the plural.

THE DIFFERENCE BETWEEN...

Disc and Disk. Spelled with a *c*, it describes removable optical media, such as a compact disc or DVD. Spelled with a *k*, it describes read-only magnetic disks, such as those inside hard drives or floppy disks. The reason: When IBM created the hard disk in the 1950s, they used the *disk* spelling; when Sony created the compact disc in 1979, they chose the *disc* spelling to differentiate their new product from magnetic disks.

The words "disc" and "disk" were used interchangeably long before the computer age, however. "Disk" came into the English language in the 17th century, modeled on words such as "whisk" and "risk." "Disc," although it entered English *after* "disk," comes from the much older Latin word *discus*, which itself came from the Greek *diskos*, meaning "platter." "Disk" is now commonly used in the U.S., while the preferred British spelling is "disc." Both spellings are acceptable for most uses today, though disc seems to be winning out in the sporting world, as evidenced by the World Flying Disc Federation (aka Frisbees). In the medical field, however, you'll find just as many doctors who treat herniated discs as those who treat herniated disks.

HOW SCISSORS WORK

When you squeeze the handles of scissors together, you are exerting force on the handles of two levers. The fulcrum of both levers is the pivot point—the spot where the two blades are joined. Squeezing the handles together forces the blades—beyond the fulcrum point—to slide past each other. When they do, anything that is between them is cut. There are four stages of cutting:

✦ *Elastic deformation* occurs when the scissors first engage the material between them and the material starts to deform. It's called "elastic" deformation because if you stop squeezing the handles and open the blades, the deformed material will "bounce back" to its original shape.

✦ *Plastic deformation* occurs when the blades apply a bit more force, enough so that the material being cut deforms to the point that, if released from the blades, the deformation will remain.

✦ *Fracture* occurs when even more force is applied and the material passes plastic deformation and breaks down at a cellular level.

✦ *Separation* occurs when the blades cut through the material.

These stages continually occur down the length of the blades as the handles of the scissors are squeezed.

THE ANGLE OF REPOSE

The *angle of repose* is a physics term that refers to the maximum angle that a slope of granular material can have and still remain stable. Steeper than that angle and the particles will roll down the slope or just collapse altogether. Most people have seen this happen on a snowy slope or sand dune—or by playing with sugar in a sugar bowl. The angle of repose is of great importance to engineers, such as those building mountain roads, ski resorts, and grain-storing units.

THE ANGLE OF DOODLEBUGS

Doodlebugs (yes, doodlebugs, a name you will have to read several more times in this paragraph) are the common name used to describe the larvae of *antlions*—voracious eaters of ants. Scientifically called *Myrmeleontidae*, these insects utilize the angle of repose when they hunt. The larvae of some doodlebug species, which resemble small beetles with large pincers, dig holes in light, sandy soil, breaking it down to fine grains. The doodlebug then removes much of the soil, leaving a conical pit— the slope of which is *just* below the angle of repose. The hunting doodlebug then conceals itself under the material in the bottom of the pit—with only its pincers and eyes sticking out—and waits until an insect lands on the slope, which causes it to collapse. The doodlebug then swiftly emerges from its hiding spot and captures its prey. (Doodlebug.)

MILTON LITTLE, ESQ.

Have you ever seen the abbreviation "Esq." after someone's name? It's not used much anymore, but "Esq." is short for "Esquire" and was once a popular way for attorneys to indicate their profession. The word is derived from "squire," an assistant hired to accompany a knight in the Medieval era. Nevertheless, "Esquire" doesn't indicate an official title (like "Sir" or "Dr."), so

you can put it after your own name if you want, even if you aren't
a lawyer (or a squire).

WHAT'S POINTILLISM?

Have you ever looked really carefully at a printed image in a
newspaper or book? At close range it seems to be composed of
many tiny black-and-white or colored dots of ink, but when you
back away from it, the dots blend to make a coherent, unbroken
picture. This phenomenon is known as *optical mixing*. In printing, the dot pattern is called halftone (first used in the reproduction of a photograph in 1880, in the *New York Daily Graphic*); in
painting, it's called *pointillism*.

Today the look of pointillism is familiar, but in the 1880s in
France, when Georges Seurat (1859–91) first laid small dabs of
oil paint side by side on his canvas in order to create an image,
it was a new concept. Before producing the large pointillist
works for which he became famous (such as *La Grande Jatte*),
Seurat systematically studied color theory to understand how to
combine the colors to get the effects he wanted. Very few other
painters were using this laborious and exacting technique, and
art critics of the time did not take it seriously. The style was so
ahead of its time that very few artists even attempted it until
modern photorealists like Chuck Close and Malcolm Morley
developed a technique very similar to 19th-century pointillism,
methodically placing small brush strokes of color in the squares
of a gridded canvas.

THEOPHILUS VAN KANNEL

On August 7, 1888, Swiss-American inventor Theophilus Van
Kannel, based in Philadelphia, Pennsylvania, was granted U.S.
Patent #387,571 for a "Storm-Door Structure." It was described
as having "three radiating and equidistant wings," which
"effectually prevents the entrance of wind, snow, rain or dust.

There is no possibility of collision, and yet persons can pass both in and out at the same time." What is it? A revolving door. The inventor started the Van Kannel Revolving Door Company in Philadelphia that year; the first door was installed in Rector's, a restaurant in New York City's Times Square. In 1889 the Franklin Institute of Philadelphia awarded Van Kannel a medal for his "contribution to society." In 1907 the company was sold to International Steel, and it survives today as the International Revolving Door Company. In 2007 Theophilus Van Kannel was inducted into the National Inventors Hall of Fame in Akron, Ohio. (Some of the doors he manufactured in his first year of business are still in use today.)

HAGFISH

Here's some information on one of the most ancient, primitive, bizarre, slimy, and disgusting creatures on Earth. Hagfish are long, tubular sea creatures that were long thought to be a kind of eel. They are actually their own class of fish (although some biologists argue that they're so unique, they shouldn't even be classified as fish). There are 65 species of hagfish found in cold ocean waters around the world. They vary in color from gray to bluish to pinkish and can grow up to 25 inches long.

Weirdness #1: Hagfish have no fins, no scales, no stomach, no jaws, a partial skull, no vertebrae, five hearts, and extremely poor eyesight.

Weirdness #2: When attacked, hagfish secrete large amounts of thick, transparent, snotlike, extremely sticky slime from glands all over their bodies. After it's given the predator a good sliming, the hagfish ties itself into a knot and pulls the knot down the length of its body, scraping the slime off as it does.

Weirdness #3: They have very slow metabolisms, allowing them to go for as long as seven months between feedings.

Weirdness #4: The hagfish commonly feeds on dead fish—but not in the normal way. It slithers into its prey's body either through the mouth, gills, or anus...and then eats it from the inside out. And because the hagfish lacks a lower jaw, it must snatch pieces of flesh with its raspy tongue. Hagfish sometimes do this to live fish as well.

FIRST LADY: CHRISTINE DE PIZAN

Etienne du Castel, a royal secretary of the court of King Charles V of France, died in 1388. That left his wife, 24-year-old Christine de Pizan, alone, poor, and responsible for the care of her three children, her mother, and her niece. Having educated herself on a wide variety of subjects since she was very young, de Pizan decided to earn money by writing—nearly unheard of for a woman at the time. Not only did she overcome that taboo, she did so openly under her own name, and even dared to write about the mistreatment of women in Europe. Over the next 30 years, de Pizan published 41 books of poetry and prose. Today she is regarded as the first professional female writer in European history, and her work is considered by many historians to be the starting point of modern feminism.

ON GENIUS

"Intellectuals solve problems; geniuses prevent them."

—Albert Einstein

"A man of genius is unbearable, unless he possesses at least two things besides: gratitude and purity."

—Friedrich Nietzsche

"The first and last thing required of genius is the love of truth."

—Johann Wolfgang von Goethe

CHAPTER 2

BIG SHIP DEFINITIONS

✦ **Merchant ships** are any large ships that are used for commercial purposes.

✦ **Tramp steamers**, one of the two types of merchant ships, ship cargo wherever and whenever the owner is paid to take it. Tramp steamers are usually independently owned.

✦ **Ocean liners** are the other principal type of merchant ship. They can be many different sizes but are generally very large. They're so named because—unlike tramp steamers—they travel a regularly scheduled "line" between two or more locations.

✦ **Cabin liners** are ocean liners that carry passengers.

✦ **Cargo liners** carry cargo rather than passengers.

✦ **Cruise ships**, or "cruise liners," are cabin liners designed exclusively for recreation travel rather than transportation.

✦ **Luxury liners** are cruise ships with an especially high standard of accommodation.

YOU ARE READING THIS

What's an ideo locator? The part of a map that says "You are here."

SECRET AGENCIES

✦ **The KGB** was the notorious Soviet spy agency during the Cold War era. KGB stands for *Komitet Gosudarstvennoy Bezopasnosti*. Translation: "Federal Security Service." Among the agency's successes as the secret international arm of the Soviets were quelling anti-Communist revolutions in Hungary (1956) and Czechoslovakia (1968). (KGB agents failed, however, to assassinate John Wayne in 1949.)

✦ **The Stasi** was both the secret police and the intelligence organization for East Germany from the 1950s to the '80s, in many ways a combination of the CIA and FBI. (Stasi is an abbreviation of *Staatssicherheit*, or "state security.") Stasi agents, many of whom were former Nazi officers, worked with the KGB to enforce and spread Communist rule in Eastern Europe. The agency funded terrorist groups in West Germany, seeking to bring that country down. In 1984 Stasi agents murdered Cats Falck, a Swedish reporter who'd uncovered East German weapons smuggling. By the late 1980s, 2% of all East Germans either worked for the agency or were unpaid informants.

✦ **Mossad** is the state intelligence agency of Israel. The full name of the agency is *Ha Mossad le Moudiin ule Tafkidim Meyuhadim* (Hebrew for "The Institute for Intelligence and Special Tasks"). Its most famous acts: tracking down Nazi war criminal Adolf Eichmann, who was living under an assumed name in Argentina in 1960 (Mossad brought him to Israel, where he was tried and executed); and locating and executing the members of Black September, a Palestinian terrorist group who murdered 11 Israeli athletes at the 1972 Summer Olympics in Munich, Germany.

SAUSAGE GUIDE

✦ The simple definition of sausage: ground and seasoned meat, usually stuffed into a casing traditionally made from an animal intestine. The first recorded mention of such a food goes back to 589 B.C.E., when the ancient Chinese referred to a semidried sausage called *lup cheong*, made from pork, salt, sugar, green onions, pepper, wine, and soy sauce. (Lup cheong sausage is still eaten around the world.)

✦ Ancient Greeks also made sausage; the poet Homer even refers to the food in *The Odyssey*. The Romans learned sausage-making from the Greeks, and they spread it throughout Europe and North Africa, with different regions developing their own sausage recipes and traditions over the centuries. The modern word "sausage" is derived from the Latin *salsus*, meaning "salted," and dates to the 15th century.

✦ Sausages come in five main categories:

Fresh: made of raw meat, uncooked and uncured; must be refrigerated and cooked before eating (e.g., most pork breakfast sausage)

Cooked: cooked during the manufacturing process; should be kept refrigerated, and then reheated before serving (e.g., braunschweiger, liver sausage)

Cooked, smoked: cooked and also smoked (smoking is a kind of slow cooking in which the food is exposed to smoke, usually from smoldering wood); should be kept refrigerated; can be eaten cold or heated (e.g., kielbasa, wieners)

Fresh-smoked: uncooked and lightly smoked; should be kept refrigerated and then fully cooked before eating (e.g., mettwurst, Romanian sausage)

Dry sausage: put through a complicated "drying" process; has a "hard" texture and very long shelf life; can be eaten hot or cold (e.g., pepperoni, Genoa salami)

✦ *Natural* casings are made from hog, sheep, or beef intestines, and sometimes stomachs or skin. *Artificial* casings are made from collagen (from the connective tissues of animals), cellulose (from cotton fibers), muslin (woven cotton fabric), or thick, inedible, synthetic casings that make refrigeration unnecessary (often color-coded, e.g., bright red for bologna).

OLDEST.COM

The first 10 domain names ever registered:

1. *symbolics.com* (March 15, 1985)

2. *bbn.com* (April 24, 1985)

3. *think.com* (May 24, 1985)

4. *mcc.com* (July 11, 1985)

5. *dec.com* (September 30, 1985)

6. *northrop.com* (November 7, 1985)

7. *xerox.com* (January 9, 1986)

8. *sri.com* (January 17, 1986)

9. *hp.com* (March 3, 1986)

10. *bellcore.com* (March 5, 1986)

DIVORCE VS. ANNULMENT

An annulment cancels a marriage. Legally, it's as though the marriage never technically existed, on the grounds that it was never valid. Those grounds must be argued, and must fall into one of these categories: one of the spouses was already married (bigamy); one of the spouses was forced into the marriage or threatened (forced consent); the reason for marrying turned out to be a lie (fraud); the marriage was incestuous; one of the spouses was mentally ill or emotionally disturbed at the time of marriage; one of the spouses was intoxicated or under the influence of drugs; the marriage hasn't been consummated; or one of the parties was under age and lacked court or parental approval to marry. When a short-term marriage is annulled, assets are not divided; if the marriage lasted several years, most states allow for some division of assets. It's usually more difficult to get an annulment than it is a divorce, which is the dissolving or cancellation of a marriage. In a contested divorce, grounds must also be proven and include (in addition to the annulment list) adultery, desertion, and abuse. But nearly all states allow "no-fault" divorces, in which one or both parties petition a judge for the right to end the marriage. If neither party wishes to contest it, no grounds have to be proven and the divorce is granted.

10 UNUSUAL TERMS FOR "MARRIAGE"

1. Adelphogamy: marriage between siblings

2. Coenogamy: a group marriage between at least two men and at least two women

3. Deuterogamy: a second marriage (after a divorce)

4. Digamy: a second marriage after the death of the first spouse

5. Hypergamy: marriage into a higher social group

6. Matrilocal: a married couple living close to the wife's parents

7. Patrilocal: a married couple living close to the husband's parents

8. Morganatic: a marriage between one spouse of high social rank and one of low social rank in which the lower-ranking spouse and any offspring bear no claim to rank or property

9. Opsigamy: a marriage late in life

10. Trigamy: having three spouses at the same time

SURVIVING A HIGH FALL INTO WATER

✦ If you're forced to jump from a bridge or a cliff into water, try to aim for the deepest part—you'll be traveling so fast that even if you survive the impact with the water, you could be injured or killed by slamming into a shallow bottom. Also, avoid areas near piers or pylons, as debris tends to collect around them.

✦ While you're in the air, keep your body as vertical as possible. Point your toes downward and protect your crotch with your hands. Also, clench your buttocks to keep water from rushing in and causing internal damage.

✦ Once you're in the water, fan out your arms and legs to slow your descent.

✦ If there were other people or objects on the bridge that may be falling down behind you, swim away as quickly as you can.

XXOO

What's the anatomical juxtaposition of two orbicularis oris muscles in contraction? A kiss.

THE PENAL COLONIES

Australia's first colony was, as most people know, a penal colony: On January 26, 1788, a fleet of British ships landed at what is now the city of Sydney, establishing the colony of New South Wales.

Among the 1,305 people aboard the ships, 736 of them were convicts, and most of the remainder were guards. Why did they go all the way to Australia? Because America wasn't available anymore. Great Britain first started shipping convicts overseas in the 1600s—while they were colonizing North America. As many as 50,000 prisoners were sent to the American colonies over a period of about 150 years. The only reason they stopped was because the Americans successfully revolted and became an independent nation in 1783. That led to the Australian program. Several penal colonies were established: the original in New South Wales, on Norfolk Island, and the largest and most notorious, Van Diemen's Land, now the island of Tasmania. When "transportation," as it was called, ended in 1868, more than 800 ships had brought more 160,000 male and female prisoners to Australia.

FOOD FOR THOUGHT. The breakdown of prisoners' nationalities: about 70% were English and Welsh, 24% Irish, and 5% Scottish. And at least 100 of them were American: In 1838 a small army of men crossed the border from New York into Upper Canada (now Ontario), which was then still a British colony, to aid a rebellion. They were captured by British troops, taken to England, and then sent as prisoners to Van Diemen's Land. The Lieutenant-Governor of the island at the time: Sir John Franklin, a nephew of Benjamin Franklin.

OLYMPIC METALS

✦ The International Olympic Committee stipulates that Olympic medals must be at least 70 mm (2.8 inches) in diameter and 6 mm (0.23 inches) thick.

✦ Gold medals are actually mostly silver: They must contain at least 92.5% silver, and are gilded with at least six grams of 24-carat gold. They weigh about 150 grams (5.2 ounces) total.

✦ Silver medals must also contain at least 92.5% silver.

✦ Bronze medals are made of bronze, which is an alloy containing varying amounts of copper, tin, and other metals. The mix for bronze medals is 97% copper, 2.5% zinc, 0.5% tin, and a very small amount of silver.

✦ The gold and copper used for the medals awarded at the 2008 Beijing Olympic Games came from a mine in Escondida, Chile. The silver came from mines in Queensland, Australia.

✦ The Beijing medals also contained inlaid jade, mined in China's Qinghai Province. They were the first in Olympic history to incorporate non-metal materials.

✦ The bronze medals awarded at the 2000 Sydney Olympics were made from melted-down 1- and 2-cent Australian coins that had been taken out of circulation in 1992.

"GENIUS" MISTAKES

✦ **Pythagoras,** the 6th century B.C.E. Greek mathematician known as the "Father of Numbers," believed the Earth was the center of the universe and that the Sun, the stars, and all the planets revolved around it.

✦ **Aristotle,** the 4th century B.C.E. Greek scholar considered one of the most important figures in the history of Western science, believed that lower forms of life, such as worms and flies, grew from rotting fruit or manure by a process of spontaneous generation.

HOW DO WHALES SLEEP?

Have you ever wondered how marine mammals such as whales, dolphins, and porpoises sleep? They all breathe air, just like we do, and they all need to sleep, just like we do. So why don't they drown? The answer is that they do sleep…but only half of their brain at a time. Researchers studying electroencephalogram (EEG) readings on bottlenose dolphins discovered that they shut down half of their brain—and close the opposite eye—while the other half, and eye, remains alert. They do this for about two hours, then switch the sleep side of their brains, repeating the half-asleep trick three or four times a day. While doing this, they either swim slowly or lie still at the surface of the water, an activity known as "logging" (because they look like logs).

THE COMMON ERA

✦ Sometime during the 6th century, a Christian monk named Dionysius Exiguus invented the calendar system that denoted dates as either before the year Jesus was born—B.C., for "Before Christ"—or after that year—A.D., for *Anno Domini* ("In the Year of the Lord" in Latin).

✦ That system was later adopted into the Gregorian calendar and is still used today. But a few hundred years ago, scientists and academics started to substitute the more secular abbreviations B.C.E ("Before the Common Era") and C.E. (the "Common Era").

✦ Christian theologians doubt that Jesus was actually born in the year "0," as the calendar suggests. The most widely accepted year for his birth is 4 B.C.E., most likely in March or April, not December.

ALLOTROPES OF CARBON

You probably know that diamonds and graphite (most commonly seen as "lead" in pencils) are made of exactly the same stuff—the chemical element carbon. So why are they so different? Because the atoms that make up each one are bonded in different configurations due to factors such as pressure, temperature, and neighboring elements. Diamonds are the result of *a lot* of pressure; graphite, not so much. This is known as *allotropy* (from the Greek *allos* for "other," and *tropos* for "manner"), and the varying substances that result from these atomic arrangements are known as *allotropes* of an element. This only relates to substances that are composed of just one element. (There are no allotropes of water, for example, which is composed of two elements: hydrogen and oxygen.) Allotropy occurs in several elements, including oxygen, nitrogen, and phosphorus, but the most common examples are the allotropes of carbon.

Diamonds. Carbon atoms in diamonds are bonded in a three-dimensional lattice configuration. Each atom is very strongly bonded to four other atoms in four different directions—on different planes. This results in all the atoms having a perfectly symmetrical, interlocking pattern throughout a given stone. That arrangement is what gives diamonds their particular physical characteristics, such as how they react to light, their distinctive hardness, and their resistance to electric current.

Graphite. Each atom in a piece of graphite is strongly bonded to three other atoms in three different directions, but, unlike diamonds, all on the same plane. They form sheets of carbon, each just one atom thick. Those sheets are bonded to each other, but only very weakly, so they're able to slip and slide over each other and easily come apart—like cards in a pack. This is what makes graphite so soft and "slippery," and is why it's used in pencils, where some of it easily slides off onto paper. (It's also used industrially as a "dry lubricant.")

Lonsdaleite. This is another allotrope of carbon (there are several), and it's an interesting combination of the two substances above. When a meteorite containing graphite strikes Earth, the heat and force of the collision cause the atoms to change configuration, resulting in an interlocking lattice formation similar to diamonds but containing graphite's three-atom bonds. It's very hard—though not as hard as diamond—transparent, and brownish-yellow. Lonsdaleite is very rare, and was named after Irish crystallographer Kathleen Lonsdale.

FOOD FOR THOUGHT. Oxygen has two allotropes, both gases. The air that we breathe contains O_2—molecules composed of two bonded oxygen atoms. Certain conditions cause three oxygen atoms to bond in one molecule—O_3—which is ozone. Some properties of the ozone molecule not seen in oxygen: We can smell it and, unlike oxygen, it's very harmful to breathe. Just 0.1 to 1 part per million of ozone in the air can cause headaches and pain to the respiratory tract.

THE FIRST RULE OF PLANT CLUB IS...

..."Nobody names a plant without their permission." Whose permission? The International Code of Nomenclature for Cultivated Plants, or ICNCP. If you find or develop a *cultivar*, a plant that has attributes unique to itself and no others within its species, you're allowed to give it a name. But you have to follow the rules: It must consist of the scientific name, genus, and species or hybrid epithet, all italicized, followed by an unitalicized *cultivar epithet* (descriptive name), with the first letter of each word of the epithet capitalized and the entire epithet in single quotes. (Epithets may not be in Latin and must be in a modern language.)

An example you may recognize: *Malus domestica* 'Red Delicious,' the Red Delicious apple. It was a "chance seedling," discovered in the 1860s on the Iowa farm of Jesse Hiatt. These days it's common to see such names without the species name—*Malus* 'Red Delicious'; or with the genus name abbreviated—*M.* 'Red Delicious.' Many interesting names have been chosen over the years. A few examples:

✦ *Ranunculus* 'Brazen Hussy': a perennial in the *Ranunculus* genus (which includes buttercups and spearworts) known for its bright, gaudy yellow petals.

✦ *Tetrapanax* 'Steroidal Giant': an evergreen shrub that grows to 25 feet high and has leaves three feet wide and five feet long.

✦ *Hemerocallis* 'Little Wart': a type of daylily.

✦ *Hydrangea* 'Pinky Winky': named by a Flemish plant breeder for his son, whose favorite *Teletubbies* character was Tinky Winky.

✦ *Hosta* 'Outhouse Delight': a lilylike plant described by North Carolina horticulturalist Tony Avent as "the ugliest hosta in the history of hostas."

3 OFFICIAL TITLES

Custodian of the Two Holy Mosques: The formal name of King Abdullah bin Abdul Aziz Al Saud of Saudi Arabia. It refers to the king's status as ruler of the land that holds Islam's two holiest sites, the *Masjid al Haram*—"Holy Mosque"—in Mecca, and the *Al-Masjid al-Nabawi*—"Prophet's Mosque"—in Medina. It's a historical term once used by *caliphs* (Muslim heads of state) who ruled the region, and was adopted for modern kings in 1986 by King Abdullah's predecessor, King Fahd bin Abdul Aziz.

His Holiness the Pope Benedict XVI: That's just one of his official names. The eight others: "Bishop Of Rome And Vicar Of Jesus Christ," "Successor Of St. Peter," "Prince Of The Apostles," "Supreme Pontiff Of The Universal Church," "Patriarch Of The West," "Servant Of The Servants Of God," "Primate Of Italy," "Archbishop And Metropolitan Of The Roman Province," and "Sovereign Of Vatican City State."

Pope of Alexandria and the Patriarch of All Africa on the Holy Apostolic See of Saint Mark the Evangelist: That's the name of the "other pope," the ruler of the Coptic Orthodox Church in Egypt. But even that's just a short version. His official title: "Pope and Lord Archbishop of the Great City of Alexandria and Patriarch of All Africa on the Holy Orthodox and Apostolic Throne of Saint Mark the Evangelist and Holy Apostle that is, in Egypt, Pentapolis, Libya, Nubia, Sudan, Ethiopia, Eritrea, and all Africa." The current pope, Shenouda III, is the 117th in the line. His name at birth: Nazeer Gayed.

BECOMING A STATE AGAIN

Readmission of the former Confederate states to the Union following the end of the Civil War in 1865 wasn't automatic: The states had to meet certain qualifications, including ratifying the 14th Amendment to the U.S. Constitution, which granted full citizenship and civil rights to former slaves.

In the case of states that were not readmitted by February 1869, when the 15th Amendment was proposed (it made it illegal to deny the right to vote on the basis of race), the states were required to ratify this amendment as well. Georgia ratified the 14th Amendment and was readmitted to the Union in 1868, only to be expelled again in 1869 after it refused to ratify the 15th Amendment. It was readmitted a *second* time after it finally ratified the 15th Amendment in 1870. The Confederate States and their readmission dates:

Tennessee	July 24, 1866
Alabama	June 13, 1868
Arkansas	June 22, 1868
Florida, Louisiana, Georgia (the first time)	June 25, 1868
North Carolina	July 4, 1868
South Carolina	July 9, 1868
Virginia	January 26, 1870
Mississippi	February 23, 1870
Texas	March 30, 1870
Georgia (the second time)	July 15, 1870

I CHING

The *I Ching* (pronounced "ee-ching" or "yee-jing") is an ancient Chinese text that translates as "Book of Changes." Utilizing a combination of Eastern philosophies, including Taoism and Confucianism, the *I Ching* uses a system of symbols and interpretations of those symbols to offer commentaries and advice about life. The system is believed to have been invented in the 28th century B.C.E. by Fu Xi, an early emperor and major figure in Chinese folklore who was thought to have had divine powers. The *I Ching* is based on three main principles: a simple, basic understructure of the universe; the inevitability of change; and a constant, central principle that persists in spite of change.

The symbols—each consisting of a stack of six horizontal lines, some broken by a gap, and some solid—are also used in the Western world for fortune-telling. After a question is asked, three coins are tossed simultaneously. The "heads" and "tails" combination (e.g., three heads, or one head and two tails) is recorded, with each combination corresponding to either a broken or solid horizontal line. The coins are tossed six times, building an *I Ching* symbol one line at a time. The reader then looks up the symbol in the book of *I Ching* (there are 64 symbols, each with its own chapter) to interpret the answer.

A WALK IN THE ARTS

A look at some of the most influential art movements that make up the period historians refer to as "Modern Art."

Impressionism (1860s–1890s). This is considered the first era of Modern Art. It began in the 1860s, when a small group of artists in Paris began rebelling against the rigid style and narrow range of "allowed" subject matter in French painting. Working primarily outdoors, they painted scenes from everyday life, primarily by using dabs or short strokes of light, primary colors, with the focus on the effects of light. The work was mocked by art critics for years, and finally accepted as an important movement of its own in the 1880s. They were first called "Impressionists" in 1874 by an art critic as an insulting reference to Claude Monet's sunset painting *Impression, Soleil Levant*. Some of the best-known Impressionists: Claude Monet, Edouard Manet, Camille Pissarro, Paul Cézanne, and Pierre Auguste Renoir.

Post Impressionism (1880s–1900s). New art movements are almost always about rejecting old art movements, and in the late 19th century a number of European artists rejected Impressionism. The everyday subject matter and vivid colors remained, but the paintings were often much darker overall, and the emphasis on the effects of light were gone. Also left behind was the strict realism, allowing for experimentation in shape and form. The movement didn't get its name until 1910, when it was coined by British art critic Roger Fry. The most famous Post-Impressionists: Vincent van Gogh, Paul Cézanne, Paul Gauguin, and Henri de Toulouse-Lautrec.

Fauvism (1900–1910). This was a loosely aligned group centered around Henri Matisse and exhibiting at the Salon d'Automne in Paris. Matisse had mastered the previous eras' painting styles, especially "Neo-Impressionism" (a transitional movement in the late 1800s), then began to experiment. He used brilliant colors in big, spontaneous, and undisguised strokes, letting color, not perspective or dimension or the proportions of the subject, lead the way. This movement also got its name from a critic: *Fauve* means "wild beast" in French, which is how the critic saw Matisse's and the others' work. Other big names in Fauvism: Maurice de Vlaminck, Andre Derain, and Kees van Dongen. (Fauvism would be one of the biggest influences on Expressionism, which emerged in the early 1900s. Go to page 265 for more on that.)

EVOLUTION WITNESSED

In 1971 an international team of biologists took five male and five female Italian wall lizards from Pod Kopiste, a tiny, rocky island off the coast of Croatia in the South Adriatic Sea, and transferred them to a nearby, lushly vegetated island called Pod Mrcaru. They monitored the lizards for more than 20 years and then were suddenly cut off from the islands when civil war broke out in Croatia. In 2004 the biologists were finally allowed back in.

Here's what they found: The transplanted lizards had thrived…beyond expectations. There were virtually thousands on Pod Mrcaru, and genetic testing proved that all of them were descendants of the original 10…but they had changed.

Italian wall lizards (at least the original ones) are small, quick-running insect-eaters who occasionally eat leaves; about 5% of their diet is vegetarian. This is logical, given that Pod Kopiste is rocky and barren of plant life. But Pod Mrcaru is lush. The biologists were stunned to find that the vegetation portion of the lizards' diet on Pod Mrcaru had jumped to about 35% in the spring and up to more than 60% in the summer. Along with this, their heads had become bigger and their jaws more powerful—something necessary for plant-eaters, since plants are tougher to eat than insects. And there was more.

The "new" lizards were equipped with *cecal valves*, a digestive feature that allows sections of the gut to close off, holding food longer and allowing for better digestion. The "original" lizards on Pod Kopiste didn't have cecal valves—in fact almost *no* lizards in the world have them. These were entirely new anatomical features.

The environmental change had affected the lizards' social structure as well. On Pod Kopiste, where the insect diet made food harder to come by, lizards staked out territories and defended them fiercely. On Pod Mrcaru, where food was abundant and easy to procure, they no longer did this—instead, they shared territories. All of these new features appeared in the species after just 30 years—and 30 generations—an amount of time most evolutionary biologists had, before the study, considered much too short a period of time to result in such drastic and demonstrable changes.

PREMATURE BURIAL

✦ With all the things there are to worry about in the 21st century—global warming, stock market crashes, and the flesh-eating virus, to name just three—it's comforting to know that some things that used to terrify the public are no longer cause for concern. One example: being buried alive. Before the invention of the stethoscope in 1816, it was difficult to determine whether a "dead" person was really dead, merely unconscious, or in a coma. One can only guess how many people woke up in their coffins six feet underground, only to die a slow, suffocating death as they desperately tried to claw their way out of their caskets.

✦ Organizations such as the Society for the Prevention of People Being Buried Alive were formed to lobby for the not-yet-dead: Undertakers were urged to let the deceased lie in their coffins for a week or longer before burial, and numerous inventors devised "safety coffins" that enabled buried people to signal for help by ringing bells, waving flags, or even setting off fireworks if they regained consciousness. One design took the opposite approach by incorporating poison gas capsules that ruptured when the lid was nailed onto the casket.

✦ Wealthy people who could afford to be buried above ground in a crypt made provisions to be interred with a key to the crypt. Those who could only afford in-ground burials were often buried with crowbars, shovels, food, and water to sustain them while they dug their way to the surface. The terror of being buried alive would probably still be with us today, were it not for two things: 1) the development of modern medicine, which makes the determination of death virtually certain; and 2) the development of modern embalming techniques. If whatever "killed" you didn't really kill you, removing all of your blood and replacing it with preservatives and dye *certainly* will.

HOUSEHOLD GENIUS

To open sealed or stuck jars, place a rubber band securely around the lid and twist. The rubber band provides friction, making it easier to open the jar. Fat rubber bands—such as those used to hold broccoli or celery stalks—work best, but thinner rubber bands can be doubled if necessary.

THUNDERSTORMS

✦ Thunderstorms are defined simply as storms that produce thunder and lightning. They have what meteorologists call "life cycles": In the *cumulus* stage, weather conditions such as sudden cold fronts contact warm, moist air, and then cause that warm air—which is less dense than cool air—to rise. As it does, it cools, causing the moisture inside it to condense, forming cumulus clouds (the vertically aligned "fluffy" clouds). The process of condensation in turn causes more heat to be released, warming the air and causing an updraft to form, pulling more and more warm, moist air upward into a tower shape. That updraft is the storm's *cell*.

✦ In the *mature* stage, the rising warm air meets a "ceiling" of even warmer air, through which it can't rise. This causes it to spread horizontally, forming an anvil-shaped *cumulonimbus* cloud. The water in the cloud freezes in droplet form, falls, and melts into rain. If the water freezes into large enough droplets, they don't have enough time to melt. Result: hail. The falling rain and/or hail creates a downdraft, which can accentuate and interfere with the existing updraft, causing very turbulent winds and often very severe weather.

✦ Lightning occurs when static electricity builds up in a cloud, caused by the interaction of water and ice. When enough builds up—Crack!—it has to be released. A lightning bolt superheats the air around it and creates a pressure wave that we hear as thunder.

✦ In the *dissipation* stage, the cool air of the downdraft pushes away the supply of warm air fueling the updraft, and the storm dissipates.

3 PHRASE ORIGINS

Cold shoulder. The first recorded use of this phrase appeared in the novel *The Antiquary*, by Sir Walter Scott, published in 1816: "The Countess's dislike didna gang farther at first than just showing o' the cauld shouther." Etymologists disagree on its origin—some claim that Scott invented it, probably referencing a dismissive movement of a shoulder. Others argue that it came from a custom going back to the Middle Ages: Dinner guests who stayed too long were given a "cold shoulder" of meat rather than a cooked one as a hint that it was time to leave.

Humble pie. In the 14th century, the Middle English word for the innards of an animal—the heart, liver, intestines, etc.—was *numbles*, and later *umbles*. Using them to make pies was common for poor people. Sometime in the 1800s, *umble* became associated with *humble*, and it became common to say that someone who had been humiliated in some way had eaten "humble pie."

An axe to grind. This comes from an early American cautionary tale whose authorship remains disputed: A man stops by a house and pretends to admire a grindstone there—and tricks the homeowner into sharpening his axe, which he happens to have handy. Someone who has "an axe to grind" has long since come to refer to someone with a hidden ulterior motive.

4 KINDS OF SUSHI

In the Japanese language, "sushi" refers only to the vinegared, sticky rice used in many traditional dishes. Around the world, it has largely come to describe the raw fish often used in those dishes, or any Japanese dish featuring rice and raw or cooked fish. There are four common types of sushi served in the United States today:

Maki-sushi. The common rolled sushi in which fillings, usually vegetables, seafood (fish, shrimp, eel, etc.), and rice are wrapped in toasted *nori*, seaweed processed into thin, paperlike sheets. There are two main types of maki: *hosomaki* contains just a little rice along with one or two other items (vegetables and/or fish); *futomaki* is much thicker, contains several ingredients, and is served with a much larger portion of rice. There is also *uramaki*, in which the fillings of seafood and/or vegetables are wrapped in nori and the nori is then rolled in rice (sometimes called an "inside-out roll" because the rice is on the outside). One order can range from four to ten pieces, and, like all sushi dishes, is commonly served with hot *wasabi* mustard (related to horserad-ish) and pickled ginger.

Temaki-sushi. Rolled sushi, but the roll is cone-shaped and held in the hand (also called a "hand roll"). One order is one roll.

Nigiri-sushi. A finger of rice topped with a slice of seafood. A thin band of nori (about ¼ inch wide) is sometimes used to "tie" the seafood and rice together. One order is usually two pieces. There is also *gunkan nigiri*, or "boat" nigiri, where a three-inch-wide strip of nori is wrapped vertically around a finger of rice, forming walls that go straight up beyond the top of the rice. (They are said to resemble boats.) This provides a compartment for ingredients, like fish eggs, to be held in place on top of the rice.

Sashimi. Three to five slices of raw (sometimes pickled or cooked) fish, usually served on *shiso* leaves (also known as *perilla*—an herb with a cinnamon-like flavor), with grated daikon radish.

SIX FLAGS OVER TEXAS

The Six Flags amusement park chain (first park: Arlington, Texas, which opened in 1961) was named for the phrase "six flags over Texas," referring to the six different governments that have ruled the state.

Spain (1529–1685, 1690–1821)

France (1685–1690)

Mexico (1821–1836)

Republic of Texas (1836–1845)

Confederate States of America (1861–1865)

United States of America (1845–1861, 1865–present)

THE OVERTON WINDOW

Joseph P. Overton was the vice president of the Michigan-based Mackinac Center for Public Policy until his death in 2003. His lasting legacy: the theory known as the "Overton Window of Political Possibilities." Picture a yardstick representing all possible political positions on any given issue, from the most extreme on the right, to the center, to the most extreme on the left. Overton theorized that only a limited section of that yardstick (the "window")—say, just eight inches from the center—will fall into the realm of political possibility at any given time. Several factors could contribute to this: public opinion, fearful politicians, failed policies, etc. Only those options within the Overton Window are politically viable. Here's how it works, using Prohibition as an example.

✦ In 1920 anti-alcohol groups were very popular in the United States—and the idea of making alcohol illegal was *inside* the Overton Window. Politicians were therefore able to pass the 18th Amendment, making the sale and consumption of alcohol illegal. (The amendment was repealed in 1933.)

✦ The consumption of alcohol is now deeply entrenched in our culture, and attempting to make it illegal would be next to impossible. It can be therefore said to be far *outside* the Overton Window.

✦ If someone wanted to make alcohol illegal again, their job would be to "shift the Overton Window," or sway public opinion (via advertisements, demonstrations, letter-writing campaigns, etc.), back to where such a thing would be possible.

TROY: FROM MYTH TO REALITY

The Trojan War between the Spartans and the Trojans was just a mythological tale, right? Wrong. Those two city-states really did battle each other, probably in the 13th century B.C.E.... but where were they? The location of Sparta has always been known: its site is the town of Sparti in southern Greece. Troy, on the other hand, and knowledge of its location, disappeared. Then, in 1870—about 3,000 years after the war—a German archaeologist excavated a site in northwest Turkey and found what most archaeologists believe is the site of the legendary city. Work continues to this day, and so far evidence of nine different settlements, built one on top of the other over many centuries, has been uncovered. One of them, "Troy VII," the seventh layer from the top, may be the city-state that fought the Spartans in the Trojan War. (They haven't found a really big, wooden horse...yet.)

TUMPLINES

If you've ever hiked in the Himalayan Mountains, you've probably seen local people, especially Sherpas, using a *tumpline*, a headstrap used to carry a load on the back. Used by Himalayan peoples for thousands of years, it consists of a leather headpiece about two feet long and two or three inches wide. Attached are two thin leather straps several feet long. The ends of these straps are affixed to the load (a sack, backpack, or a collection of branches) at or near the bottom. The headstrap is then put across the top of the head—not on the forehead—while crouching, and lifted, with the weight coming down directly in line with the spine. The pack is meant to be carried quite high on the back, with the top often extending well above the head.

It may seem odd to backpack-carrying Westerners, but this is a remarkably efficient way to carry a load. In 2005 researchers at the Catholic University of Louvain in Belgium studied Sherpas from 11 to 68 years old carrying tumplined loads on a footpath. Women's loads averaged 66% of their body weight—equivalent to a 120-pound woman carrying an 80-pound pack. For men, the average jumped to 93%—and some carried 183% of their body weight—that's equivalent to a 150-pound man carrying about 275 pounds. (And the footpath was at an elevation of over 9,000 feet.)

Tumplines were also used in other areas of the world, including by Native Americans before the arrival of Europeans. This led to their use by the infamous Voyageurs, Indian and European (mostly French) porters of the 17th- and 18th-century North American fur trade. The Voyageurs were famous for their strength and endurance, regularly carrying 90-pound packs full of pelts...for 14 hours per day.

VICTOR HUGO ON THINKING

"There are thoughts which are prayers. There are moments when, whatever the posture of the body, the soul is on its knees."

WORD SEARCH: *BIGWIG*

In 17th-century France, when King Louis XIII began to lose his hair, he started wearing a wig. His successor, Louis XIV, the "Sun King," followed suit and sparked a fashion trend. Wigs were expensive to produce, though, and only the wealthy could afford them. Plus, the larger the wig, the more it cost. So commoners started using the term "bigwig" to describe members of the upper classes.

THE HISTORY OF NUNAVUT

✦ Around 800 C.E., the Thule society developed in far eastern Siberia, on islands in the Bering Strait and in northwest Alaska on the coast of the Bering Sea. The small civilization was built around the hunting of sea mammals, primarily whales.

✦ In about 1160, a warming trend in the Northern Hemisphere shrank the polar ice cap, which resulted in less ice on the Arctic Sea. The Thule people took advantage of that open sea, and the subsequent access to new fishing waters, to expand eastward. Within just 200 years, they inhabited a region that stretched all the way across northern Canada and into Greenland. (The name "Thule" comes from an ancient site found in Thule, Greenland.)

✦ Their descendants still live there today. Their Canadian neighbors, the Algonquin Indians, called them the *Eskimo*, which is believed to refer to snowshoes, but they called themselves the *Inuit*, meaning "The People."

✦ The area was named the Northwest Territories in 1859 and fell under the control of Canada on its formation in 1870. Over the following decades, huge chunks of the area were lost to the new provinces of Saskatchewan, Alberta, and the Yukon Territory.

✦ In the 1960s, a movement to form an Inuit-controlled area

first arose. It took more than 30 years, but on April 1, 1999, a triangle-shaped territory in north-central and eastern Canada—more than 800,000 square miles (roughly the size of Western Europe)—officially became the Inuit-controlled territory of *Nunavut*, which means "Our Land" in Inuktitut, the Inuit language.

✦ About 31,000 people now live in Nunavut; 85% of them are Inuit.

✦ Nunavut is the largest area in the world to be governed by aboriginal people.

THE X PRIZES

In 1995 American entrepreneur and inventor Dr. Peter Diamandis proposed that a series of prizes—*big* prizes—be offered to teams of scientists in order to promote technological progress in areas that benefit humanity. Over the next year, Diamandis worked with a number of innovators and philanthropists, and in 1996 they announced the opening of the X Prize Foundation, with Diamandis as its chairman.

The Ansari X Prize. This first prize was an offer of $10 million to the first private organization to launch a reusable manned spacecraft into space twice within two weeks. Twenty-six teams from around the world competed; the Tier One project, a team financed by Microsoft cofounder Paul Allen won the prize in October 2004.

The Archon X Prize offers $10 million to the first team that reduces the time and cost necessary to sequence human genomes, an accomplishment that could have dramatic benefits for medicine. (Nobody's won that one yet, but seven teams are currently working on it.)

The Automotive X Prize. Announced in 2005, it promises $7.5 million to the first team that designs a vehicle that can seat four people, accelerate from 0 to 60 mph in 12 seconds, drive at least

200 miles between fuelings—and get 100 mpg. (Nobody's won that one, either—but more than 60 teams have signed up so far.)

The Google Lunar X Prize. The largest X Prize announced to date. Sponsored by Google, it offers $20 million to whoever successfully lands and operates a rover on the surface of the Moon. (Twelve teams have signed up to compete.)

FOOD FOR THOUGHT. To win the $20 million Google Lunar X Prize, you must reach the Moon by December 31, 2012. After that date, the prize drops to $15 million. The final deadline is December 31, 2014, so get cracking!

AN ANIMAL ODDITY

Velvet worms, the name given to several species of worms that make up the phylum *Onychophora* (meaning "claw-bearers"), are found all over the world. They look more like caterpillars than worms, having many small, leglike appendages on their sides, and they even have antennae. They're also voracious carnivores, eating ants, moths, and spiders, upon which they squirt a sticky substance from their foreheads that entangles the prey's legs and/or wings, allowing for easy capture. But the velvet worm's real oddity comes from its mating habits. The male ignores the fact that a female has a convenient opening through which sperm can be transferred, and instead deposits a "sperm packet" onto her back or side. The packet contains biochemicals that dissolve the female's skin, allowing the sperm to penetrate her body and then search for her ovaries, where they will fertilize her eggs. (In some velvet worm species, the males have specialized spikes on their heads, on which they carry their sperm packets as they wander in search of females.)

PRUNE HANDS

You've probably noticed the phenomenon known as "prune hands" or "prune fingers": When you're in the bath or swimming pool for a long time, the skin on your palms, fingers, and soles of your feet becomes wrinkled. This is due to the fact that the outermost layer of human skin, called the *stratum corneum* (or "horny layer") is made up of dead skin cells. If submerged for long periods, these dead cells absorb a great deal of water, which causes them to expand. Because this expanded outer layer of skin is attached to the inner layers that *haven't* absorbed water and expanded, it must wrinkle to accommodate its increased surface area. The "prune" effect shows up primarily on the palms of the hands and soles of the feet because those areas need more protection than other parts of our body, and therefore have a much thicker stratum corneum.

WHISKEY

There are four main types of whiskey in the world: Irish, Scotch, American, and Canadian. They're all made from a *mash* of hot water and crushed grain, to which yeast is added to induce fermentation. They are then soaked in wooden barrels. Irish and Scotch whiskeys also use *malting* before making the mash— soaking the grain in water until it begins to germinate, then stopping that germination by heating and drying it. (Malting results in more sugar content in the mash for fermentation and flavor.)

✦ **Irish whiskey** is believed to be the oldest type, originating sometime around the 12th century (legend says that monks brought it to the island in the 4th century). It's made from a mash of malted and unmalted barley, along with corn and rye (and sometimes other grains in lesser amounts). The whiskey is then triple-distilled in copper stills and aged for at least three years in used sherry, brandy, bourbon, or rum oak casks. It comes in "single malt," from barley only and from one distillery, and "blended," a mixture of products from different distilleries. Irish whiskeys are very refined (due to the triple-distilling), full-bodied, and have a smooth, malty flavor.

✦ **Scotch whisky** is made only in Scotland, and has been made there since at least the 14th century. Single-malt Scotch is made from 100% malted barley mash dried over peat fires (peat is partially decayed vegetation common in wetland areas), which gives it a smoky, "earthy" flavor that Irish whiskey doesn't have. Also, it must be aged for at least three years in used sherry or bourbon casks, adding yet again to the whisky's flavor. There are also Scotch "grain whiskies," made from different grains, and many types of blended Scotch.

✦ **American whiskey** has been made since the 1700s and comes in two main types: bourbon and rye whiskey. Bourbon must be made in the U.S. from a grain mixture containing between 51% and 79% corn (over 79%, and it must be called "corn whiskey"). It can be no higher than 160 proof and it must be aged in charred American oak barrels. If the whiskey is aged for more than four years, it can be called "straight bourbon." Bourbons are made with a "sour mash" process, which means that each new batch of mash is mixed with some from the previous batch. Rye whiskey has also been made in the United States since the 1700s (George Washington made his own). It must be at least 51% rye (corn and barley make up the rest), and several current distillers make 100% rye. American whiskey was once very popular, especially in the East, but has become less so since Prohibition, when Canadian blended whiskeys (often called "rye whiskey" even though they often have little or no rye in their mash) got the upper hand. Rye whiskey is lighter, more bitter, and less sweet than bourbon.

✦ **Canadian whisky** is a blend of corn, rye, wheat, and barley grains, with no rules regarding percentages. (It's still often called "rye whisky" in Canada, but cannot be sold in the United States with this label.) Canadian whisky must be aged in a wood barrel in Canada for at least three years. It is known for its light body and "crisp" taste. Popular brands include Crown Royal and Canadian Club.

FOOD FOR THOUGHT. Is it spelled "whiskey" or "whisky"? We weren't drunk when we wrote this—actually, it's spelled both ways. Irish and American whiskey are spelled with an e; Scotch and Canadian whisky are always spelled without one.

HEAVENS TO MURGATROYD!

If you've ever watched the Hanna-Barbera cartoons from the 1960s, you've probably heard the phrase "Heavens to Murgatroyd." It's a derivation of the more well-known "Heavens to Betsy," which goes back to the 1890s and is meant to express shock or dismay. It was made famous by the character Snagglepuss in *Yogi Bear* cartoons, but it goes back further than that: It was first uttered by a character in the 1944 Lucille Ball film, *Meet the People*. The character who said it: the Commander, played by Bert Lahr, best known as the Cowardly Lion in *The Wizard of Oz* (after whom Snagglepuss was partly fashioned—which is why the phrase was chosen for him). It's unknown whether the film's screenwriters, Sig Herzig and Fred Saidy, made the phrase up or heard it somewhere else, but they would have been familiar with the name: It was the family name of several characters in the 1887 Gilbert and Sullivan comic opera *Ruddigore*. And it really is a family name: According to Murgatroyd genealogists, it goes back to England circa 1371. When a man named John Warley was made constable of a district in the moors around Yorkshire, he took a titular name meaning "John of Moor Gate Road"—which became "Johanus de Morgateroyde." It's been the family name ever since. (The spelling has changed a few times over the years: Murgatroyde, Murgatroid, Mergatoryde, and Mergatoid are just a few variations seen today.)

LANDSLIDES

Landslides are an important part of a natural erosion process that geologists call "mass wasting." The mass being moved is rock and *regolith*—all the material that makes up the Earth's surface that isn't rock, such as soil, sand, and sediment. Mass wasting is separated into five categories:

Slumps describe when a section of a slope breaks away and slides downward in one piece. The released piece moves in a downward and rotational direction—leaving behind curved cliffs that look like they've been scooped out with a large spoon. You've probably seen slumps on river, lake, and ocean banks.

Falls occur when at least one rock falls off a cliff face and falls freely to the ground, or bounces, rather than rolling or sliding, down a steep slope. You've probably seen the result of rockfalls in a *talus*, a sloping pile of rocks at the base of a steep cliff.

Slides are collections of loose surface rocks or debris that *slide* down a slope, usually in one movement. It seems obvious, but this is an important distinction to geologists working on mountain road construction, where they must take into account all types of possible slope movements.

Avalanches are the extremely rapid—up to 200 miles per hour—movements of a huge amounts of snow, rocks, or debris (or all of the above).

Mudflows (often called "mudslides") are concrete- to soup-textured landslides. These are most often triggered by heavy and sustained rain, and can pick up rocks, boulders, trees, houses, and whatever gets in their way as they travel, sometimes for many miles.

ON LANGUAGES

Q: "What makes languages change so often, so that scarce any nation understands what their ancestors spoke or writ 2 or 300 years ago?"

A: "The same that makes the fashion of cloaths alter. When the vulgar are got into the fashion, the gentry invent somthing new to diversifie and distinguish themselves from them." (Sir John Lowther's *Memorandum Book*, 1677).

COMMON DIAMOND RING SETTINGS

There are four main sections of a diamond gemstone: the *table*, *crown*, *girdle*, and *pavilion*. The table is the flat top of the stone. The crown, or the upper portion of the stone, angles up and in from the girdle toward the table and includes the table. The girdle is the thin outer edge of the widest part of a diamond. The pavilion is the lower portion of the diamond from the bottom point extending up to the girdle. There are five main setting styles used to mount a diamond onto a ring:

Prong setting. The most commonly used setting, this has three or more narrow metal prongs that extend up from the band and bend slightly over the girdle and just onto the crown. This allows for maximum light exposure of the entire stone.

Bezel setting. A metal ring encircles the entire stone at and just above the girdle, holding it on the *bezels* (the crown facets that angle up from the girdle to the table). Full-bezels circle the entire stone and allow no view of the girdle or pavilion. Semi- or half-bezels encircle only portions of the stone and partially expose both the girdle and the pavilion.

Channel setting. This is a stone or stones set into a channel or groove cut directly into the band. They are held in place simply by hammering the upper edges of the channel walls very slightly inward.

Pavé (pa-VAY) setting. From the French word meaning "to pave," this is when a ring's band or crown, or both or any parts thereof, are completely covered in a "paving" of tiny diamonds. This is done by setting tiny stones into small holes. They are held in place by a tiny bead of metal (usually gold or platinum) placed carefully where the stones meet.

THE HUMAN BODY
AND THE EARTH'S CRUST

The 20 most prevalent chemical elements in the human body, and in the Earth's crust, by percentage.

HUMAN BODY	EARTH'S CRUST
1. Oxygen: 65%	1. Oxygen: 46.71%
2. Carbon: 18%	2. Silicon: 27.69%
3. Hydrogen: 10%	3. Aluminum: 8.07%
4. Nitrogen: 3%	4. Iron: 5.05%
5. Calcium: 1.5%	5. Calcium: 3.65%
6. Phosphorus: 1%	6. Sodium: 2.75%
7. Sulfur: 0.25%	7. Potassium: 2.58%
8. Potassium: 0.2%	8. Magnesium: 2.08%
9. Chlorine: 0.15%	9. Titanium: 0.62%
10. Sodium: 0.15%	10. Hydrogen: 0.14%
11. Magnesium: 0.05%	11. Phosphorus: 0.13%
12. Iron: 0.006%	12. Carbon: 0.094%
13. Fluorine: 0.0037%	13. Manganese: 0.09%
14. Zinc: 0.0032%	14. Sulfur: 0.052%
15. Silicon: 0.002%	15. Barium: 0.05%
16. Zirconium: 0.0006%	16. Chlorine: 0.045%
17. Rubidium: 0.00046%	17. Chromium: 0.035%
18. Strontium: 0.00046%	18. Fluorine: 0.029%
19. Bromine: 0.00029%	19. Zirconium: 0.025%
20. Lead: 0.00017%	20. Nickel: 0.019%

SOUND LIKE A GENIUS

It's a common grammatical mistake for someone to use "lay" when they actually mean "lie," and vice versa. What makes it so confusing is that these two similar words have similar definitions and some identically spelled forms, but each has its own specific rules.

✦ Here's the best way to remember it: "lay," a verb meaning "to put or set down" is followed by an object: "You lay *something* down on the table, but *you* lie down on the couch." The definition of "lie," also a verb, is "to rest in a horizontal position."

✦ Making it even more confusing, the past tense of "lie" is "lay," which makes this sentence correct: "Earlier, Brian came in and lay down on the couch, so go lay this blanket over him." It's not correct to say "Brian laid down on the couch," nor is it correct to say "Brian lied down on the couch."

✦ To clarify, here are the correct tenses of "lay."

Present: "Now I *lay* me down to sleep." (In this case the object is "me." Technically, the object should be "myself.")

Past: "Last night I *laid* me down to sleep."

✦ Here are the correct tenses of "lie."

Present: "Now I *lie* down to sleep." (Notice that there's no object.)

Past: "Last night I *lay* down to sleep."

KNOW YOUR BEAKS

✦ All birds have beaks, also known as *bills* or *rostrums*.

✦ Beaks are comprised of an upper jaw, called a *maxilla,* and a lower jaw, called a *mandible* (these are the terms for jaw parts in other animals as well—even humans). Beaks are comprised of bone covered by a thin sheath of hardened *keratin* (the same stuff that hair, fingernails, and horns are made of). The keratin sheath, like horns and fingernails, continues to grow throughout a bird's life.

✦ On the top of the beak and near where it joins the head are two nostril openings called *nares*. In some species, such as hawks and parrots, a fleshy or waxy area on the beak called the *ceres* houses the nares.

✦ Beaks appear in a huge variety of colors, shapes, textures, and sizes, and have numerous uses, varying among species, including eating, preening, grasping, digging, climbing, fighting, and impressing prospective mates.

✦ The shapes and sizes of beaks evolved according to what food the birds ate. Examples: Birds of prey such as owls and hawks have short, thick, curved beaks that are well-suited for ripping flesh. Parrots have short, stout, curved beaks that can crack the hard outer shells of nuts. Birds that catch insects in flight, such as swifts, have short, wide beaks. And water birds such as cranes have long, narrow beaks for probing the floors of bodies of water.

✦ The pelican's lower beak resembles a narrow needle, allowing for the large elastic *gular sac* that runs from nearly the tip of the beak down to the pelican's throat area. Several other related species have gular skin, such as cormorants and frigatebirds, the males of which use the sac in mating rituals, inflating it with air and making it look like a bright red balloon.

✦ Crossbills have what appear to be deformed beaks: the upper and lower jaws curve in opposite directions—one to the right and one to the left, so the ends overlap. They're perfect for prying open pine cones to get the seeds, the crossbill's favorite food.

LETHOLOGICA

You know that feeling when you're trying to find the perfect word, but can't think of it? The technical name for that is *lethologica*. (Now, don't forget.)

FAITHLESS ELECTORS

In the United States, voters don't directly elect the president. The winner is actually decided by the Electoral College. The College is made up of delegates from each state, the number of which is the same as their congressional delegation, plus three for the District of Columbia. For instance, Oklahoma has five representatives and two senators, so it gets seven electoral votes. There are a total of 538 electoral votes, of which 270 are needed to win a presidential election. Electoral College voters (appointed at the state level by the two major political parties) are expected to cast their votes according to how their state voted in the general election. And it's a winner take-all-system: The candidate who received the most popular votes in a state gets *all* the electoral votes. The College usually votes as their constituents have directed...but they don't always. Here are a few "faithless electors":

2004: A Minnesota elector made a slip-up on his ballot. He accidentally cast his presidential vote for John Edwards, who was the Democratic candidate for vice president, and his vice presidential vote for John Kerry, the candidate for president.

2000: A Washington, D.C., elector cast no electoral votes to protest the District of Columbia's lack of statehood.

1976: A Washington state elector pledged a presidential vote for Ronald Reagan, who had been defeated in the primaries by Gerald Ford.

1968: A North Carolina elector was supposed to pledge for the Republican ticket of Richard Nixon and Spiro Agnew but voted for independent candidates George Wallace and Curtis LeMay instead.

1960: Fifteen electors who were supposed to pledge for Nixon voted for independent candidate Harry Byrd.

1948: A Tennessee elector cast a vote for States' Rights Democratic Party (segregationist) candidate Strom Thurmond, not Harry Truman, who had won the state.

1836: Richard M. Johnson was the Democratic nominee for vice president, but Virginia's 23 electors abstained due to the rumor that Johnson had once lived with an African-American woman. That meant a lack of majority in the vice presidential contest, so according to the Constitution, the nominee was decided by the Senate. They chose Johnson.

HOW TO BUILD A RAIN BARREL IN 10 STEPS

What's a rain barrel? It's a way to accumulate rain that you can later use to water plants. A typical rain barrel has a hole at the top, a sealed lid, an overflow pipe, and an on/off spigot at the bottom.

Tools and Materials: Drill; 6" hole saw; $^{29}\!/_{32}$" drill bit; $^{3}\!/_{4}$" pipe tap; louvered screen; $^{3}\!/_{4}$" brass faucet; teflon tape; $^{3}\!/_{4}$" hose adapter

1. Use the saw to cut a perfectly round 6" hole on the top of the barrel.

2. Drill two $^{29}\!/_{32}$" holes in the barrel—one near the top for an overflow and one near the bottom for the faucet.

3. Twist the $^{3}\!/_{4}$" pipe tap into the upper hole and then untwist and back it out of the hole. Repeat the same process for the lower hole.

4. Twist the threaded side of the hose adapter into the overflow hole.

5. Prepare the threaded side of the brass faucet; wrap the threads tightly with Teflon tape.

6. Twist the prepared end of the faucet into a $^{3}\!/_{4}$" hole at the bottom of the barrel.

7. Cover the 6" hole in the top by placing the 6" louvered screen onto the barrel with the louvered side up and the screen side down. (The screen will help keep mosquitoes, critters, and small children out of the barrel.)

8. Elevate the barrel on three cinder blocks and attach a hose to the hose adapter at the top of the barrel to direct overflow water *away* from the foundation of your home.

9. Cut your downspout about 4" above the top of the barrel, add an elbow if necessary, and make any final adjustments to the base and barrel.

10. Attach a hose to the faucet and keep it available to fill a watering can for your garden. Caution: Direct the overflow water *away* from the foundation of your house, and don't use the water for cooking, bathing, or drinking.

THREE RUNNY NOSES

The answer to the oft-asked question, "Why does my nose run?" is explained by the mucus glands in your nose and sinuses.

Reason #1: When you have a cold or an allergic reaction to something like pollen, the membranes go into mucus production overdrive to fight germs and wash out your nose.

Reason #2: When you cry, some of the tears from the ducts underneath your eyelids empty back into your nasal cavity and mix with mucus.

Reason #3: When it's cold outside, the tiny blood vessels inside your nose dilate in an attempt to warm the air passing through the nose before it reaches the lungs. The extra blood flow causes increased mucus production…causing a cold-weather runny nose. One other factor: The warmth inside your nose causes the water vapor in cold air to turn to steam, which then mixes with mucous and drops out.

CHAPTER 4

HOW FROSTBITE HAPPENS

Frostbite is characterized by damage to skin and other tissues
due to exposure to below-freezing temperatures. Three separate
biological processes are simultaneously called into play when
frostbite occurs:

1. Tissue freezing. Ice crystals form inside skin cells, damaging
and eventually killing them.

2. Tissue hypoxia. Capillaries in extremities become narrow and
draw blood away from the skin into the body's core in order to
protect vital organs. The ensuing lack of oxygen-carrying blood
in the extremities can lead to skin cell death. Narrowing of capillaries also causes blood clots.

3. Inflammatory mediators. These are produced by frostbite-
damaged cells, and aid in the immune system's inflammation

process. Normally that's a good thing, but in frostbite conditions inflammation unfortunately causes additional damage to skin cells.

Frostbite is classified by degree of damage:

✦ First degree: also called "frostnip"; skin turns white and stiff but is still soft beneath; damage is reversible.

✦ Second degree: skin turns white and/or blue and feels frozen; blisters form; partially reversible.

✦ Third degree: skin turns white/blue and becomes very hard; deep, blood-filled blisters; permanent damage.

✦ Fourth degree: white/blue to purple/black and completely frozen skin; deeper tissues, such as muscles, tendons, nerves, and bones are also damaged; tissue can mummify and fall off; permanent damage.

Warning: Never rub or massage areas affected by frostbite. This exacerbates tissue damage and causes severe pain. And do not put the victim or affected areas near a heat source such as a campfire unless refreezing of the area can be absolutely avoided. Partial thawing and refreezing causes repetition of the three processes above, which may lead to a more severe injury.

SPEAK LIKE A GENIUS

Between or Among? Technically speaking, "between" is used to set off two, and only two, things; "among" is used to set off three or more things.

"Help me, I can't decide between these two muffins."

"I can't help you, I'm trying to decide among all these cakes."

As far as choosing between "between" and "in between" when describing where an object is located, both can be grammatically correct, so use the one that sounds less awkward. (There is no such word as "inbetween.")

TOOTHPASTE: A HISTORY

✦ As early as 3000 B.C.E., ancient Babylonians (in modern-day Iraq) recorded the use of "chew sticks"—twigs with frayed ends—to clean their teeth.

✦ Hieroglyphs reveal that in about 2000 B.C.E. the Egyptians were making a tooth powder consisting of crushed ashes, cattle hooves, myrrh, eggshells, and pumice (volcanic rock).

✦ By 1000 B.C.E., Persians were making toothpastes similar to the Egyptians, but with burned and crushed snails and oysters added.

✦ Roman physician Scribonius Largus wrote in 47 C.E. that teeth should be scraped with a metal blade and the mouth rinsed with pure wine.

✦ Perhaps anecdotal, another story about ancient Roman dental care says that wealthy Romans bought other people's urine to clean stains from their teeth. (The uric acid in urine actually makes this plausible.) According to some historians, the Romans considered urine from Portugal the best.

✦ In the 7th century, a quote attributed to the Muslim Prophet Muhammad says: "The Siwak is an implement for the cleansing of teeth and a pleasure to God." The siwak is a chew stick made from twigs of the *Salvadora persica* tree. Commonly called the "toothbrush tree," it's an evergreen shrub found in Africa and Asia. It is still used today, and contains natural compounds proven to prevent tooth decay.

THE ORIGIN OF PURPLE

Purple *cloth*, that is. In around 1800 B.C.E., someone in the Phoenician city of Tyre (on the Mediterranean coast of what is now Lebanon) extracted and mashed up the mucus-producing *hypobranchial* glands of the Murex mollusk, a small, spiral sea snail. The mixture proved to be a powerful and long-lasting dye—and the color was something that had never been seen before in a cloth: a bright, vibrant purple. It became so popular that it spawned the first chemical dye industry in the world, and the Phoenicians became a regional powerhouse selling it all throughout the Middle East. (The name *Phoenicia* comes from the Greek for "Land of the Purple.")

Making the dye was an incredibly tedious process: It took more than 12,000 of the tiny shellfish (they grow to just 2 or 3 inches in length) to make 1.4 grams—less than a teaspoon—of dye. That made it extremely expensive: At its peak, it cost the equivalent of about $20,000 for a pound of dyed cloth, much more than the price of gold at the time. The color became known as "Tyrian Purple," and the industry flourished for nearly 3,000 years, changing hands several times as various empires—Persian, Egyptian, Greek, and Roman—took control of the Mediterranean region. During that time, it was the official color of several royal houses and became known by the name we still know it by today, "royal purple."

In the 1400s, a newer, less expensive dye (made from *Kermes* insects) of a similar color put the Murex dye makers out of business for good. That one became known as "Cardinal's Purple," as it was officially adopted by the Catholic Church and is still the color Catholic cardinals wear today.

PISTOL SHRIMP

Pistol shrimp, also called *snapping shrimp*, are a family of about 600 shrimp species known for their very peculiar hunting method. When one of the shrimp spots likely prey, usually a member of another shrimp species, it points its one enlarged claw at it. A specialized pincer on the claw is then drawn back and "clicks" into position, almost like the hammer on a gun. When it's ready, the shrimp releases the pincer and it flies shut (in less than one thousandth of a second), emitting a loud snapping noise. This causes a stream of bubbles to be shot at the unwitting prey; the shockwave can knock it unconscious...or even kill it. Then the prey is quickly dragged to a safe place and eaten.

It was long thought that the act of the pincers slamming together was the source of the loud snap (which can be easily heard through fishtank walls), but high-speed photography has since proven that this is not the case. Pistol shrimp pincers are formed in such a way that when they close, a stream of water shoots out from between them so rapidly that the water reaches, for a very tiny moment, a temperature of more than 8,500°F. This causes a phenomenon known as *cavitation*: production of an extremely low-pressure bubble that instantly collapses. That implosion is what gives the pistol shrimp its snap.

THE 5 KINDS OF MARINE SEDIMENT

Geologists classify all the sediment found on ocean floors into five types. They are:

Terrigenous: particles of land-based rock that, due to erosion, have become gravel, sand, or mud and are then transported to the oceans by water and wind

Biogenic: organic particles from decayed plants and animals, primarily bones and shells of marine organisms

Authigenic: minerals created through chemical interactions of particles on the seafloor

Volcanogenic: particles derived from volcanic eruptions, primarily ash and glass

Cosmogenous: particles from cosmic dust and meteorites from outer space (the least abundant sediment type)

WHERE'S YOUR PREPOSITION AT?

It's commonly taught in middle-school English classes that you can't end a sentence with a preposition. Sure you can. What you can't do is use a preposition without an object, at least not in formal English. The actual reason that "where are you at?" is incorrect is because "at" has no object in the sentence. You wouldn't say, "At where are you?" Besides, it's redundant; "Where are you?" works just fine. However, this sentence is correct: "What level are you at?" It could be turned around to say, "At what level are you?"

This sentence, which ends with a preposition, is also correct: "Which course did you sign up for?" The object of the preposition "for" is "which course," so the sentence could be written, "For which course did you sign up?" Both are correct. Where did this misconception come from? According to *The American Heritage Dictionary*, it was 17th-century English poet John Dryden:

Dryden first promulgated the doctrine that a preposition may not be used at the end of a sentence, probably on the basis of a specious analogy to Latin. Grammarians in the 18th century refined the doctrine, and the rule has since become one of the most venerated maxims of schoolroom grammar. But sentences ending with prepositions can be found in the works of most of the great writers since the Renaissance. Efforts to rewrite such sentences to place the preposition elsewhere can have stilted and even comical results, as Winston Churchill demonstrated when he objected to the doctrine by saying, "This is the sort of English up with which I cannot put."

CPR UPDATE

Ever worried that you might "catch" something if you had to give someone mouth-to-mouth resuscitation? So has the American Heart Association. In 2008 they unveiled new research that shows that chest pumps alone could be used in many instances in which *cardio pulmonary resuscitation* (CPR) is needed. Unconscious adults, the research revealed, are most likely to have suffered a cardiac arrest or similar heart problem—and usually still have plenty of air left in their lungs. That means that mouth-to-mouth is usually unnecessary. Unconscious children, on the other hand, are more likely to have suffered some kind of breathing obstruction and still require mouth-to-mouth. (This is also true of victims of non-heart-related events such as near drownings, exposure to carbon monoxide, and drug overdoses.) The AHA believes these new rules will likely save many lives, simply because people who would otherwise not perform *any* CPR—due to their fear of infection from mouth-to-mouth breathing—would at least be willing to do chest compressions. (The new technique, called Hands-Only CPR, consists of about 100 deep chest pumps per minute.)

C.I.A. CRYPTONYMS

The Central Intelligence Agency uses *cryptonyms*, or code names, to identify different countries, organizations, people, and entities in internal documents so as not to arouse suspicion or expose state secrets if the documents are ever leaked. Here are some real-life cryptonyms (although since they've been leaked, they've probably been replaced):

AMQUACK: Che Guevara

AMTHUG: Fidel Castro

RTACTION: C.I.A.

KMFLUSH: Nicaragua

PBPRIME: United States

ODUNIT: U.S. Air Force

ODOATH: U.S. Navy

LCPANGS: Costa Rica

KUFIRE: Intelligence

KUGOWN: Propaganda

THE DIFFERENCE BETWEEN...

Musical and Revue. Both feature performers acting and singing on a stage, but a musical—which originated in ancient Greece—is a play in which the narrative is interrupted by songs. A revue, which was developed in the U.S. in the 19th century, consists of a series of skits and music numbers that often take on a topical and satirical tone.

THE SURREALISTS

Surrealism was an organized intellectual, political, and cultural movement that began in Paris in 1924 with poet/critic Andre Breton's *Manifesto of Surrealism* and disbanded at the onset of World War II. It emerged from Dadaism, an earlier art and literary movement that reached its height between 1916 and 1920. Dadaists (often called "nihilistic") vehemently protested World War I and the "bourgeois," capitalist Western culture that had produced it. They rejected traditional aesthetic values, described their own output as "anti-art" and "anti-rational," and deliberately tried to shock viewers into political awareness with work that appeared to be chaotic and anarchic.

This paved the way for surrealism, a movement that included visual artists, writers, and musicians. The surrealists believed that art must express the imagination, without regard for convention, tradition, logic, or even comprehensibility. Much of their work was based on dreams and dream analysis (influenced by Sigmund Freud), and on visual imagery and symbols that came from the subconscious mind. Probably the best-known surrealist was painter Salvador Dalí, whose dream-inspired images included melting clocks, jumbles of objects, distorted figures, and strange landscapes. Other surrealists were Man Ray, Yves Tanguy, Max Ernst, René Magritte, Jean Cocteau, Eugène Ionesco, Marcel Duchamp, Jacques Prévert, Joan Miró, and Paul Éluard.

ANCIENT DATING TECHNIQUES

The techniques used by archaeologists to date ancient artifacts are divided into two types: *relative* and *absolute*. Relative dating can give only approximate dates, in most cases, and dates an artifact relative to other finds. Absolute dating is much more modern and much more specific. Relative techniques include:

Biostratigraphy. This is the oldest technique, dating to the 1700s. Simply put: new rock layers have been continuously created out of sediment on the Earth's surface for more than four billion years. Each layer contains fossils of the plants and animals that lived when that layer was created. For example: *Tyrannosaurus rex* fossils are found all over western North America—but only in rock layers corresponding to when T. rex existed (which modern testing has shown to be between 68 and 65 million years ago). So, if a new T. rex fossil is found, it, and fossils around it, can be relatively dated to that era. Biostratigraphy can be used to date artifacts from thousands to billions of years old, and was one of the key discoveries that led to Charles Darwin's theory of evolution.

Seriation studies deposit layers, too, but at sites inhabited by humans. The Beaker people, for example, lived in many areas of Europe. Sites occupied by them can be identified by their distinctive beakerlike pottery style—which has been dated using more specific techniques to the 3rd millennium B.C.E. That means that wherever Beaker pottery is discovered, the layer in which it is found can be relatively dated to that same era. Seriation is used to date sites up to about 12,000 years old.

Pollen analysis studies pollen layers. Every flowering plant species produces uniquely-shaped, microscopic pollen grains. They're also very hard, so they stick around for thousands of years, and can even become fossilized. Therefore, studying pollen deposits in core samples taken from the ground can reveal which plants lived in an area over many millions of years. That information can then be compared to other areas for relative dating. Pollen analysis was the technique used to solve the mystery of Easter Island, famous for the huge, carved stone heads that dot its barren landscape. The analysis showed that the island was once covered by a subtropical forest, which supported a large human population, and that deforestation by those people finally decimated the island's plant life by around 1500 C.E., along with most of the civilization that occupied it.

Fluorine dating is used to date skeletal remains. How it works: When a body (human or otherwise) is buried, its bones absorb minerals, like fluorine, from groundwater. Fluorine content is consistent over given areas, and bone absorbs it at a known rate. So if two bodies are found in the same vicinity, they can be dated relative to each other by measuring how much fluorine each has absorbed. One of fluorine dating's most famous uses was in regards to "Piltdown Man," the supposed 500,000-year-old remains (a skull and jawbone) of a man found in East Sussex, England, in 1912. In 1953 fluorine testing helped prove that the skull and jawbone were different ages, and both were less than 50,000 years old. Subsequent radiocarbon dating tests found the skull was only about 630 years old (and the jawbone turned out to be from an orangutan).

Obsidian hydration analysis (OHA) was developed in 1960. Obsidian is a natural glass formed from volcanic magma. It was a favorite of ancient tool makers, making it a favorite of archaeologists. How OHA works: When a piece of obsidian is broken or chipped (when an ancient hunter is sharpening it into a spear head, for example), it begins to absorb water from the atmosphere, and does so at a very consistent rate. Using OHA, an ancient tool is examined under a microscope, the saturation depth is determined, it's compared to other samples, and a relative age is determined. OHA can provide relative ages for tools from 200 to 200,000 years old.

Patination is similar to OHA, but involves measuring the *patina* of an artifact (how much of its surface has been altered in color or texture) and comparing it to others. An example would be measuring the depth of the green crust that grows on bronze artifacts and comparing it to others that have been dated conclusively with other methods.

Thermoluminescence dating takes advantage of the fact that most minerals are *luminescent*: When they're exposed to radiation (like UV light from sunlight), they absorb and store it. This happens at a regular rate over time. When such a substance is then heated (to at least 500°F), such as in a kiln, it releases that stored energy as light, ie., it glows, is emptied of that energy, and starts absorbing and storing it again. With thermoluminescence dating, archaeologists heat an artifact, such as a piece of ancient pottery, and measure how much energy it releases. That amount tells them how long ago it was made. Age range: between 1,000 to 200,000 years. (For absolute dating techniques, go to page 352.)

THE SEVEN SEAS

The seven seas, as they were known to explorers in the Middle Ages: the Mediterranean Sea, Red Sea, East African Sea, West African Sea, China Sea, Persian Gulf, and Indian Ocean.

BENEDICT ARNOLD

His name is now synonymous with "traitor," but what exactly did Benedict Arnold do that was so bad? In 1780, at the height of the American Revolution, he conspired with the British government to surrender the American military fort at West Point, New York. Not long before he switched allegiances, Arnold was a major general in the Continental Army, leading his troops to decisive victory in the Battle of Saratoga in 1777, which turned the tide to the Americans' favor. But Arnold suffered a leg wound in the battle and spent a year recovering, during which time he grew bitter toward the American government because they refused to pay him for his wartime service. In a show of good faith in 1780, the government offered Arnold a job as commander of West

Point. Arnold, still bitter, took the job…because the British army had offered him £20,000 (and the rank of brigadier general) in exchange for the fort. Before the surrender could occur, a British spy was arrested, carrying documents disclosing Arnold's involvement in the plot. Arnold evaded arrest and defected to the British side. He died in England in 1801, penniless.

2 WAYS TO REMEMBER WHICH MONTHS HAVE 31 DAYS

1. This old poem: "30 days hath November / April, June, and September / February hath 28 alone / And all the rest have 31."

2. Make a fist and look at your knuckles. Going across from knuckle to knuckle "valley," and so on (omit the thumb), each knuckle is a month with 31 days. Your pinky knuckle ends on July, so start over on the first knuckle with August.

THE FIVE PILLARS OF ISLAM

The five pillars of Islam are the five specific tenets and duties expected of every practicing Muslim. While not in the Koran, the Muslim holy text, the five pillars are mentioned in the *Hadith*—oral traditions derived from the collected sayings of Islam's chief prophet, Muhammad.

✦ *Shahada*: The Muslim profession of faith which must be recited during daily prayers. In English: "I testify that there is no God but God, and Muhammad is the messenger of God."

✦ *Salat*: The recitation of prayers five times each day—at dawn, noon, mid-afternoon, sunset, and nightfall—while facing the direction of the holy shrine (the Kaaba) in Mecca, Saudi Arabia.

✦ *Zakah*: The practice of giving charity to the poor; it's obligatory for all who can afford it.

✦ *Sawm*: Ritual fasting from dawn to dusk each day during the holy month of Ramadan. This includes abstaining from food, drink, and sex.

✦ *Hajj*: The requirement that every able-bodied Muslim make a pilgrimage to Mecca at least once during his or her lifetime.

SNUFF

Nobody knows for sure how long people have been cultivating and using tobacco, but most experts believe it began with the Mayans at least 3,000 years ago. From their empire in modern-day Mexico, tobacco use spread through much of the Americas by the start of the first millennium. Crushing the leaves into powder form—"snuff"—and inhaling it into the nose, or "dipping" it between the teeth and gums, were certainly among the earliest forms of its use. Here's a timeline of the use of snuff:

1493: Ramon Pane, a Spanish friar who accompanied Columbus on his second voyage to the New World, writes extensively about snuff. Pane is the person commonly credited with introducing tobacco to Europe.

1561: The French ambassador to Portugal sends snuff to former French queen Catherine de Médicis to treat her son's chronic headaches. She becomes a regular user and a proponent of medical snuff. The ambassador's name: Jean Nicot de Villemain, after whom the scientific name of the tobacco genus, *Nicotiana*, will later be named.

1620: The first snuff mill in Europe opens in Seville, Spain. (This date is an approximation and may actually be much earlier.)

1700s: Snuff use spreads through Asia, becoming especially popular in China. It has also become the favored tobacco of the aristocracy in Europe and the American colonies. Users include Napoléon and Queen Charlotte (known as "Snuffy Charlotte"), wife of King George III of England.

1730: The first American tobacco factories open as small snuff mills in Virginia.

1761: English physician John Hill publishes "Cautions Against the Immoderate Use of Snuff," believed to be the first clinical study of the effects of tobacco, warning that snuff can cause cancers of the nose.

1794: The first tax on tobacco in the U.S. is imposed on snuff. One of those opposed to the tax was future president James Madison of the tobacco-growing state of Virginia. (He had just married his wife, Dolley, a frequent user of snuff.)

1800s: Production of snuff is far higher than smoking tobacco until the end of the century and the invention of the prerolled cigarette. The manufacture of snuff boxes, bottles, and other paraphernalia is a huge industry, especially in China, where intricately designed and painted snuff bottles are made by the millions.

1900s: The era of snuff use largely comes to an end.

2000s: Wait! It may be coming back. With more and more cities around the world outlawing smoking in public places, nicotine addicts have few alternatives. One of them: snuff.

SUPERHEROES AND THEIR ALTER EGOS

Captain America: Steve Rogers, delivery boy

Aquaman: Arthur Curry, king of the sea

The Flash: Barry Allen, police scientist

Green Hornet: Britt Reid, newspaper publisher

Green Lantern: Hal Jordan, test pilot

Wonder Woman: Diana Prince, army major

Supergirl: Linda Lee Danvers, college student

Spider-Man: Peter Parker, photographer

Iron Man: Tony Stark, inventor and industrialist

The Incredible Hulk: Bruce Banner, physicist

MOST COMMON AMERICAN NAMES

These are the top ten American surnames as listed by the 2000 U.S. Census, along with their countries of origin. Some people with these names didn't get them from their home country. The name Miller, for example, was brought to the U.S. primarily by the Scots, but immigrants from Germany, France, Italy, and Slavic countries with similar names had them "Millerized" on arrival. In those cases, only the most prominent country origin is listed.

1. Smith (England)

2. Johnson (England)

3. Williams (Wales)

4. Brown (England)

5. Jones (Wales)

6. Miller (Scotland)

7. Davis (England)

8. Garcia (Mexico)

9. Rodriguez (Mexico)

10. Wilson (Scotland)

FOOD FOR THOUGHT. The 2000 Census listed 151,671 different surnames in the United States. The only name in the top 100 not of European or Latin American origin: the most common Vietnamese name, Nguyen, at #58. (The pronunciation of Nguyen is usually given as "win," though some pronounce it "nu-yen.")

Name #54,321: Hrovat. It's a Croat name, used by an estimated 356 people in the U.S. in 2000.

THE AMERICAN POET LAUREATE

The British tradition of having a poet laureate—a "national" poet to write commemorative verse—began with John Dryden's appointment in 1670. The American poet laureateship is much more recent—it was established in 1937, though the position was originally called "Consultant in Poetry to the Library of Congress." The "Poet Laureate Consultant in Poetry," as it's now known, is appointed annually by the Librarian of Congress (taking advice from the current and former poets laureate and from respected poetry critics) and serves for eight months, from October through May, receiving a stipend of $35,000. The laureate's official duties are to present one public lecture and one reading of his or her work, as well as to promote the reading, writing, and appreciation of poetry. The first poet laureate was Joseph Auslander, followed by such eminent poets as Robert Frost, Howard Nemerov, William Stafford, Robert Penn Warren, Joseph Brodsky, Rita Dove, Louise Glück, and Robert Pinsky. Oldest poet to hold the title: Stanley Kunitz, at age 95.

STORKS AND BABIES

Here's the origin of a popular folk tradition. Before Christianity became the dominant religion in Europe, pagan worship prevailed. The summer solstice, the day with the most hours of sunlight, which normally falls on June 20 or 21 in the Northern Hemisphere, was a hugely important holiday. Festivals were held, often lasting days and frequently involving lots of alcoholic beverages and, evidence suggests, plenty of sexual activity. The evidence: the sudden boost in the number of babies born nine months after the yearly events, in the following April. In northern Europe, something else arrived every year around that time: European white storks (*Ciconia ciconia*), flying in for their springtime mating season. Storks get along remarkably well with humans, to the point of making their nests on the tops of houses, something still seen there today. The simultaneous arrival of the birds and the babies led to the folk tale of storks delivering babies, and delivering them by dropping them down chimneys. When the legend began is unknown, but it's believed to have originated in northern Germany.

MOTHER-OF-PEARL

The largest pearl ever found is the Pearl of Lao-tze, which weighed 14 pounds, 1 ounce (6.37 kg). It was found in a giant clam off the Philippine island of Palawan in 1934.

KNOW YOUR NATO

NATO—the North Atlantic Treaty Organization—is a military and political alliance of European nations plus the United States and Canada. It was created in response to the 1948 Soviet blockade of Berlin and was designed to protect Western Europe from an attack by the Soviet Union or its allies. Its mission: "to safeguard the freedom and security of its member countries by political and military means."

✦ The 12 original members of NATO were Belgium, Canada, Denmark, France, Iceland, Italy, Luxembourg, the Netherlands, Norway, Portugal, the United Kingdom, and the United States.

✦ In 1952 Greece and Turkey joined.

✦ In 1955 West Germany was admitted.

✦ In 1982 Spain became the 16th member.

✦ In 1999 the first three former Communist countries after the fall of the Berlin Wall joined NATO: the Czech Republic, Hungary, and Poland.

✦ In 2004 seven more former Communist countries joined the alliance: Bulgaria, Estonia, Latvia, Lithuania, Romania, Slovakia, and Slovenia, bringing the total number of NATO members to 26.

✦ In 2008 Albania and Croatia were invited to join NATO and are expected to become members in 2009.

FOOD FOR THOUGHT. An American military officer is always commander-in-chief of NATO forces so that U.S. troops never come under control of a foreign power.

MORE FOOD FOR THOUGHT. To retaliate against NATO, in 1955 Communist countries banded together to form the Warsaw Pact, which originally consisted of the USSR, Albania, Bulgaria, Czechoslovakia, Hungary, East Germany, Poland, and Romania. The Warsaw Pact ended in 1991 after the dissolution of the Soviet Union.

CHINA TIME

What's the largest country with just one time zone? China. It had five until 1949, when the new Communist regime reduced it to one. That means that on a given day, "solar noon," when the sun is at its zenith, can arrive before 12:00 noon in Shanghai, in the far east of the country, and after 3:00 p.m. at the Tajikistan border, in the far west.

REMEMBERING WHAT YOU READ

Tips from memory researchers:

✦ **See what you read.** Form pictures in your mind of the subject you're reading (if it's not too abstract to do so). Visualizing employs more areas of the brain and requires greater concentration than simply reading the words, so you retain more of the information.

✦ **Read out loud.** Speaking and hearing the words also requires much greater concentration, and gives more for the brain to "latch onto" when trying to remember something.

✦ **Take notes.** Stopping and thinking about what you've read and writing notes to flesh out a subject gets you involved more deeply, making for a more memorable experience.

✦ **Chew gum while you read.** Nobody knows why, but research done in the U.K. in 2002 found that people who chewed gum scored up to 36% better on memory and attention tests than people who did not.

SCRAPIE

Scrapie is a disease that affects sheep and goats. It is the most common type of *transmissible spongiform encephalopathy* (TSE), a family of rare diseases that damage the central nervous system, especially the brain, of mammals. Like all TSEs, scrapie causes degeneration of the brain tissue (it appears spongelike in autopsies), resulting in function impairment and eventually death. Scrapie has been known since the 1700s and gets its name from one of the disease's symptoms—the afflicted animals' obsessive rubbing against hard objects such as fences or rocks, which "scrapes" off its fur or wool. It is not believed to spread to other species, but there are similar diseases. Some: chronic wasting disease in deer (first recognized in the late 1960s); "mad cow" disease in cattle (first recognized in 1986); feline spongiform encephalopathy in cats (first reported in 1990); and Creutzfeldt-Jakob disease in humans (first noted in the 1920s). The cause of all of these diseases remains a mystery, and to date, none of them has a cure.

INSTANT KNOWLEDGE

Before air travel, jet lag was referred to as "boat lag."

THE MYSTERY OF
DARWIN'S PROBOSCIS

No, it's not a science-fiction-mystery film; it's the story of an animal whose existence Charles Darwin predicted in 1862. He had been studying the *comet orchid* of Madagascar, a "moth loving" flower that is pollinated by moths when they come to feed on its nectar. The odd thing about this flower is that its *nectary*—the part that produces nectar—is a narrow, tubelike spur more than 11 inches long, but the nectar is stored in its base. For a moth to be able to drink it, it would need a *proboscis* (tongue) nearly a foot long. Such an insect had never been heard of, but Darwin said it must be so: If no such creature had evolved a proboscis that could access the nectar, the orchid would not be pollinated and would have gone extinct long ago. He published the theory in 1862...and was ridiculed by his peers. It would take four decades —21 years after Darwin's death—to prove him correct. In 1903 the Morgan's Sphinx Moth, with a tongue more than three times the length of its 3-inch-long body, was discovered in Madagascar. It's known today as the "Long-Tongued Night-Flying Hawk Moth"—as well as the "Predicted Moth."

Update: In 2008 entomology professor and *National Geographic* partner Phil de Vries journeyed to Madagascar to film the moth feeding from the flower. Just finding the *flower* was hard enough: The comet orchid is an *epiphyte*—it attaches itself to trees rather than grows in the soil. And it grows high up in trees in the deep jungle. But de Vries did find it, and he set up a night vision camera…and waited…and waited…and waited…at the base of the tree, keeping his eye on the monitor. At 4:34 a.m., the tired scientist noticed something—and watched in awe as a large moth flew up to the orchid, uncoiled a very thin, very long proboscis, carefully inserted it into the blossom, and shoved it down the 11-inch nectary. The moth then sat there, flapping and drinking away. It was the first time that Darwin's Predicted Moth had been captured doing just what Darwin predicted it would do.

LIST OF LISPS

A lisp is defined broadly as a functional speech disorder, which is a difficulty pronouncing certain sounds, and specifically *sibilant* sounds—"s," "z," "ch," and "th." They're caused primarily by irregular tongue placement. There are four types:

Interdental (frontal) lisp. This is when the tongue protrudes between the upper and lower teeth, directing air forward through the teeth, making both "s" and "z" sound like "th."

Dentalized lisp. This happens when the tongue rests on or pushes against the insides of the front teeth, also directing the air forward. (Try saying "seashore" with your tongue pressed against your teeth.) The sound produced is similar to the interdental lisp, but is a bit more muffled. Both interdental and dentalized lisps are characteristic of normal childhood development, and are common in children until they grow out of it at about the age of four.

Lateral lisp. This is not part of normal speech development, and is often the result of abnormal physical development of the jaw or tongue. It causes the tongue to be in the approximate position it is when an "l" is pronounced, i.e., with the tip of the tongue up on the palate. When making sibilant sounds with the tongue in that position, air flows over the sides of the tongue and into the cheeks, resulting in a "wet" or "slushy" sound. (Try making an "l" sound and holding it while trying to make an "s" sound.)

Palatal lisp. Also not typical and often with similar causes as the lateral lisp, this is when the middle section of the tongue lifts and makes contact with the palate. To produce it, make an "h" sound, then a "y" sound—and try making an "s" sound.

THE NORTH CELESTIAL POLE

If you stood exactly on the spot that is Earth's geographic North Pole and looked straight up into the sky, you would be looking at what astronomers refer to as the North Celestial Pole (NCP).

✦ Very near to that imaginary pole in the sky, with a little varia-tion due to Earth's rotational tilt, you would find the star Polaris, also known as the "North Star" or the "Pole Star." It's part of the constellation Ursa Minor, the "Little Bear," also known as the "Little Dipper." (Polaris is the last star in the dipper's handle.)

✦ Because of its location relative to Earth's rotation, Polaris appears to us to stay in the same spot all night long, every night (in the daytime, too, if we could see it). And because, from our perspective, Earth rotates clockwise relative to that pole star, all the other stars in the sky seem to move around it in a counterclockwise direction. That phenomenon is known as *diurnal* motion—from the Latin for "daily" (and it can be seen graphically in time-lapse photography).

✦ This made Polaris extremely useful for ancient navigators (it still does), since no matter where you are, if you draw a line down from Polaris to the horizon—that point is almost exactly north. It is, however, only visible from the Northern Hemisphere.

✦ Polaris was not always nor will it always be our North Star. For various reasons concerning the movement of celestial bodies, our positional relationship to the stars changes on an approximately 25,765-year cycle. Two thousand years from now, the star known as *Gamma Cephei* will become our North Star. And about 3,000 years after that, *Iota Cephei* will take its place.

✦ To find Polaris, first locate the Big Dipper (Ursa Major, which is often easier to spot than the Little Dipper). The two stars that make up the front of the cup (farthest from the handle) are known as the "pointer stars." Follow them out from the cup, and the next bright star you see is Polaris.

THE SOUTH CELESTIAL POLE

The Southern Hemisphere doesn't have a proper pole star. The closest it has to a Southern Celestial Pole star is Sigma Octantis, located in the constellation Octans, but it's more than a full degree off the pole and is not very bright. For that reason, the constellation known as Crux, or the "Southern Cross," is more commonly used by navigators, as it is a very distinctive constellation and not far from the pole. How to use it: Locate the "top" and "bottom" stars of what makes up the vertical part of the cross. Draw a line from the top star, through the bottom star, and longer still, about 4.5 times the distance between the two stars—and you're very close to the SCP.

✦ Because Earth's rotation relative to the SCP appears as counterclockwise, all the stars in the sky in the Southern Hemisphere appear to revolve around the SCP clockwise—the opposite of the Northern Hemisphere.

VINEGAR POWER

If you've ever seen the label on a bottle of vinegar and read something like "40 grain," you probably wondered, "What does that mean?" It refers to the acid content of the vinegar: 10 grains equals 1% acid, so "40 grain" is 4% acid content, "50 grain" is 5% and so on. Those are normal contents for food use, but you can get vinegar as high as 200 grain—or 20% acid. Want some? Put on some gloves—it'll eat your skin away. And if you're spraying it on weeds, which many people do, cover your car because it can also eat through paint and metal.

TV ADVERTISING SECRETS

Advertising guru Donald Gunn of the Leo Burnett agency (creators of such icons as the Jolly Green Giant, the Marlboro Man, and Tony the Tiger) divides "effective" TV ads into 12 categories:

1. The demo: A straightforward visual demonstration of the product's capabilities (often used in vacuum cleaner and stain remover ads).

2. Show the need or problem: Shows consumer how something is missing (or wrong) in their life and how the product takes care of it ("I've fallen, and I can't get up!").

3. Symbol, analogy, or exaggerated graphic to show the need or problem: Variation of #2, but as the title states, a symbol, analogy, or graphic is used to represent the consumer's problem (a person's head is replaced by a giant nose to illustrate congested sinuses).

4. Comparison: Simply shows how the product is superior to a competitor's (the "Pepsi challenge").

5. The exemplary story: Creates a narrative showing the product's benefits (kids driving down a road talking about a movie and—BAM!—they get hit by a truck—but they're okay because "Safe Happens," the ad tells us, in a Volkswagen)

6. Benefit causes story: Shows perceived benefits of the product and then reveals the product (women fawn over a man...in an ad for a body spray).

7. Tell it: A presenter, usually a sympathetic character such as a kindly grandmother, tells how the product helped her ("I used to forget things all the time; now I take Fredo's Gingko Beloba Juice").

8. Ongoing characters or celebrities: Easily recognized in examples such as "Mr. Whipple" or the "Geico cavemen."

9. Symbol, analogy, or exaggerated graphic to demonstrate the benefit: Like #3, but the exaggerated part is the benefits rather than the problem (Verizon wireless ads that show hundreds of support people following a Verizon user).

10. Associated user imagery: Shows the type of people who would benefit from the product (athletes for Gatorade; the elderly for Metamucil).

11. Unique personality property: Highlights something unique about the product (the "Irishness" of Guinness beer; the "oldest brewery in America" for Budweiser).

12. Parody or borrowed format: Parodies a film, novel, sporting event, another ad, or some other well-known reference (the Fred Flintstones Geico ad).

THE DIFFERENCE BETWEEN...

Porcupines and hedgehogs. They both have quills—but that's where their similarities end. They're completely different *orders* of mammal: porcupines are members of *Rodentia* (the rodents); hedgehogs are members of *Erinaceidae*, which consists of just them and a few other shrewlike mammals. Porcupines are generally larger, up to 36 inches long and weighing up to 45 pounds.

Also, they have large, squarish heads and long, barbed quills that they can easily detach. The several North American varieties spend most of their time in trees, and they're herbivores. Hedgehogs are generally small, the largest growing to 17 inches long, have small, pointy-nosed heads, and they have short, unbarbed quills. They don't climb trees, and they eat insects, frogs, mushrooms, fruit, and grass, among other things. Porcupines are found in Europe, Asia, Africa, and North and South America, while hedgehogs are found in Europe, Asia, Africa, and New Zealand, and there are none in the Americas.

POSTNOMINAL LETTERS

CPA: Certified Public Accountant

D.D.: Doctor of Divinity

D.D.S.: Doctor of Dental Surgery

D.M.D.: Doctor of Dental Medicine

D.O.: Doctor of Osteopathy

D.V.M.: Doctor of Veterinary Medicine

Ed.D.: Doctor of Education

J.D.: Juris Doctor

LL.D.: Doctor of Laws

M.D.: Doctor of Medicine

O.D.: Doctor of Optometry

Ph.D.: Doctor of Philosophy

R.N.: Registered Nurse

CNP: Certified Nurse Practitioner

D.C.: Doctor of Chiropractic

DMin: Doctor of Ministry

D.M.A.: Doctor of Musical Arts

PharmD: Doctor of Pharmacy

PsyD: Doctor of Psychology

LCSW: Licensed Clinical Social Worker

LP: Licensed Psychologist

RA: Registered Architect

PE: Professional Engineer

POISON IVY MYTHS

You've probably heard that you can "catch" poison ivy by touching the blisters of people afflicted with the condition. Not true:

The rash associated with poison ivy (as well as with poison oak and poison sumac) is caused by the plant's production of an oily substance known as *urushiol*, which causes an allergic reaction in nearly 90% of humans. It does not, as is commonly believed, spread through the bloodstream. Only the area or areas that have come into direct contact with the oil are affected; the fluid inside the blisters is mostly water and cannot cause the reaction. This myth has probably spread due to the fact that if someone with a rash still has the oil on their skin or clothing, *that* can cause someone else to become infected.

FOOD FOR THOUGHT. Most animals, excluding some higher primates, are immune to urushiol. Several, such as birds, rabbits, and deer, eat the plants that produce it with no ill effects.

CANYONS

Canyons are valleys carved into rock, primarily by moving water. Their sizes can range from dozens to thousands of feet deep and from dozens of feet to miles long. There are two main types: *Plateau canyons* are V-shaped canyons formed by the constant flow of large rivers over plateaus. Their shape is determined by the material being worn away: the harder the rock, the steeper the walls. The Grand Canyon, formed by the Colorado River over many millennia, is an example. *Slot canyons*, on the other hand, are much deeper than they are wide. Many are just a few feet wide at the surface but are more than 100 feet deep. They're commonly formed by processions of flash floods over the years, rather than the constant flow of rivers, and are later aided by wind concentrated in their channels. One of the best known in North America is Antelope Canyon in Arizona. In some spots it's 100 feet deep—and just a few feet wide—with beautifully sculpted and colored sandstone walls that were carved out by water millions of years ago.

A subclassification of slot canyons is a *tension fracture*. These are simply "cracks" in the Earth's surface resulting from earthquakes or volcanic activity, and some are very deep and long. Normally they don't last long; further seismic activity usually fills them with rubble in about a century. An example is the appropriately named Crack in the Ground in the central Oregon lava fields. Just 3 to 10 feet wide at the top, its curving walls extend 70 feet down to the narrow floor—and it stretches for more than 2 miles. Geologists believe that the Crack in the Ground is a rarity, as evidence shows that it opened roughly 1,000 years ago. Adventurous hikers can walk the length of the crack, where on summer days the temperature can reach more than 100°F on the surface—and in the 60s on the canyon floor.

BUNIONS

A *bunion* is the result of a structural defect in the joint between the foot and the big toe. The defect causes the big toe to lean increasingly toward the next toe, and that in turn results in the joint being pushed out away from the foot. The result is a bump on the instep of the foot near the joint...commonly called a bunion. The cause is most often hereditary.

NOTES ON NOTES

✦ Of the 180 or so nations that issue their own currency, the U.S. is the only one whose paper money is all the same size.

✦ Ecuador and El Salvador don't have a national currency (they use American dollars).

✦ Panama has been using the American dollar alongside its *balboa* since 1904, with an exchange rate of 1:2.7.

✦ The Southeast Asian nation of East Timor made the U.S. dollar its currency after gaining independence in 2000.

✦ Paraguay has no coinage, only paper money.

✦ Eight Caribbean nations have used the East Caribbean dollar since 1965. It's pegged to the U.S. dollar 1:1.

✦ Vatican City has its own currency, the Vatican Euro, instituted in 1999. Before that it had the Vatican Lira.

✦ The Isle of Man is a British "Crown Dependency" (see page 15) and has issued its own version of the British pound, the *manx pound*, since the 1600s.

SPIDER FEET

In 2006 researchers in Germany were working with zebra tarantulas to determine how they manage to adhere to vertical surfaces. When one was placed on an inclined glass plate and started to slip, very fine strands of spider silk were emitted from the end of each of the tarantula's legs. Further study found microscopic openings on the spider's feet, through which it could emit silk. It was a phenomenon never before witnessed (or at least never before recorded). Prior to this discovery, spiders were believed to produce silk only in glands in their abdomens and secrete it through spinnerets (see page 250 for more on that). Scientists now postulate that silk production in spiders might have actually begun in their feet for increased traction and later evolved to the many better-known uses, such as web production.

THE 4 MAJOR TYPES OF VERTEBRATE TISSUE

1. Epithelial tissue is characterized by tightly packed cells that form continuous sheets. Epithelial tissue makes up the membranes that line the organs and helps to keep them separate and in position. Examples include the skin, the inside of the mouth, and the lining of the stomach.

2. Connective tissue supports, protects, and "connects" other tissues, and comes in many forms. These include tendons, ligaments, cartilage, bone, and adipose tissue, or fat, which, among other duties, "cushions" internal organs. Surprisingly, blood is also considered a type of connective tissue.

3. Muscle tissue is contractible and contains specialized proteins that allow layers to slide past one another. Those traits allow it to create force and, with that, movement. The group includes *skeletal* muscle, which is attached via tendons to bone; *smooth* (or involuntary) muscle, found in structures such as the stomach, intestines, and blood vessels; and *cardiac* muscle, found only in the heart.

4. Nerve tissue is composed of neurons, which generate and conduct nerve impulses, and neuroglia (or glial cells), which protect and provide nutrients for neurons. They comprise the nervous system and include the brain, the spinal cord, and all the nerves. Their function is to provide a means of communication between different parts of the body.

MOLL FLANDERS...

Daniel Defoe wrote two enduring classics of English literature: *Robinson Crusoe* and *Moll Flanders*. But that's not the latter's actual title. As printed on the title page of the first edition of the book in 1722, the novel's full title is *The Fortunes and Misfortunes of the Famous Moll Flanders, Etc. who was born at Newgate, and during a Life of continu'd Variety for Threescore Years, besides her Childhood, was Twelve Year a Whore, five time a Wife (whereof once to her own Brother), Twelve Year a Thief, Eight Year a Transported Felon in Virginia, at last grew rich, liv'd Honest, and died a Penitent. Written from her own Memorandums.* (It sort of kills the suspense, doesn't it?)

SPAM

As a nickname for mass quantities of junk e-mail, "spam" probably comes from early Internet message board users quoting a 1970 *Monty Python's Flying Circus* sketch where a couple goes into a café and can't get anything on the menu that doesn't have SPAM (the canned meat). They are ultimately silenced by a horde of Vikings who love SPAM and sing a repetitive song about it. Hormel, the manufacturer of SPAM, does not object to the casual use of the term, but requests that anyone referring to junk mail use the lower-case "spam" rather than the trademarked upper-case "SPAM."

8 MASSACRES DEPICTED IN THE BIBLE

1. With the jawbone of a donkey, Samson beats 1,000 men to death. (Judges)

2. Shamgar uses an ox goad (a pointed stick) to kill 600 Philistines. (Judges)

3. A captain of King David kills 300 men with a single spear. (1 Chronicles)

4. Abishai kills another 300 men with a spear. (2 Samuel)

5. For the right to purchase his wife (the price is 200 human foreskins), King David kills 200 Philistines. (1 Samuel)

6. Elijah, with God's help, burns 102 religious leaders to death. (2 Kings)

7. Abimelch kills 69 of his 70 brothers "upon a stone." (Judges)

8. Because 42 children made fun of his baldness, Elisha convinces God to send two bears to kill them. (2 Kings)

MONKEY SEE, MONKEY DON'T

In 2003 Dutch primatologist Frans de Waal and American psychologist Susan Brosnan performed a study to determine if primates had a basic sense of "fairness." They used capuchin monkeys, natives of Central and South America, which are often used in studies due to their highly social nature and intelligence. In the study, two monkeys were given simple tasks to perform and were rewarded upon completion with either grapes or pieces of cucumber. The grapes were considered the better prize, as capuchins favor them. They never knew beforehand which one they would get. When both monkeys received the same reward, there was no problem. But if they each got different rewards for the same tasks, the monkey that got the cucumber would soon stop cooperating, either by refusing to complete a task or refusing to eat the cucumber. In one case, one monkey was given a piece of cucumber after a task, and the other was given a grape after completing no task at all. The first monkey got angry and refused to continue until it was offered grapes again.

De Waal claimed that the study revealed that even lesser primates—not just humans—have a basic understanding of fairness. Not only that, but the cucumber-receiving monkeys had figured out that they were being taken advantage of, and even though it meant going hungry, they'd throw away what they had and hold out until they got a better deal—not unlike workers who form unions and go on strike.

RUMBLE RUMBLE RUMBLE

The term for the growling or rumbling sound your stomach makes: *borborygmus*. It's actually caused by fluid and gas moving in the intestines, not in the stomach. *Borborygmus* is an *onomatopoeic* word, meaning it was formed by imitating what it attempts to describe.

THE LIFE OF OYSTERS

Some oysters are male, some are female, and some are *protandric* —meaning that they begin life as male and later in their lives become female. During the first year of its life, a young oyster releases sperm into the water, which fertilizes eggs released by older oysters. For the next two or three years, it releases eggs, which are in turn fertilized by younger oysters.

✦ Once fertilized, the larvae, or *spat*, feed at the surface of the ocean for about three weeks and then attach to a hard surface, such as a rock, a pier pylon, or another oyster. Their average life span is just 5 to 10 years in the wild; domestic freshwater oysters have been known to live as long as 80 years.

4 UNUSUAL UNITS OF MEASURE

British thermal unit (Btu). The amount of heat energy needed to raise the temperature of one pound of water at sea level (or equivalent atmospheric pressure) one degree Fahrenheit—specifically, from 60° to 61°F. Btus are used in air conditioning, refrigeration, heating, and cooling.

Ell. 1¼ yards of cloth. (A bolt is 40 yards of cloth, which means that an ell is ¹⁄₃₂ of a bolt.)

Chain or Gunter's Chain. A unit of measure used by surveyors: One chain is 20 meters, or 66 feet long, and is divided into 100 links. The chain isn't used much in surveying anymore, but another unit of measure based on it is still in wide use—the acre, which is equal to 10 square chains or 100,000 square links. (There are 640 acres in a square mile.)

Hogshead (hhd). Two barrels of wine. Two hogsheads are known as a pipe.

WEASEL WORDS

Weasel words are defined as words in writing or speech that purport to seem straightforward and truthful while actually being deliberately misleading. The term first appeared in New York lawyer Stewart Chaplin's short story "Stained Glass Political Platform," published in *The Century Magazine* in 1900. "Why, weasel words are words," Chaplin wrote, "that suck the life out of the words next to them, just as a weasel sucks the egg and leaves the shell." Modern examples include well-known phrases like "downsizing" or "right-sizing," euphemisms for firing employees, and "Some people say..." followed by outrageous statements falsely attributed to political opponents.

COUNTRIES THAT NO LONGER EXIST

Austria-Hungary. Now Austria and Hungary, but the 1867–1918 empire (broken up during World War I) also included parts of what are now the Czech Republic, Poland, Italy, Romania, and Serbia.

Bengal. A kingdom from the 6th century C.E. to the late 18th century, it's now split between India and Bangladesh.

Catalonia. Now a part of Spain, it was independent from 1932 to 1934 and 1936 to 1939.

Champa. An independent kingdom from the 2nd century to the 15th century, it's now part of Vietnam.

Corsica. Once an independent island nation, it's now part of France.

Gran Colombia. The large South American nation that included what's now Colombia, Panama, Venezuela, and Ecuador from 1822 to 1830, fractured into separate states in 1830 after Venezuela and Ecuador seceded.

Hawaii. Inhabited since 300 C.E., the islands were united under King Kamehameha in 1810, and annexed by the United States in 1898. Hawaii became a state in 1959.

Sikkim. An independent monarchy from the 17th century to 1975, this region near Tibet is now part of India.

Tanganyika and Zanzibar. These two African countries merged in 1964 to become Tanzania.

Tibet. It was established as a kingdom in the 7th century but was taken over by China in 1951.

United Arab Republic. Despite not bordering each other, from 1958 to 1961 Syria and Egypt comprised this singular entity. Syria left the alliance in 1961, but Egypt called itself the United Arab Republic for another decade.

Vermont. During the American Revolution, Vermont seceded from the British Empire. It remained an independent republic from 1777 to 1791, when it became the 14th state in the Union.

21ST-CENTURY ANIMALS

It's pretty amazing to think that, even though humans have vehicles driving around on Mars, there are still new species of animals being discovered regularly right here on Earth.

Glass tulips. Between 2002 and 2005, researchers from New Zealand's National Institute of Water and Atmospheric Research discovered hundreds of previously unknown creatures deep in the ocean off Antarctica. One of them looked like blown-glass tulips growing on the seafloor—slender, translucent tubes rising to a height of about three feet, topped by bulb-shaped "heads" with openings at the top. They were a new species of *tunicates*, often called "sea squirts." These primitive creatures are actually born as free-swimming tadpolelike larvae. Early in their lives, glass tulips fix themselves to the seafloor, lose their tails, and become completely immobile, surviving on organisms such as the plankton that they "catch" by filtering water through their sievelike bodies.

Monster cockroaches. Biologists searching through caves in Borneo jungles discovered several new insect species in 2004. One was a cockroach more than four inches long. That makes it the largest (and scariest) cockroach species on Earth.

New macaques. Macaques are a genus of monkey found from Africa to Japan, and a new species of the type hadn't been discovered since 1903. In 2004 that changed when a stocky brown-furred macaque with a short tail—something no other macaques have—was discovered in a remote Himalayan region of northeast India. They were extremely shy and unknown to the scientific world—but the locals knew of their existence, calling them *mun zala*, or "deep-forest monkeys."

Cosmetic bacteria. Japanese scientists discovered a species of bacteria...that can live in hair spray. Genetic testing showed that it was an entirely new species (and one that may be infectious to humans). They named it *Microbacterium hatanonis* in honor of microbacterium expert Dr. Kazunori Hatano.

Crawling fish. A species of fist-sized, fleshy, tan-and-peach-colored fish—that would rather crawl in rocky underwater crevices than swim—was discovered in the sea near Indonesia's Ambon Island in 2008. Among its many peculiarities is a flattened face and eyes that appear to see forward—something never before seen in fish. It's being called the "frogfish" for now, and fish experts believe DNA study will reveal it to be an entirely new family of fish, something discovered only five times in the last 50 years.

FATHER'S DAY

In 1909 Sonora Smart Dodd, a housewife in Spokane, Washington, was in her local church on Mother's Day, listening to a sermon about mothers. But all that Dodd could think about was her father, William Jackson Smart, who was forced to raise six children alone after Dodd's mother died. Dodd wanted to do something to let her father know that he—and the rest of the world's fathers—were just as selfless and loving as mothers. She lobbied local religious leaders and a year later, church leaders around Spokane held the first Father's Day celebration. (It took place in June because her father was born in that month.) A National Father's Day Committee was formed in 1926, and Congress recognized Father's Day as a holiday in 1956. But it wasn't until 1972 that President Richard Nixon made it an officially observed holiday celebrated on the third Sunday of June.

MONSTER SNOWFLAKES

According to *Guinness World Records*, the largest snowflakes ever recorded fell on January 28, 1887, in Fort Keogh in Montana. One was measured at 8 inches thick and 15 inches in diameter.

THE INFIELD FLY RULE

This baseball rule has an undeserved reputation for being hard to understand. But it's actually very sensible and straightforward, and should make sense to anyone who already knows the basic rules of the game, especially how outs and double plays are made. Simply put, the rule prevents fielders from dropping easy fly balls in order to facilitate double or triple plays. It only applies when there are fewer than two outs with runners on first and second base, or fewer than two outs with the bases loaded. In these situations, according to the rules of Major League Baseball, a batter is automatically out if he hits "a fair fly ball (not including a line drive nor an attempted bunt) which can be caught by an infielder with ordinary effort."

Before the rule was put in place in 1895, easy infield pop-ups left baserunners with no options. If they took off for the next base, the infielder could catch the ball for one out, and then throw it back to the recently vacated base for a double play. If the runners stayed put, the infielder could intentionally miss the pop fly—turning it into a ground ball and setting up the standard, force-out type of double (or even triple) play.

Now, when a batter hits a pop-up to the infield and the umpire calls the infield fly rule, it doesn't matter whether the infielder catches the ball or not—the runners must remain on their bases, and the batter is automatically out.

CHAPTER 6

15 BROKEN BONES

There are many classifications of broken bones. Fifteen of them:

Closed fracture: A fracture with no broken skin

Comminuted bone fracture: A fracture in which two or more fragments break completely off the bone

Butterfly fracture: A fracture in which the bone breaks in such a way that the fracture site is vaguely butterfly-shaped. This is also a comminuted fracture—and the fragments that come off the bone are also butterfly-shaped.

Complex fracture: When a broken bone severely damages surrounding soft tissue

Compression fracture: Generally entailing vertebrae fractured by compressing each other as the result of a fall

Double fracture: Multiple bone breaks or multiple breaks of one bone

Fissure fracture: Also known as a "hairline fracture," this is a crack but not a break of a bone, with no or little damage to the surrounding tissue

Fracture-dislocation: When a bone breaks in combination with the joint nearest it becoming dislocated

Fragmented fracture: Many broken bones with many bone fragments in the patient's body

Greenstick fracture: Only one side of the bone breaks, commonly with bones that are "bent," with the break on the outside of the bend

Impacted fracture: When the edges of broken bones become wedged together

Oblique fracture: A break not perpendicular to the length of bone, but at an angle of at least 45 degrees

Spiral fracture: Usually caused by a twisting motion, which results in a bone breaking in a spiral up its length

Transverse fracture: The break is straight across the affected bone

Compound bone fracture: When fragments of broken bone penetrate through the skin...as witnessed by the millions who saw the outline of Washington Redskins quarterback Joe Theisman's tibia and fibula (lower leg bones) through his football pants after he was sacked during a 1985 *Monday Night Football* game. (Theisman never played again.)

AN ANIMAL ODDITY

In the early 1800s, celebrated French naturalist Georges Cuvier was studying a female argonaut, a small kind of octopus, when he discovered a strange parasitic worm inside its abdomen. He named the worm *hectocotylus*, "one hundred cups," for the many suckerlike structures on it. It wasn't until the 20th century that biologists discovered that it was the male argonaut's penis, and it was *supposed* to be inside the female. Nearly all cephalopods—the class of marine animals that includes octopuses, squids, and cuttlefish—have similar devices. They are actually a specialized type of tentacle that detaches once the job is complete. With the argonaut and similar species, it can actually break off *before* contact with the female...and swim over to her to do its business.

CAN A CELL PHONE CAUSE A PLANE CRASH?

Probably not, but nobody really knows for sure. Cell phones were first banned on airplanes in 1991, not for safety reasons but for terrestrial communications reasons. When you make a call from a cell phone on the ground, a radio signal is created that travels to a cell antenna. Because radio waves travel in straight lines, those transmissions are blocked by buildings, hills, mountains, and so forth—so you can't contact several antennas at once. When you're in a plane, however, the signal can travel downward from the plane to many antennas simultaneously. Cell networks aren't built to handle such traffic; it could overload the system. That's never been proven, but in 1991 the Federal Communications Commission decided that it was enough reason to institute the ban. The Federal Aviation Administration believes cell phones *might* interfere with communications and navigation systems on planes. But they don't know that for sure either, and *they* don't have a ban of cell phones on planes. They simply comply with the FCC's ban.

FOOD FOR THOUGHT. So if cell phones are potentially dangerous, why are airlines allowed to install them on planes (and charge you a lot of money to use them)? Because the signals are transmitted from a special antenna on the bottom of the plane, and are sent to special antennas on the ground. (And you *can* use cell phones on a plane…if you own the plane. They're perfectly legal on private aircraft.)

THE BIG CHEESE

All cheese is born the same way: Fresh milk, usually from cows, sheep, or goats, is heated up and a curdling agent is added to it. That causes the milk to separate into a thin liquid called *whey* and white, lumpy *curds*. The curds are what become the cheese. They go through a huge variety of processes that turn them into all the different kinds of cheeses. Some are pressed, which squeezes out the whey, and then aged for anywhere from weeks to years. The natural color of cheese ranges from white to deep yellow, which is a product of fats, the color deepening with age. Other colors come from additives; the vegetable dye annato is a common one, and gives cheddar and many other cheeses their "cheddary" color. The cheese families:

Fresh unripened cheese. These are made by lightly pressing and aging for a very short time, usually just a week or so, giving them a mild flavor and a soft, creamy texture. Examples: cream cheese, Neufchatel, goat cheese, and Cabrette.

Feta. This is a fresh unripened cheese, but it's *brined*—soaked in salt water—for months. That's how feta gets its flaky texture and salty taste. (Real feta is always made from sheep's and/or goat's milk.)

Cottage cheese. This is also a fresh unripened cheese, but it deserves its own mention. The white lumps are the curds that formed in the original cheese-making process, with little or nothing done to them after that. The liquid is simply the whey, making cottage cheese the simplest of the cheeses. (You can actually make it at home—or in a *cottage*—in just hours.)

Bloomy rind cheese. Also called "soft-ripened," these are cheeses with white "skins"—naturally occurring mold that protects the *pate*, the inside of the cheese, which allows it to maintain a creamy, soft texture. They're aged from between one month to a year. Examples: Brie and Camembert.

Washed rind cheese. These are related to bloomy rind cheeses, but their surfaces are washed repeatedly during aging with ingredients such as beer, wine, brandy, and brine, which adds flavor and causes bacteria to grow on the surface. This gives rinds their distinctive colors, from bright orange to brown—as well as their distinctive pungent odor. Examples: Limburger, Stinking Bishop, and Muenster.

Uncooked/pressed. This is the largest family. They're made by repeated pressings, which gets rid of most of the water, and then aged from between three months to five years. Examples: Gouda, cheddar, Havarti, and jack.

Cooked/pressed. The curds are cut into tiny pieces (grain-sized), soaked in hot water or dry-heated, and pressed into molds. Like the uncooked variety, they're aged for months or years. Examples: Parmesan, Gruyère, and Raclette.

Stretched curd cheese. This is a variety of cooked/pressed, but in this case the curds are cut and molded together several times, then soaked in heated whey, bringing it to a taffylike texture. It's then stretched and kneaded until soft, giving it a "stringy" texture. Examples: mozzarella and provolone.

Blue cheese. How does it get its blue/green veins? The same way it gets its taste: from regular injections—with needles—of penicillium mold. It's then aged for a few months, normally in cool caves. Examples: Roquefort, Gorgonzola, and Stilton.

Processed cheese. This isn't cheese in the traditional sense. It's made with scraps from cheese factories and can also include dyes, gums, emulsifiers, and other ingredients. The most famous kinds are American cheese and Cheez Whiz. And the French have a kind called *La Vache Qui Rit:* "The Laughing Cow."

FOOD FOR THOUGHT. The curdling agent most often used is *rennet*, a digestive enzyme taken from calf intestines, though more and more companies are making vegetable rennet for vegetarians (it's not vegetable-based—it's microbe-based). Other curdlers include vinegar, lemon juice, wine, and buttermilk. Cheese can be made from almost any milk, and is made from the milk of llamas, yaks, bison, reindeer, and moose (on a farm in Sweden; it's $500 a pound).

OLDEST KNOWN MUSICAL INSTRUMENTS

In 1999 researchers excavating a site in the Yellow River Basin in Henan Province in China discovered six complete flutes made from the *ulnae*, or wing bones, of red-crowned cranes. Carbon-14 dating proved them to be between 7,000 and 9,000 years old. They have from five to eight finger holes, their patterns closely corresponding to the Western diatonic ("do re mi") scale, something that musicologists believed wasn't developed until several thousand years later (and in the West). Best of all: The flutes are still playable. They now reside in the Henan Museum in Zhengzhou and are the oldest confirmed musical instruments in the world.

OLDEST (UNCONFIRMED) MUSICAL INSTRUMENT

Humanity's first music maker may have been a hollow section of a bear's femur with four small puncture holes. It was found in a cave in Slovenia in 1998. (The bone is broken and about five inches long.) According to some musicologists, the fact that the holes are equally sized, in a line, and roughly where they'd have to be to play a diatonic scale, prove that it's a man-made, 45,000-year-old flute. That would make it the oldest known instrument by more than 30,000 years. Some archaeologists, however, have a different theory: The holes were put there by the teeth of a carnivore, likely a wolf, after the bear died.

SURVIVING BEING TIED UP

Although this rarely occurs outside the movies, it does happen. If it happens to you, here's a magician's trick (Houdini used it): While your captor is tying you up, make yourself as large as possible by inhaling and pushing your chest out. Flex any muscles that are being tied up, but do it as subtly as possible so as not to raise suspicion. When your captor leaves, relax. You'll get at least a half an inch of slack in the ropes, which may be enough to wiggle your way to freedom.

3 PHRASE ORIGINS

Donnybrook. In the year 1204 C.E., the village of Donnybrook in County Dublin, Ireland, was granted a license to hold an annual fair. It grew to become a huge, carnival-like event, complete with fortune-tellers, musicians, jugglers, dancers, food, and lots of drink. The drinking led to the regular occurrence of fights, and the Donnybrook Fair became a notoriously violent event known all over Europe. In 1855 the city of Dublin closed it down, and all that lives on is the name "donnybrook," which has become synonymous with any type of brawl or noisy uproar.

Fishwife. This is defined as a woman who sells fish, or simply a lower class, vulgar woman. It goes back to the 16th-century women who sold fish at Billingsgate Fish Market, the largest in London. They were notorious for various reasons: They smelled bad (no surprise; they sold fish all day), drank, and swore like sailors. One of the earliest references called them "oyster-wives"; others called them "Billingsgate wives"; but "fishwives" is the one best known.

Keep your nose to the grindstone. Beginning in the early 1400s, grains such as wheat, corn, and barley were ground into flour between two counter-rotating grindstones. If the stones were set too close together, heat from friction would scorch the flour and ruin it. To keep this from occurring, the miller frequently sniffed—or kept his nose to—the grindstones. The phrase was first used sometime in the 16th century.

CHOOSE YOUR VICE

George McGovern was the Democratic nominee for president in 1972, and on the third day of the four-day Democratic National Convention, he still hadn't selected a vice-presidential running mate.

First choice: Edmund Muskie, Maine senator (and one of McGovern's opponents in the primaries). He declined.

Second choice: Hubert Humphrey, Minnesota senator and 1968 presidential nominee. He declined.

Third choice: Massachusetts senator Ted Kennedy. He declined, but suggested Thomas Eagleton, a first-term Missouri senator who had been actively campaigning in the media for the VP slot. McGovern dismissed the idea—he felt he didn't know Eagleton well enough.

Fourth choice: Sargent Shriver, Kennedy's brother-in-law and director of the Peace Corps. One problem: Shriver was in the Soviet Union and couldn't be reached, so he was eliminated as a possibility.

Fifth choice: McGovern then asked Minnesota senator Walter Mondale. Like Kennedy, Mondale declined and also recommended Eagleton.

Sixth choice: Connecticut senator Abe Ribicoff. Still unsure about Eagleton, McGovern asked Ribicoff, who would have been the first Jewish candidate on a major party ticket, but doing so would mean he'd have to cancel his honeymoon. He declined.

Seventh choice: Kevin White, the mayor of Boston. McGovern's campaign manager Gary Hart suggested White, who actually accepted the position. But Ken Galbraith, a McGovern crony and leader of the Massachusetts convention delegation, threatened a walkout because White had publicly endorsed Muskie in the primaries, so McGovern withdrew the offer.

Eighth choice: Hearing a news report that CBS news anchor Walter Cronkite was "the most trusted man in America," McGovern briefly, but somewhat jokingly, considered him. (McGovern told Cronkite about it years later—Cronkite said he would have accepted.)

Ninth choice: He asked Wisconsin senator Gaylord Nelson. He didn't want the job, and recommended Eagleton.

Tenth choice: McGovern gave up and offered the job to Thomas Eagleton. At that point, there was no time to vet him, but Eagleton assured McGovern that there was nothing in his past that he would find troublesome or embarrassing.

Bad choice: Reports quickly surfaced that Eagleton had once undergone shock treatments for depression. Eighteen days after the selection, McGovern replaced Eagleton with one of his earlier picks, Sargent Shriver. The pick and subsequent replacement of Eagleton may have made McGovern look incompetent to voters. He lost the popular vote to Richard Nixon, 61% to 38%—one of the biggest landslides in history.

SIMPLE GENIUS:
THE BIRDMAN OF MONTANA

In 1973 Montana insurance agent and longtime conservationist Art Aylesworth decided to do something about his state's mountain bluebirds. He remembered how common they were when he was a kid...and how rare they had become over the intervening decades. So he built five nesting boxes and put them up near his home in the town of Ronan. The next year he counted five *fledglings*—birds successfully grown to flight ability. Aylesworth then started recruiting people to do the same, and convinced local lumberyards to donate scrap wood for the nesting boxes. His simple idea grew into a movement. Aylesworth died in 1999 at the age of 72, but his Mountain Bluebird Trails project is still going strong, with 600 volunteers—and nearly 340,000 fledgling bluebirds have hatched in the more than 35,000 bluebird houses the project has given away since 1974.

SUPERWORDS

Merriam-Webster's Collegiate Dictionary contains more than 200 legitimate words that begin with the prefix "super-" (which we think is supercool). They include:

superaccurate	superhot	supersecret
superbitch	superjock	supersinger
supercheap	supermacho	supersmooth
superclass	supermassive	superspecial
supercolossal	supermind	superspy
supercop	supernutrition	superstud
supercute	superorgasm	supersurgeon
superfan	superperson	superterrific
superfarm	superpolite	superthin
superfast	superrace	superweapon
supergood	superromantic	superwife

IS GLASS A LIQUID?

You may have heard that old glass windows are thicker at the bottom because glass is a liquid and it actually flows downward slowly over long periods of time. That's not true. Any deformities seen in old windows are simply the results of old window-making processes. Unless it's melted into molten glass or vaporized into gases, glass is a solid.

INSTANT SHAKESPEARE:
MUCH ADO ABOUT NOTHING

Every instant genius should be familiar with the plays of William Shakespeare. There are 37 in all; in this book we've provided the synopses of four. They represent the broad spectrum of plays written by the man whom many scholars consider the finest writer in the history of the English language.

Much Ado About Nothing (1598) is Shakespeare's signature comedy—in that it involves mistaken identity, the plot hinges on an intricate web of lies, and it all ends happily with a wedding.

The plot: A nobleman named Leonato lives in the Italian village of Messina with his daughter, Hero, his niece, Beatrice, and his brother, Antonio. At the beginning of the play, Leonato welcomes some soldiers returning home from a war. They are the prince Don Pedro, the nobleman Claudio, the comedian Benedick, and the cynical Don John. Claudio meets Hero and the two fall in love and decide to marry.

Don John, just for the heck of it, decides to try and break up the romance. First, he gets his friend Borachio to sleep with Hero's servant, Margaret. Then, Don John brings Claudio to watch them sleeping together (through a window, from the street), and tells him that it's Hero sleeping with Borachio. On their wedding day, Claudio confronts Hero about the alleged affair and leaves her at the altar. Knowing the truth and wanting to make Claudio feel bad, Leonato spreads the false news that being left at the altar made Hero die suddenly of shock. A few night watchmen overhear Borachio talking about his involvement in Don John's scheme, leading the police to arrest Borachio.

When the truth—that Hero was innocent—gets to Claudio,

he falls deeper into mourning and guilt. Leonato convinces him to tell the entire town of Messina that Hero was innocent and that he is sorry for what he did. As a show of good faith, Leonato arranges a marriage between Claudio and his "niece," who looks a lot like Hero. It is, of course, actually Hero—and the lovers are reunited.

Memorable line: "Some Cupid kills with arrows, some with traps." (Hero, Act III, Scene 1)

TYPES OF U.S. PATENTS

There are three main types of patents issued in the United States. Here they are, with their official definitions from the U.S. Patent and Trademark Office.

✦ **Utility Patent.** "Issued for the invention of a new and useful process, machine, manufacture, or composition of matter, or a new and useful improvement thereof, it generally permits its owner to exclude others from making, using, or selling the invention for a period of up to 20 years from the date of patent application filing, subject to the payment of maintenance fees. Approximately 90% of the patent documents issued by the PTO in recent years have been utility patents, also referred to as 'patents for invention.'"

✦ **Design Patent.** "Issued for a new, original, and ornamental design for an article of manufacture, it permits its owner to exclude others from making, using, or selling the design for a period of 14 years from the date of patent grant. Design patents are not subject to the payment of maintenance fees."

✦ **Plant Patent.** "Issued for a new and distinct, invented or discovered, asexually reproduced plant including cultivated sports, mutants, hybrids, and newly found seedlings, other than a tuber propagated plant or a plant found in an uncultivated state, it permits its owner to exclude others from making, using, or selling the plant for a period of up to 20 years from the date of patent application filing. Plant patents are not subject to the payment of maintenance fees."

THE BRAZIL NUT EFFECT

Fill a bucket with several different sizes of granular material, such as sand grains, salt crystals, BBs, marbles, and golf balls, and put a lid on it. Now shake it vigorously for ten seconds. Open it up and you will find that the smallest particles—the sand grains in this case—have fallen to the bottom of the bucket, and the largest—the golf balls—are sitting at the top. Shake it long enough and all the particles will order themselves from smallest to largest from the bottom to the top. Even if you start with all the golf balls at the bottom, they'll still end up at the top.

This is known as the "Brazil nut effect," named for the large nuts commonly found at the top of a jar of mixed nuts, and it has been studied by scientists for decades…and they still don't quite understand it. In the above experiment, golf balls were by far the heaviest items in the bucket, so you'd think they'd be the ones to fall to the bottom. But not only do they not fall, they rise. A long-held theory as to why this happens is that larger-grained items have larger spaces between them, allowing the smaller grains to fall past them and fill the bottom of the container. Shaking the container allows the smaller particles to take full advantage of this and fill up spaces under the larger ones while they are being shaken.

Experiments done in the early 1990s revealed that there was more to it than that: Shaking causes a *convection flow* to occur in the container—all the particles rise up through a channel in the center of the container, then fall at the edges. The larger particles, it turns out, travel easily up the center channel, but are too large to fit down the narrow channels at the sides—and thus become stuck at the top. The experiments also showed that the larger particles actually rose in the center channel faster than the smaller ones. Nobody knows why.

REGIONAL DRINKS

Everyone knows about Mexican tequila and Scotch whisky. Here are a few other traditional drinks that aren't so well known:

Akvavit (AH-qua-veet) is a traditional Scandinavian drink distilled from potatoes or grain. It can be clear like vodka or colored, depending on the variety; has an alcohol content of 40%; and is flavored with caraway seed, anise, dill, and a variety of other herbs. Its origins go back to at least 1531, when a Danish lord sent a sample to the archbishop of Norway with an accompanying note that said the package contained "some water which is called Aqua Vite and is a help for all sort of sickness which a man can have both internally and externally." Akvavit is served cold, straight, and in a small glass. It is meant to be imbibed with food and is usually the drink of choice for big celebrations. (It's said to go well with the traditional Icelandic dish of hákarl—putrefied shark.)

Metaxa is a Greek beverage invented by a silk trader named Spyros Metaxas in 1888. It's often classified as a brandy, but it's actually a unique mix of double-distilled brandies and aged muscatel wines, along with a secret recipe of herbs, all of which is allowed to "marry" in oak casks for at least three years. Metaxa is 80 proof (40% alcohol), and comes in Three Star, Five Star, and Seven Star versions, the number of stars equaling the number of years aged. Longer-aged varieties exist—up to 30 years in "Grand Reserve"—but are much harder to find. It's served in many different ways, either straight or with mixers (often in coffee drinks).

Chang, also spelled *chhaang* and often pronounced "chong," is a traditional drink made throughout the Himalayas—in Tibet, Nepal, Bhutan, and northern India. Although it's sometimes called a beer, it doesn't taste like Western beer at all. Chang is made from grain—millet, barley, and sometimes rice—that is cooked and cooled. Yeast is then added and the mixture is allowed to ferment for several days. (Honey or sugar is sometimes added.) The cloudy, milky drink is served at room temperature. It has a low alcohol content, usually around 5%.

Feni is produced in small, traditional pot distilleries in the state of Goa in southern India. It's made by double- or triple-distilling either palm sap or the juice of the cashew fruit. (Cashew trees have a yellow-orange "apple.") Feni is about 40% alcohol, and is drunk straight with a slice of lime, or mixed with cola or lemonade. The cashew version (the preferred variety) is said to have a slightly fruity flavor.

Insamju has been a traditional drink in the Kumsan region of South Korea for 2,000 years. Kumsan is called the "Ginseng Capital of the World," and insamju is a "ginseng wine." It's made traditionally by fermenting a mix of ginseng, rice, pine leaves, mugwort, and water, which gives it its brownish-yellow, almost beerlike color and its unique, earthy flavor.

THE DOPPLER EFFECT

In 1842 Austrian physicist Christian Doppler developed a theory concerning *binary stars*—two stars that orbit each other. Astronomers had been trying to figure out why stars in a binary system seemed to change color: One would be blue and the other red, and then they'd switch. Doppler theorized that it was because of two things: 1) The stars were moving alternatively away from and toward us, and 2) because light moves as a wave. The star moving toward us appears blue, and the one moving away appears red.

✦ To help you understand it, try this thought experiment: You're standing still, and someone standing 20 feet away from you starts throwing tennis balls at you, one every second. Now the person runs toward you very fast while still throwing one ball per second at you. The frequency at which the balls hit you seems to increase, even though the thrower is still throwing one ball a second. Reverse it: The person runs very quickly away from you while throwing one ball a second toward you. The balls now seem to hit you less frequently.

✦ This is basically what's happening with light. The light waves from a star moving toward Earth appear to be of a higher frequency than light waves from one that is moving away. We perceive high-frequency light as the color blue, so the star appears blue. Light from a star moving away from us appears as low-frequency light—which we perceive as red.

✦ It's the same with sound: You're on a sidewalk and an ambulance comes down the street, siren blaring. As it approaches, the siren seems to get higher and higher in pitch, and then lowers in pitch after it passes you. That's the Doppler Effect, too. As the ambulance is approaching you, the sound waves emanating from it are getting bunched up, appearing as higher and higher frequencies—which you hear as a higher pitch. As it passes and begins moving away from you, the waves become more spread out and thus have a lower frequency—which you hear as a lower pitch.

BAMBOOZLING BEAR

Giant pandas live exclusively in bamboo-rich forests in central and western China. Even though—anatomically-speaking—they are carnivores like other bears, pandas eat almost nothing but bamboo, which makes acquiring enough nourishment to survive difficult. Herbivores—such as deer, cattle, and sheep—have highly specialized digestive systems that allow them to break down and absorb nutrients from vegetation. Carnivores don't—their digestive tracts are short, because meat is easy to digest. So how do pandas do it? Partly by having huge molars and extremely powerful jaw muscles (this is the reason their heads are so round). That allows them to pulverize bamboo culms, stems, and leaves, making them that much easier to digest. But it only helps so much, and most of the bamboo pandas eat goes undigested…and exits their bodies as bam*poop*.

That's why they have to eat for 10 to 16 hours and ingest from 20 to 40 pounds of bamboo per day. Also: Pandas don't hibernate, so they don't need to build up as much extra fat as most bears.

FOOD FOR THOUGHT. About 1% of a panda's diet is made up of fruit, insects, fish, small mammals, and even carrion.

HOUSEHOLD GENIUS

To keep dairy products fresher longer, store them at the back of the refrigerator, where it's coolest.

WHAT LOVING'S ALL ABOUT

In June 1958, African American Mildred Jeter, 19, and caucasian Richard Loving, 25, of Central Point, Virginia, were married in Washington, D.C. A few weeks later, they were arrested...for getting married. They had violated Virginia's Racial Integrity Act of 1924, a law prohibiting racially mixed marriages (or, more specifically, interracial marriages involving a white person; the law didn't refer to marriages between other races). They pled guilty to the charges and were each sentenced to one year in prison, but avoided jail time by agreeing to leave Virginia—the only home either had ever known—for at least 25 years. They moved to D.C., hired a lawyer, and in 1963 filed a motion with the State of Virginia to have their convictions vacated. In 1967 the case made it to the U.S. Supreme Court and, in one of the most important civil rights cases in U.S. history, *Loving v. Virginia*, the justices unanimously found Virginia's law unconstitutional. That law—along with similar laws in 17 other states—was immediately rendered powerless. Result: The Lovings were the last couple in U.S. history arrested for breaking such laws.

Richard Loving died in 1975 at the age of 41; Mildred Loving died in 2008 at the age of 68. Before her death, in 2007, the 40th anniversary of the decision, Mildred wrote a letter that was carried in newspapers around the world. The last paragraph:

"I am still not a political person, but I am proud that Richard's and my name is on a court case that can help reinforce the love, the commitment, the fairness, and the family that so many people, black or white, young or old, gay or straight, seek in life. I support the freedom to marry for all. That's what Loving, and loving, are all about."

21 POSTAL SVCE. ABBRS.

You know that "street" is abbreviated as "St.," and "Blvd." is short for "boulevard." Here's how some other street *designators*, or suffixes, should be abbreviated in postal addresses:

Alley: Aly.	**Grove:** Grv.	**Pines:** Pnes.
Bluff: Blf.	**Harbor:** Hbr.	**River:** Riv.
Cove: Cv.	**Island:** Is.	**Shoals:** Shls.
Creek: Crk.	**Lake:** Lk.	**Spring:** Spg.
Dam: Dm.	**Meadows:** Mdws.	**Summit:** Smt.
Field: Fld.	**Neck:** Nck.	**Trail:** Trl.
Forest: Frst.	**Orchard:** Orch.	**Viaduct:** Via.

GEGENSCHEIN

Have you ever looked up into clear, dark night sky—and seen a large patch of light? That's a phenomenon known as *Gegenschein* (GAY-guhn-shine)—German for "counter-glow." It's always exactly 180° opposite the Sun, and appears as a very faintly glowing, oval-shaped light. Its cause is a light phenomenon called *back-scattering*, the scattering in this case involving reflections of sunlight off millimeter-sized dust particles that orbit the sun.

✦ A similar phenomenon known as *zodiacal light* appears as a roughly triangular-shaped glow, but only near the horizon, and not opposite the sun.

CHAPTER 7

7 NEUTRAL NATIONS

Over the last two centuries, several countries have declared
themselves neutral; they choose not to enter into any foreign war
on any side, hoping thereby to avoid invasion, and to provide a
"neutral" location where conflicts might be avoided or halted
by diplomatic means. The following seven neutral nations are
members of the United Nations, all but one have standing armies
for defense, and most participate in United Nations peacekeep-
ing missions.

Austria: Neutral since 1955, Austrian law states "in all future
times Austria will not join any military alliances and will not
permit the establishment of any foreign military bases on her
territory."

Costa Rica: Neutral since 1949, the year it became the first modern nation to abolish its army. Members of the small "civil guard" are bound to form a national army in case of invasion.

Finland: Sharing a border with the USSR put it in a precarious position as World War II ended, and it declared neutrality shortly thereafter to alleviate Cold War tensions.

Ireland: Neutral since gaining its independence in 1922, Ireland possesses a small army and, unlike most neutral nations, allows foreign military aircraft to fly over the country and refuel at some Irish airports.

Sweden: Sweden hasn't fought a war since the Napoleonic War of 1814, making it the longest-running neutral nation on Earth.

Switzerland: Neutral since 1815.

Turkmenistan: It's been neutral since it gained independence from Russia in 1992. It does have a standing army, but doesn't participate in UN missions.

CAROLINA FLYTRAP

The Venus flytrap, infamous as the plant that acts like an animal, trapping and "eating" insects and spiders, is native only to a tiny geographic region about 200 miles in diameter around Wilmington, North Carolina. One of the reasons that they developed their singular animal-like ability: They grow in nutrient-poor soils, especially in bogs that lack sufficient supplies of nutrients like nitrogen. They get those missing nutrients from the bugs they eat.

✦ A small patch of flytraps has been found in northern Florida. It is speculated that they ended up there via birds that ate the seeds in North Carolina and expelled them in their dung in Florida.

✦ However, some people speculate that these odd plants live only in this isolated area because they were brought here by meteors...and are actually alien life-forms. The theory is easily dispatched by the fact that there are more than 600 species of carnivorous plants found in similar, nutrient-deficient soils around the world. (But it's still a fun theory.)

HOW CAFFEINE KEEPS YOU AWAKE

Not all of the physiological reasons we become drowsy after being awake for several hours are understood—but some are. One involves *adenosine* (uh-DEN-uh-seen). When you're awake, adenosine molecules are being produced in your brain. There, they bond with specialized receptors on neurons (brain cells) and basically shut the neurons off. The longer you're awake, the more neurons are shut off, and the result is that you feel sleepy. When you're asleep, production of adenosine drops, so after sleeping for some time you feel alert again.

It just so happens that caffeine molecules are very similar to adenosine molecules. When we consume caffeine, those molecules find their way to the brain and attach to neurons just like adenosine does—except that they don't have the effect of making us drowsy. Take in enough caffeine, and the molecules "crowd out" the adenosine—and we feel more awake.

ENTOPTIC PHENOMENA

Have you ever rubbed your eyes and seen lights and colors? What you were experiencing was an *entoptic phenomenon*, a visual effect whose source is inside rather than outside the eye. (That's not the same as an optical illusion, the source of which is the brain rather than the eye.) A few types:

Phosphenes. This is when you see "light" that is not actually light. Many things can cause it, including pressure on the eyes, which stimulates the cells of your retinas, causing "light" signals to be sent to your brain's visual center. Another phosphene event is when you "see stars" when you stand up too fast or get hit in the head. It's believed to be caused by the retinas, the light-sensitive part of the eyes, responding to chemicals produced by the sudden movement or blow.

Floaters. These are the odd shapes and "little creatures" that sometimes appear to be inside your eyes. They actually are. They're leftover cells from veins that supplied blood to your eyes as they were forming when you were a fetus. Having completed their jobs, they broke down...and will stay trapped in the vitreous fluid in your eyes forever. (Well, until you die.)

Blue field entoptic phenomenon. BFEP is common but is difficult for some people to see. It appears as tiny dots of light moving in squiggly lines when you look into blue light, such as the sky. What's happening? White blood cells are moving inside tiny capillaries in the front of your retina. Red blood cells, which far outnumber the white ones, absorb blue light and would show up as dark lines if our brains didn't cancel them out so we can see. White blood cells don't absorb blue light very well—the result being that they show up as bright white dots as they move across your retina. Also, BFEP doesn't occur in the center of your field of vision. Why? Because you don't have any capillaries there.

PROBLEM 14

In 1893 a Russian Egyptologist purchased a scroll found in a tomb near the Nile River city of Luxor. Dated to approximately 1850 B.C.E., the scroll (now called the Moscow Mathematical Papyrus) is among the oldest known mathematics texts in the world. Written in *hieratic script* (a cursive form of hieroglyphics) are 25 math problems. Most are fairly simple, such as finding the area of a triangle. (Another calculates the amount of grain needed to make a certain amount of beer.) However, one problem stood out: "Problem 14," as it's called by modern mathematicians, roughly translates to this:

Given a truncated pyramid of height 6, base 4, and top 2, you are to square the bottom, multiply the bottom by the top, square the top, and add all these to give 28. Then you are to multiply this by a third of the height to give the right answer, 56.

What is it? An equation for finding the volume of a four-sided pyramid with a flat top (a type of *frustum*). For reasons still not understood, such mathematical skill was completely lost and not rediscovered until Ancient Greek mathematicians began using it more than 1,500 years later.

(NOT) BEST PICTURE

There are 26 movies on the American Film Institute's 2007 list of the "100 Greatest American Movies of All Time" that were not nominated for Best Picture at the Academy Awards. They are (with their AFI ranking in parentheses):

✦ *Toy Story* (99)

✦ *Blade Runner* (97)

✦ *Do the Right Thing* (96)

✦ *Sophie's Choice* (91)

✦ *Swing Time* (90)

✦ *Bringing Up Baby* (88)

✦ *A Night at the Opera* (85)

✦ *Easy Rider* (84)

✦ *Spartacus* (81)

✦ *The Wild Bunch* (79)

✦ *Modern Times* (78)

✦ *The African Queen* (65)

✦ *Sullivan's Travels* (61)

✦ *Duck Soup* (60)

✦ *North by Northwest* (55)

✦ *Rear Window* (48)

✦ *King Kong* (1933) (41)

✦ *Snow White and the Seven Dwarfs* (34)

✦ *Some Like It Hot* (22)

✦ *The General* (18)

✦ *2001: A Space Odyssey* (15)

✦ *Psycho* (14)

✦ *The Searchers* (12)

✦ *City Lights* (11)

✦ *Vertigo* (9)

✦ *Singin' in the Rain* (5)

SKYSCRAPERS

For a building to be technically classified as a skyscraper, it has to be supported by an internal skeleton made of iron or steel. That metal core must bear the weight. If the structure's main support comes from weight-bearing outer walls, it is not a skyscraper.

INSECT LIFE STAGES

Several insect species go through the biological process known as *metamorphosis*, during which they change form. The word comes from the Greek *meta*, for "change" and *morph*, for "form."

✦ Most insects go through one of two types of metamorphosis: *hemimetabolous* ("simple" metamorphosis) or *holometabolous* ("complex" metamorphosis).

✦ Some go through neither: *Ametabolic* insects are the most primitive type—they emerge from eggs looking physically like adults in every way except size. Examples include bristletails and silverfish.

✦ *Hemimetabolic* insects go through three life stages: They begin as eggs and are born as nymphs or larvae. In this stage they grow and shed their exoskeletons, or *molt*, several times, each time emerging more like their adult form, and with their last molt they emerge as an adult. Examples include dragonflies, grasshoppers, cockroaches, and cicadas.

✦ *Holometabolic* insects make up about 85% of all modern insects. They have four distinct life stages, during which they can drastically change their body structure, habitat, and feeding habits. They begin as an egg; hatch into a larva (e.g., grub or caterpillar), go through an inactive period as a pupa (e.g., in a cocoon), and emerge as an adult. These include flies, bees, wasps, ants, beetles, moths, and butterflies.

FOOD FOR THOUGHT. Some insects are viviparous, meaning they give birth to live young. They still have eggs, but the mothers develop and hatch them inside their bodies. An example is the blood-sucking African tsetse fly. They not only hatch inside their mothers, they go through two molts inside her, during which they feed on a secretion…similar to a human mother's milk. (It's even white.)

MIDHUSBANDS?

You've heard of midwives: women who help other women with childbirth. But have you heard of *male* midwives? They're out there. A few dozen are officially certified in the United States; many more exist around the world. Why aren't they called "mid-husbands"? Because the "wife" in the term refers to the woman giving birth, not the person helping her. It was derived from a Middle English term that meant "with wife," or "with woman."

PARTS OF A SHOE

✦ **Sole:** the complete bottom piece

✦ **Insole:** the interior bottom

✦ **Outsole:** the part that makes contact with the ground

✦ **Midsole:** between the insole and the outsole

✦ **Heel:** the rear outside part of the shoe

✦ **Shank:** the supportive center section of the sole between the ball-of-foot line and the front of the heel

✦ **Shankpiece:** a finger-length piece of material for reinforcement inside the shank—made of wood, plastic, or metal

✦ **Sock lining:** the interior lining of the shoe

✦ **Inlay:** the removable lining upon which the foot directly sits

✦ **Upper:** the part above the sole that (mostly) covers the foot

✦ **Vamp:** the forepart of the upper, from the instep to the toe box

- ✦ **Toe box:** the part of the vamp that covers the toes
- ✦ **Tongue:** The strip behind the laces on a laced shoe that protects the top of the foot from the laces
- ✦ **Throat:** where the foot enters
- ✦ **Collar:** the top rim of the throat, also called the "top line"

DRINKING SEAWATER: BAD

If you're ever lost at sea with no freshwater available—bummer. Trying to stay hydrated with seawater for a long period of time is fatal. The 3.5% salt content of seawater is far too high for our bodies to handle. The kidneys regulate salt content, and if it's above about 0.9% in the blood, the kidneys make you urinate—which makes you need more water. So the more seawater you drink, the more seawater you *have* to drink. Keep drinking it and your kidneys won't be able to keep up. Your salt content will rise to the point that all the cells in your body will empty of water in an attempt to dilute the salt content, which can cause them to cease functioning. And the blood cells will keep ferrying salt to the kidneys, which will finally give up and just stop working altogether. You will then go into convulsions, experience heart attacks, and eventually die.

DRINKING SEAWATER: GOOD

If you bump into an iceberg or a polar ice cap, then you have a good chance of obtaining drinkable water. Seawater freezes at about 28.5°F, and when it does, the salt leaches out beneath it. This is because as a liquid, H_2O molecules freely move around each other, and salt molecules (NaCl) have "room," so to speak, to be there. As a solid, H_2O molecules are pulled tightly together in a neatly structured crystal lattice—and there's just no room for NaCl molecules. As water freezes, they are pushed out into the liquid water beneath the ice, or into gaps in the ice. On top of that (literally), as seawater freezes, it creates a surface upon which to "catch" precipitation in the form of ice and snow—both of which are freshwater. Result: Much of the polar ice caps and icebergs are freshwater.

TYPES OF SENTENCES

There are four basic kinds of sentences: declarative, imperative, interrogative, and exclamatory.

✦ **Declarative** sentences make a statement: "You are a genius."

✦ **Imperative** sentences make a command or request: "Say something smart."

✦ **Interrogative** sentences ask a question: "Are you impressed?"

✦ **Exclamatory** sentences show strong feeling: "Yes, I am!"

Parts of a sentence: A complete sentence must have both a subject and a verb, (sometimes called a *predicate*). The subject is the word or phrase doing the action described in the sentence, and the verb is the action word or phrase. Simple example: "You ran." To find the subject in this or any sentence, ask *who* or *what* followed by the verb, i.e., "Who or what ran?" The answer is "you"—the subject of the sentence. The verb is obviously "ran."

In some sentences, the subject is understood, meaning that the sentence contains no subject, but its presence is implied, for example, "Run!" That sentence, if directed at you, implies "(You) run!"

THE THIRD NIPPLE

It is estimated that 1 in 18 people have an extra or *supernumerary* nipple on their body, which can look like a nipple, mole, or freckle. While still embryos, humans develop "milk lines," strips of tissue that run from the areas that will become the armpits, to the chest, and then downward to the groin. At about six weeks, they develop into slightly risen "milk ridges," and after another ten weeks or so they recede, leaving only, normally, the two nipples behind. People who have supernumerary nipples will always have them somewhere along the path of those milk lines.

FOOD FOR THOUGHT. In 2005 British researchers discovered a gene involved in breast formation that they believe could help determine what causes the development of breast cancer. They named the gene Scaramanga, after Francisco "Pistols" Scaramanga, the villain and title character in the James Bond film *The Man with the Golden Gun*. Bond's assignment in the story is to find and kill Scaramanga, an assassin. Scaramanga's only identifiable physical feature: a third nipple on his chest, so Bond disguises himself as the killer—by wearing a fake third nipple.

SWEETS AND SOURS

According to an old Pennsylvania Dutch custom, every meal should have a mix of "seven sweets and seven sours," and to a large degree, this custom is still observed. The sweets are represented by homegrown fruits such as currants, apples, quinces, watermelon, cherries, and strawberries; the sours by foods such as pickles, pickled onions, beets, coleslaw, relishes, and horseradish sauce. Want a taste? You can get it at the Seven Sweets and Sours Festival, held every September in the town of Intercourse, Pennsylvania.

PEKING TO BEIJING

A few years after China became the Communist nation known as the People's Republic of China in 1949, the government adopted a new method of translating its proper names into Western languages—the *pinyin* method. It used the Latin alphabet (the ABCs) to more closely approximate the actual pronunciation of the names of people and cities in the primary Chinese dialect of Mandarin. This created the misconception in the West that the name of the capital city of Peking was changed to Beijing("bay-jing"). It turns out "Peking" was a goof—the correct pronunciation (using the pinyin method) is Beijing. Other changes included Nanking to Nanjing and Chunking (the name for mainland China) to Chongqing.

THE APOLLO MISSIONS

In 1961 President John F. Kennedy proposed to Congress that the government increase funds to the National Aeronautics and Space Administration (NASA) with the goal of landing men on the Moon by 1970. That began the Apollo Moon program. The first mission, in January 1967, never launched—while the spacecraft was still on the ground, a combination of substandard wiring and too much oxygen led to a fire that tore through the command module of Apollo 1, killing all three astronauts onboard. The Apollo name was retired (although NASA's next projects were still informally referred to as "Apollo" missions) until it was re-adopted for Apollo 4. Apollo 2 through 6 were all unmanned missions, undertaken to test the launch rockets, command module, and lunar-landing module. The rest of the missions, Apollo 7 through 17, were all manned, and each had different objectives.

Apollo 7 (October 1968). An 11-day mission to test the service module (where all the machinery is housed) in Earth's orbit.

Apollo 8 (December 1968). This is the first mission to approach the Moon. While Apollo 8 doesn't land on the Moon, it does orbit it and take photos of the far side.

Apollo 9 (March 1969). A 10-day mission to test the lunar module (where the crew sits and operates the spacecraft) in Earth's orbit.

Apollo 10 (May 1969). A test of the lunar module in the Moon's orbit.

Apollo 11 (July 1969). The crew of Buzz Aldrin, Neil Armstrong, and Michael Collins (who remained in orbit) lands on the Moon.

Apollo 12 (November 1969). Astronauts land on the Moon again to collect pieces of rock and data from *Surveyor 3*, an exploratory probe sent in 1967.

Apollo 13 (April 1970). Astronauts were set to explore the Fra Mauro highlands and crater but were forced to abort the mission after an oxygen tank exploded in the service module on the way to the Moon.

Apollo 14 (January–February 1971). Astronauts land on the Moon to collect 25 million-year-old rocks and soil samples.

Apollo 15 (July–August 1971). Astronauts land on the Moon and drill below the surface to obtain samples. They also travel around on the Lunar Roving Vehicle.

Apollo 16 (April 1972). An exploration of the lunar highlands. Astronauts collect rock samples, proving the highlands were formed by meteorite impacts and not volcanic activity, as previously thought.

Apollo 17 (December 1972). Harrison Schmitt, a geologist who was the first civilian scientist to visit the Moon, helps collect more than 240 pounds of Moon rocks.

WHAT'S A POLYMER?

You've probably heard the word in reference to plastics, but it actually has a much broader meaning. A *polymer* is simply a substance, natural or synthetic, composed of very long, chainlike molecules with many repeating units, those units being joined in the same way. These very long molecules get tangled up with themselves and each other, which makes them difficult to pull apart—making substances made of polymers flexible but very tough.

✦ Some well-known naturally occurring polymers include proteins, DNA, cellulose, rubber, and starch. Synthetic varieties:

Bakelite, nylon, Teflon, and the thousands of kinds of plastic, such as polyethylene.

✦ What makes synthetic polymers so popular also makes them problematic. They're easy to make, light, and very strong. But that strength, due to the properties of polymers, makes them stick around long after they've outrun their usefulness. Example: A plastic soda bottle, which can take centuries to break down in a landfill.

SLAM BOOKS

Making "slam books" is an American high school tradition that goes back to the 1940s. They were spiral notebooks that students would fill, anonymously, with harsh words for one or more of their classmates, "slamming" them with insults that they wouldn't say to their faces. They're not as popular today as they once were, although their equivalents may exist…on the Internet.

VANISHING LAKES MYSTERY

In April 2008, oceanographers in Greenland solved a mystery that had been bugging them for decades: How did the large lakes that form during the summer on top of the island's ice sheets vanish in less than 24 hours? And where did the water go?

✦ The appearance of summertime lakes, known as *supraglacial* or *meltwater* lakes, has increased in recent years, as has their size. Thousands of them, some covering up to a few square miles, show up each summer. And many of them do the baffling disappearing act. Where could so much water go so quickly?

✦ The answer came when a team of oceanographers placed seismic instruments around one of the lakes in 2006…and waited. That particular lake covered 2.2 square miles and was as deep as 40 feet in some places, giving it in the neighborhood of 11.6 billion gallons of water. The team got lucky in July—when 90% of the lake disappeared in 90 minutes. It had drained through massive cracks that the weight of the water had made in the ice. That explanation had been considered before, but such cracks would have to reach the bottom of the ice sheet to allow all the water to disappear, and that had been deemed impossible. It wasn't. The cracks opened up to a depth of more than 3,200 feet—all the way to where the glacier sits on bedrock and slowly makes its way to the ocean. That allowed the millions of tons of water to drain almost at once—with more force than Niagara Falls—to the bedrock underneath the ice, which actually caused a huge section of the ice to rise some 20 feet as the water surged beneath it.

LEARN SOME JAPANESE

In general, vowels are pronounced as they appear in these words: w**a**sh, mach**i**ne, **e**gg, g**o**, t**u**be. Pronounce each vowel separately.

Anata: You (formal).

Watakushi: I.

Kudasai: Please (when requesting something).

Domo arrigato gozaimasu: Thank you very much.

Dozo: Please (when offering something).

Gomen nasai: Pardon me

Eigo ga wakarimasu ka? Do you understand English?

Hai: Yes.

Hai, wakarimasu: Yes, I understand.

Iie: No.

Iie, wakarimasen: No, I don't understand.

Ohayou gozaimasu: Good morning (before 10 a.m.).

Konnichi wa: Good afternoon (after 10 a.m.).

Konban wa: Good evening.

Moshi moshi: Hello (when using the phone or calling out to a stranger).

Nanji desu ka? What time is it?

Ryoogae suru: To exchange money.

Sayonara: Good-bye.

Sumimasen: Excuse me.

Toire wa doko ni arimasu ka? Where is the toilet?

ON GENIUS

"Geniuses are like thunderstorms. They go against the wind, terrify people, cleanse the air."

—Søren Kierkegaard, philosopher

"Philosophy becomes poetry and science imagination, in the enthusiasm of genius."

—Benjamin Disraeli, British prime minister

WHAT'S POP ART?

When you hear "pop art," you probably think of Andy Warhol's paintings of Campbell's Soup cans and silkscreens of Marilyn Monroe's face repeated in neon colors. But Warhol was just one of many pop artists whose work became well known to Americans from the late 1950s through the '60s. Robert Indiana, Roy Lichtenstein, Jim Dine, Marisol, Red Grooms, Claes Oldenburg, George Segal, James Rosenquist, Tom Wesselmann, and many more artists produced works of art that drew inspiration from artifacts of everyday life, mass-produced objects, consumerism, celebrities, and the imagery of TV, magazines, and comics. Pop artists glorified the "low art" of popular culture and disdained the sophisticated "high art" of abstract expressionism, which they considered to be elitist and overly serious. At the time, many critics thought pop art—with its references to sign painting, billboards, comic strips, and magazine illustrations—was crass, kitschy, and not "real" art. But pop artists believed their work democratized art and made it accessible to ordinary people.

4 WAYS TO PREDICT THE FUTURE

✦ **Scarpomancy:** predicting someone's future by studying their old shoes

✦ **Tiromancy:** studying the shape, holes, mold, and other features on a piece of cheese

✦ **Haruspication:** studying the guts of a sacrificed animal

✦ **Pynchonomancy:** throwing darts at a paperback copy of *Gravity's Rainbow* by Thomas Pynchon, then reading the sentence on the deepest page penetrated by the dart

COMMON CYANIDE SOURCES

Five popular foods that contain trace amounts of cyanide: cassava root, sorghum, spinach, almonds, and lima beans.

60,000 WORDS

If you stopped reading right now and wrote down 200 words—depending on how fast you can type or print, it would take you anywhere from five to ten minutes—and if you did that tomorrow, and the next day, and the next day...in 300 days you'd have written 60,000 words, the average number of words in a modern novel. These words would, of course, have to tell a compelling story of some kind for your book to be successful. But you'd have done the minimum amount of work required to write a novel. (So get started!)

CHAPTER 8

WHAT BEATS A ROYAL FLUSH?

The ranks of the 10 possible hands in traditional poker:

1. Royal flush: A ten, jack, queen, king, and ace of the same suit (no suit ranks higher than another).

2. Straight flush: Five cards of the same suit in numerical order.

3. Four of a kind: Four cards of the same rank.

4. Full house: Three cards of one rank, two of another, e.g., three aces and two eights. (If two players both have a full house, the hand with the highest three of a kind wins.)

5. Flush: Five cards of the same suit not in numerical order.

6. Straight: Five cards in numerical order, not of the same suit.

7. Three of a kind: Three cards of the same rank.

8. Two pairs: Two pairs of cards with different ranks.

9. One pair: Two cards of the same rank.

10. High card: If none of the hands even has a pair, then the player with the highest card wins. (If the high cards are the same, then the second-highest card wins, and so on.)

So what beats a royal flush? Nothing...unless you're playing with wild cards, in which case a *five* of a kind beats it.

HIBERNATION

Many animal species have developed the ability to *hibernate*, a form of sleep accompanied by extremely low metabolic activity that allows them to survive climate extremes and the food shortages that accompany them. In the most common form, the animal, most likely spurred by biological reactions to changes in temperature and hours of daylight (nobody knows for sure), spends the late summer and fall gorging on food in order to store up the body fat on which it will live while dormant. Then it finds a safe place, like a burrow or den, curls up, and goes to sleep. In cases of true hibernation (there are other categories) the animal doesn't merely sleep, it falls into a deep, comalike state. Both the heart and breathing rates drop to almost undetectable levels (chipmunks' heart rates go from about 350 beats per minute to as low as 4 within hours of lying down), and the body temperature falls until it is nearly the same as the air around the animal—as low as a few degrees above freezing in many cases. Unlike sleep, there is no movement and very little brain activity. The animal appears dead; it can be touched, prodded, or subjected to loud noises and it still won't come out of its slumber.

✦ The duration of hibernation varies among animals and according to how harsh the winter is, lasting from several days to more than half the year. Nearly all hibernators come out of their sleep every few weeks for a day or so, during which they will drink a little water, eat a little food, and urinate and defecate to rid the body of natural toxins that build up due to lack of movement. At the end of the hibernating period, probably again spurred by changes in temperature and sunlight, the animal's temperature and heart rate rise over several hours as it slowly awakens. Some warm-blooded, mammalian true hibernators: badgers, chipmunks, dormice, ground squirrels, woodchucks, hamsters, hedgehogs, and skunks.

✦ Many biologists don't classify bears as true hibernators. During their *torpor*, as some call it, a bear's body temperature lowers about 10°F, and its heart rate slows to about 20% of normal. And bears can, as some unfortunate explorers have learned, be easily awakened during their winter slumber. While this may not be true hibernation, it allows bears, if undisturbed, to go through entire winters, sometimes up to seven months, without once getting up to eat, drink, urinate, or defecate. They may not even change position.

✦ Many cold-blooded animals hibernate or go into periods of torpor that last from just hours to several weeks, including some snakes, lizards, turtles, frogs, toads, bees, and shrimp.

✦ Poorwills, relatives of the whip-poor-will and native to western North America, are the only birds known to hibernate. For days at a time, the perfectly camouflaged birds sit among rocks in desert regions. Their body temperatures drop as much as 35°F, and they can be picked up and won't awaken.

✦ *Estivation* is a form of hibernation that takes place in summer months in order to survive the heat and the lack of water. Many different kinds of animals do it, including tortoises, crocodiles, turtles, salamanders, lungfish, and snails.

✦ Fat-tailed lemurs are native to the island of Madagascar off the eastern coast of Africa. In 2004 researchers were surprised to discover that they hibernate, some for as long as six months, in reaction to long dry seasons. It was also a surprise because it made lemurs the only known primate species that hibernates. (After gorging, they live off the fat stored in their long tails.)

JEWISH ANGELS

The *Jewish Encyclopedia* lists 10 orders of angels in the Jewish angel hierarchy. They are:

1. Chayot Ha Kadesh	**6.** Malakhim
2. Ophanim	**7.** Elohim
3. Erelim	**8.** Bene Elohim
4. Hashmallim	**9.** Cherubim
5. Seraphim	**10.** Ishim

MEDICAL HISTORY

The Egyptian "Kahun Medical Papyrus," a hieroglyphic document dating to around 1850 B.C.E., reveals that ancient Egyptian women used elaborate insertable contraceptive mixes—among the earliest known contraceptives. They were made from mixes of various substances, one of them containing the mineral sodium carbonate, honey…and crocodile dung. (Other cultures in northern Africa substituted elephant dung.)

ARISTOTLE ON POETRY

"The distinction between historian and poet is not in the one writing prose and the other verse…the one describes the thing that has been, and the other a kind of thing that might be. Hence poetry is something more philosophic and of graver import than history, since its statements are of the nature rather of universals, whereas those of history are singulars."

SINGLE-PAYER

Single-payer healthcare refers to any health insurance program, whether community-based, state, national, or private, that has one administrative source of funding used to pay health-care providers. All hospitals, doctors, and other health-care providers in this system bill just one entity for their services. In terms of national health care, this runs in opposition to systems (such as the one currently used in the United States) in which there are literally thousands of payers in the form of insurance companies, HMOs, billing companies, and so on. Examples of existing single-payer programs: the Canadian, British, and Australian national health-care systems, as well as the American Medicare program for disabled children and the elderly.

THE CALORIC REFLEX TEST

Doctors have long known that it's possible to glean information about the functioning ability of an unconscious person's brain by performing a remarkably simple test: squirting water into the ears and noting the reaction of the eyes. What's this test used for? It's an important part in diagnosing vision disorders, balance problems...and whether or not someone is "brain dead." The technique, known as the *caloric reflex test*, relies on the body's *vestibulo-ocular reflex* (VOR), which gives you your sense of balance.

✦ The VOR's job is to allow you to see images clearly even when your head is moving. How it works: The *semicircular canals*, located in the ears, contain fluid and are lined with hairs (cilia) connected to nerves. As your head moves, the fluid in the ears moves, too. That makes the hairs move, which in turn sends nerve signals to the *vestibular nuclei*, located in the brain stem. Those signals are interpreted, and messages are sent to muscles around the eyes—resulting in corresponding eye movements. That allows you to keep images in focus. For example: If you turn your head sharply to the left for just a moment while reading this, a signal will be sent to the muscles around your eyes to very quickly move to the right, allowing you to keep the page in focus. (Without the VOR, we wouldn't be able to read at all, since our heads are constantly moving enough to make focus impossible without it.)

How the caloric reflex test works: A small amount of cold or warm water is squirted into one ear and onto the eardrum. If it's cold water (below 86°F), it thickens and slows down the fluid in that ear canal relative to the other ear. This has the effect of signaling that the head has turned the opposite direction of the squirted ear—and the eyes reflexively turn toward the squirted ear. With warm water (about 110°F), the opposite happens, and the eyes reflexively turn away from the squirted ear. Monitoring how the eyes react to the test determines the state of the vestibular nuclei and the brain stem—and therefore your brain.

THE FACTS OF FIRE

The next time you gaze into a fireplace, here's something to ponder:

✦ Fire is a very rapid form of a process known as *oxidation*, a chemical reaction between a *fuel* and an *oxidizing agent*, most commonly oxygen. (A slower form: rusting.)

✦ When something burns, oxygen atoms in the air rapidly combine with the atoms of whatever's burning.

✦ For example, *hydrocarbons*, organic substances that consist entirely of carbon (C) and hydrogen (H), burn very easily because both carbon and hydrogen combine very easily with oxygen. Gasoline is a hydrocarbon; propane is another. Burn these substances, and the oxygen in the air combines with the carbon and hydrogen in the fuels to form the two most common by-products of fire: CO_2 (carbon dioxide), which is released as gas, and H_2O (water), which is released as steam.

✦ In order for any substance to burn, it has to be heated to its *ignition temperature*, which is different for different substances. The source of the heat can be any number of things, for example, lightning, friction (as when striking a match), or a chemical reaction. Once a fuel reaches its ignition temperature, *combustion* occurs, then fire. If enough fuel and oxygen remain, the fire itself provides the heat necessary to keep the fire burning.

✦ The chemical reaction that is fire occurs only between gases—even when solids or liquids burn. This is because when a fuel is heated to its ignition temperature, it decomposes and begins to give off flammable gases known as *volatiles*. Those volatiles are what react with the oxygen.

✦ Using a candle as an example: When you apply a burning match to the wax on the wick (the fuel), at a certain temperature (its ignition temperature) the wax evaporates and releases gases (*volatiles*), which then react with the oxygen in the air and ignite (combustion). The heat from the fire then keeps the wax melting and moving down the wick, continuously evaporating and igniting.

✦ How do you put out a fire? Take away one or all of the three necessary components: the fuel, the oxygen, or the sufficient heat. Blow a candle out, and you've cooled the wax below its ignition temperature. Press the wick between your thumb and finger, and you've taken away the fuel by stopping the wax from climbing up the wick. Put a glass over the candle, and you've taken the oxygen away—and the fire will be extinguished after it burns up all the oxygen under the glass.

✦ Other oxidizing agents: fluorine and chlorine. Both can cause rapid oxidation reactions, thereby causing fire without oxygen.

WHO YOU GONNA CALL?

Blennophobia is an abnormal, unwarranted fear of slime. It can cause, among other symptoms, shortness of breath, irregular heartbeat, nausea, severe anxiety, and panic attacks. The condition is common in people with obsessive-compulsive disorders as well as those with schizophrenia, and can be triggered by contact with or just proximity to any slimy substance, such as snail slime, or even just images on TV or in films (like *Ghostbusters*).

EASY SLIME RECIPE

Ingredients: 2 cups water, ½ cup cornstarch, food coloring.

Instructions: Bring water to a boil in a medium-size saucepan. Add cornstarch and food coloring while stirring constantly. Remove from heat and allow to cool. You now have a gooey, messy slime that's fun for the whole family. (Eating it is not recommended.)

THE DOGS OF WAR

Shortly after the bombing of Pearl Harbor in 1941, the U.S. military set up a program called Dogs for Defense to begin training dogs to assist soldiers in the battlefield. People all over the country donated their pets to the program, including a family from Pleasantville, New York, who contributed their German Shepherd-Collie-Husky mix named Chips. During the invasion of Sicily in 1943, Chips and his handler were pinned down on the beach as soldiers fired on them from a camouflaged pillbox. As soon as the shooting started, Chips broke free from his handler and attacked the pillbox, forcing all four of the gunmen inside to surrender, saving his handler's life in the process.

For his bravery, Chips was awarded the Silver Star; for the scalp wound and powder burns he suffered, he was awarded the Purple Heart. The novelty of a dog receiving medals normally awarded to soldiers received a lot of newspaper attention, and that, in turn, caused Chips to be stripped of his medals when the Commander of the Order of the Purple Heart complained that such awards were an insult to their human recipients. Dogs have fought in every war the U.S. has fought in since then, but none have been awarded any official decorations—Chips was the last. (He survived the war and returned to his family in Pleasantville.)

TIDAL BORE

A *tidal bore* is an aquatic phenomenon in which an incoming tide is funneled into a shallow, narrow river (usually from a bay), forming a wave that travels up the river and rapidly raises the water level. The largest bore in the world is on the Qiantang River, which flows into the East China Sea through Hangzhou Bay. When the tide comes in against the river, it can form a wave 30 feet high that travels 25 miles per hour. (The term comes from the Old Norse *bara*, meaning "wave.")

VAN NESS ROTATIONPLASTY

The "Van Ness Rotationplasty" is a rare type of procedure performed on cancer patients who have a leg amputated above the knee. The lower leg and foot are removed (in one piece) from the amputated leg, and are reattached at the thigh in a reversed position. The ankle bone basically becomes the patient's knee, and the foot is used as a stump to which a prosthetic limb can be attached. The procedure was first performed by Dr. J. Borggreve in Germany in the 1930s, and was named after a Dr. C.P. Van Ness, who wrote about, improved, and began performing the procedure in the 1950s.

A FAMOUS LIPOGRAM

A *lipogram* is a work of writing in which a particular letter (or letters) is purposely not used. It comes from the Greek *lipagrammatos*, meaning "missing letter." Probably the most famous (and longest) lipogram is the 1939 novel by Ernest Vincent Wright, *Gadsby*, subtitled *A Story of Over 50,000 Words Without Using the Letter "E."* Wright died in 1939 at the age of 66—on the day the book was published. It went on to become reasonably well known—not for its writing in particular, but for the odd absence of the letter "E" in its content.

HOME REMEDIES

Ammonia. To waken an unconscious person, here's a substitute for smelling salts: Open a bottle of ammonia and hold it underneath the unconscious person's nose so that they get a whiff of the ammonia fumes. (Make sure they don't drink or inhale the liquid.)

Powdered or dry mustard. One to three teaspoons dissolved in a glass of warm water can be used to induce vomiting. Two teaspoons of table salt dissolved in a glass of warm water will have the same effect.

Seawater. In a pinch, clean seawater can be used to clean wounds if you are injured at the beach.

CLASSIFICATIONS OF SUICIDE

According to the World Health Organization, there are three main classifications of suicide:

✦ **Violent:** hanging, shooting, burning, planned accidents

✦ **Nonviolent:** drug overdose, poisoning, inhaling exhaust fumes, suffocation

✦ **Passive:** refusing to accept treatment for an injury or illness

KING WILLIAM THE BASTARD

Before he altered the course of European history by invading England in 1066 C.E. and leading the Normans to victory over the Anglo-Saxons, William the Conqueror was known as William the Bastard. The future King William I was the illegitimate son of Robert I, Duke of Normandy, and Herleva, the daughter of a tanner. According to legend, when William laid siege to the city of Alençon (in modern-day France), the citizens taunted him and mocked his humble origins by hanging animal hides from the city walls. (Embarrassing nicknames ran in the family: William's great uncle was called Ethelred the Unready.)

FURRY CROCODILES

According to evolutionary biologists, life began in the water. After millions of years, many aquatic species made the transition to land. Millions of years later, some of those land animals returned to the water.

✦ Among them are the animals in the order *Cetacea*—all whales, porpoises, and dolphins.

✦ The most compelling signs that they were once land-dwellers are the characteristics they share with each other, but not with their aquatic neighbors: They're warm-blooded, breathe air rather than extracting oxygen from water through gills, produce milk to feed their young, have skin rather than scales, and have hair.

✦ The earliest known cetaceans: the extinct *pakicetids*, 50-million-year-old fossils of which were found in Pakistan in the 1980s. They were small, doglike animals that lived near, and presumably hunted in, water. The evidence for their relation to modern cetaceans is found in peculiarities in their ear bones and the shape of the cusps of their molar teeth, features found today only in cetaceans.

✦ Another early cetacean: the 12-foot-long *Ambulocetus natans*, which existed about 49 million years ago. The name means "walking whale that swims," and it is described as resembling a four-legged, furry crocodile that breathed air but spent most of its time in the water.

✦ Between 35 and 41 million years ago came the *basilosaurids* (king lizards). These full-time sea creatures were huge, up to 60 feet long, and had *flukes*, horizontally configured tails. By this time their front limbs had evolved into flippers, but they still had tiny hind legs. And their nostrils had begun the migration up the head—toward the location of the modern cetacean *blowhole.*

✦ There are about 80 cetacean species known to exist today. The largest: the Blue Whale, which can grow to more than 100 feet and 300,000 pounds. The smallest: the Vaquita, a species of porpoise endemic only to Mexico's Sea of Cortez. (The name means "little cow.") They grow to only 5 feet long and 120 pounds. Vaquitas are among the most endangered cetaceans, with possibly as few as 100 alive today.

✦ Why do cetaceans have flukes rather than the vertically aligned tails that all fish have? Because they were once land mammals, and their spines reflect it. Watch a dog or cat when it runs: Their spines move up and down rather than side to side. When similar animals took to the water all those millennia ago, that trait went with them; all cetaceans propel themselves by moving their tails up and down. The horizontal design of their tails, for obvious reasons, aids that type of propulsion. Fish, on the other hand, evolved from full-time sea creatures whose propulsion method was side-to-side motion, and for that reason they developed their vertical tails.

CONSILIO ET ANIMIS

A motto is a short statement of beliefs or ideals. The ancient Romans were prolific motto makers, which is why the tradition of translating mottos into Latin persists throughout the Western world today. Here are a few notable mottoes from the days of the Roman Empire:

> **Consilio et animis.** "Wisdom and courage."

> **Veritas vos liberabit.** "Truth will free you."

Alis volat propiis. "It flies with its own wings."

Ut aquila versus coelum. "As an eagle against the sky."

Amor ac studio. "By love and by study."

Veni, vidi, vici. "I came, I saw, I conquered."

Fiat lux. "Let there be light."

ISAAC NEWTON ON UNDERSTANDING

"A man may imagine things that are false, but he can only understand things that are true, for if the things be false, the apprehension of them is not understanding."

CLASSIFICATIONS OF THUNDERSTORMS

On page 40 we wrote about the life cycle of a thunderstorm. Here are the different kinds.

Single-cell storms. As the name implies, these have just one cell that goes through one life cycle; lasts from 20 to 30 minutes; and can produce moderate to heavy rainfall, moderate downbursts (strong downward wind bursts that spread out in all directions upon contact with land or water), and hail.

Multicell cluster storms. The most common type of thunderstorm, these happen when the downdraft of cool air formed by a thunderstorm cell, which can kill *that* cell, pushes warm air into *another* cell just forming. That cell then goes through its cycle and does the same thing to another new cell, forming several clustered cells, each in a different stage of the storm cycle. They can produce hail, moderate downbursts, flash floods, and weak tornadoes.

Multicell line storms. These are similar to cluster storms, but rather than clusters, the cells are arranged in a line, forming one continuous front. These fronts can be hundreds of miles long;

they can produce very strong winds and downbursts, heavy rain, moderately sized hail, and weak tornadoes.

Supercells. The most dangerous kind of thunderstorms. They're characterized by having a continuously rotating updraft, or *mesocyclone*, and can produce torrential rainfall, massive and very strong downbursts, baseball-sized hail, flash floods, and violent tornadoes—and they can last for hours.

FOOD FOR THOUGHT. Although all thunderstorms produce rain, it doesn't always make it to the ground. Dry thunderstorms form high above a layer of very dry air—and the rain evaporates before it hits the ground. They're common in the American West, and the lightning they produce often causes forest fires.

THE # SYMBOL

There are many different theories regarding the origin of this symbol, called the "number sign," the "hash mark," the "octothorpe," or the "pound" sign. One of the most common is that it derives from the abbreviation for "pound" (the weight measurement), "lb.," which comes from the Latin word *libra*, meaning "balance." Shipping clerks, this theory continues, used to draw a line through "lb." on packages if it referred to the weight in pounds, to clearly differentiate it from some other use (the initials "LB" for someone's name, for example). The cross-through resembled the # symbol, leading to its widespread use.

TYPES OF STEAKS

Steaks, generally speaking, are tender cuts of beef that taste best when grilled or roasted for a relatively short time. The finest steaks come from the section of the cow with the tenderest muscles—the midsection between the front and back legs, toward the spine: rib, short loin, sirloin, and tenderloin.

Rib steak: bone-in; very tender, marbled, and flavorful.

Rib-eye steak: boneless version of rib steak.

Filet mignon: boneless; thick-cut from the small end of the tenderloin; prized for its tenderness, but definitely not the most flavorful steak.

Sirloin steak: general term that includes pin-bone, flat-bone, round-bone, and wedge-bone steaks; sold bone-in or boneless; sometimes on the chewy side, but still full-flavored.

Strip steak: also called shell steak, club steak, strip loin steak, New York strip, or Kansas City strip steak; usually boneless; very tender.

T-bone steak, porterhouse: nearly identical (the porterhouse has a thicker tenderloin); bone-in; hearty flavor; usually cut thick.

Flank steak: cut from the underside of the loin; boneless; a little chewy but quite tasty; often used for fajitas.

Skirt steak (or hanger steak): cut from the underside of the ribs; boneless; cheaper and less tender, but very flavorful.

PANGAEA

Approximately 225 million years ago, all the land that makes up the seven continents was combined in one massive, roughly *C*-shaped "supercontinent" now called Pangaea. The vast ocean that surrounded it is called Panthalassa (the two names mean, respectively, "All Earth," and "All Seas"). Due to shifting tectonic plates, about 200 million years ago, Pangaea began to separate, eventually forming the continents Laurasia, to the north, and Gondwana, to the south. Laurasia later broke up to become what is now Asia (minus India), Europe, and North America. Gondwana broke up to become Antarctica, South America, Africa, Australia, Madagascar, the Arabian Peninsula, and the Indian subcontinent.

CHAPTER 9

TATTOO YOU

When you're looking at someone's tattoo, you're actually looking *inside* their skin. Whether made by a thorn, needle, or tattoo machine, tattoos endure because the ink is deposited into the *dermis*, the inner layer of skin. The outer layer, the *epidermis*, is constantly creating new cells, which soon die and flake off. The dermis, on the other hand, is much more stable, and allows the ink to stay in place for decades.

FAMILIAR ALLUSIONS

An *allusion* is an indirect reference to a well-known person, place, or thing—real or fictional—often brought up to make a point.

Walter Mitty. This is a character in James Thurber's 1939 short story "The Secret Life of Walter Mitty." He is an ineffectual man who spends a great deal of time imagining himself in adventurous situations, such as a fighter pilot in a dogfight or an assassin on assignment. The name is now commonly used to describe an ordinary or boring person who seeks escape in daydreams, or someone with allusions of especially daring grandeur, as in, "That new rent-a-cop is a real Walter Mitty."

Abelard and Heloise. Peter Abelard was a French philosopher in the 11th and 12th centuries. Heloise (family name unknown) was the brilliant niece of Fulbert, Canon of Notre Dame. A brief version of their true and tragic story: While still a teenager, Heloise and her tutor, Abelard, then around 30 years old, fell in love. She became pregnant, and the two were secretly married. Fulbert found out and had Abelard castrated. Heloise became a nun and abbess (a female abbot) as well as a respected writer and scholar; he became a monk and respected philosopher. For many years after their separation, they corresponded through moving letters, expressing their love and sorrow. They are believed to have eventually been buried together. "Abelard and Heloise" are often alluded to as representatives of passionate but tragic love.

ATOMS AND ELEMENTS: THE BASICS

All the matter in the universe—you, all animals, plants, oceans, mountains, stars, planets, and galaxies—is made of the exact same stuff: atoms. And every single atom is made of the same stuff, too.

✦ Atoms are made up of atomic particles: protons, neutrons, and electrons.

✦ Protons are positively charged, whereas neutrons have no electrical charge—and together they make up the very dense nuclei of atoms. Electrons are extremely small compared to protons and neutrons, having almost no mass at all. Physicists often describe them as wisps of negatively charged electrical energy that orbit an atom's nucleus, pulled there by the positive charge of the protons. This is essentially what every atom "looks like."

✦ There are 94 naturally occurring atom types, their only difference being the number of protons, neutrons, and electrons.

✦ These are the chemical elements, such as hydrogen, oxygen, sulfur, silver, gold, and uranium. Again: There are just 94 that occur in nature and make up all matter. (Another 23 artificial elements have been created in nuclear reactors.)

✦ The elements oxygen and gold? They are made up of the exact same stuff: atoms. Silver and hydrogen? Same stuff. Aluminum and calcium? The very same stuff. So what makes them different? The atoms that make them up have different amounts of atomic particles.

✦ Atoms of hydrogen, for example, have just one proton, one neutron, and one electron. Hydrogen therefore has the *atomic number* 1.

✦ The next simplest element is helium—atomic number 2. Its atoms have two protons, two neutrons, and two electrons each. The next, lithium, has three of each particle and has the atomic number 3. This continues, covering every number, until you get to the heaviest natural element, plutonium, made up of 94 protons, neutrons, and electrons in each atom.

✦ The reason this makes elements so different is that the number of atomic particles an atom contains determines how it behaves chemically. It's what makes, for example, gold act like gold (very dense, yellowish, and malleable), and oxygen act like oxygen (a colorless, odorless, tasteless, and highly flammable gas).

✦ That's the basic description of atoms and their atomic particles—but there are variations. Atoms of the same element (and the same atomic number) can have varying numbers of neutrons and electrons, called isotopes and ions. For more on that, go to page 253.

SNAP! CRACKLE! POP!
IN OTHER LANGUAGES

Afrikaans: *Knap! Knaetter! Knak!*

Spanish: *Pim! Pum! Pam!*

Danish: *Piff! Paff! Puff!*

Dutch: *Pif! Paf! Pof!*

Finnish: *Riks! Raks! Poks!*

German: *Knisper! Knasper! Knusper!*

ROOSEVELT (MARCH OF) DIMES

Why is there an image of President Franklin Delano Roosevelt on the American dime? Because of his connection to the National Foundation for Infantile Paralysis (NAIP). Roosevelt contracted infantile paralysis, also known as polio, in 1921 at the age of 39, eventually becoming permanently paralyzed from the waist down. Back then, thousands of people in the U.S. were paralyzed or killed every year by polio, yet there was very little spent on its treatment or cure. Roosevelt helped change that, founding the Warm Springs Institute for Rehabilitation in 1927, and then the NAIP in 1938, later renamed the March of Dimes. (Their first act was a public plea for people to donate one dime to the cause.) When Roosevelt died in 1945, requests that his image be used on U.S. currency flooded the United States Treasury. The dime was the natural choice, and the new coin debuted on Roosevelt's birthday, January 30, in 1946.

SURVIVING A HOUSE FIRE

✦ Indoor fires can spread quickly, so don't waste precious seconds looking for valuables. Get everyone out of the house as soon as possible.

✦ Do not try to put out a grease fire with water; this will cause it to spread. If you think it's containable, try to smother it with a non-flammable object, such as a pan lid.

✦ Wherever possible, keep all doors and windows closed. This will slow the spread of the fire.

✦ If your only hope for escape is through a closed door, open it very carefully. Use a piece of clothing to touch the doorknob and slowly open the door, using it as a heat shield. If you've determined that it's safe to move through the doorway, do so quickly and close the door. If you have to break down a door, your foot is far more effective than your shoulder. Aim your kicks right next to the doorknob.

✦ Once outside, get a safe distance from the fire and call 911.

HERBS OR SPICES?

People tend to lump herbs and spices together, but they're different.

✦ **Herbs** come from the fragrant leaves of *herbaceous*, or non-woody, plants, which means they have tender stems that die back to the ground in winter. These grow mostly in temperate climates and include oregano, parsley, sage, thyme, rosemary, tarragon, savory, marjoram, mint, and basil.

✦ **Spices** come from the bark, seeds, berries, roots, or flowers of either woody or non-woody plants that grow mostly in tropical or subtropical zones. Examples: cinnamon, cloves, allspice, nutmeg, cardamom, ginger, saffron, cumin, fennel, and peppercorns.

Some herbaceous plants yield both herbs *and* spices: dill weed, for example, yields feathery green dill leaves and also dill seeds; coriander yields leaves (called cilantro) and seeds, too. Herbs are usually associated with savory foods and flavors; most spices are associated with sweet foods, and some (such as ginger and pep-percorns) are hot to the taste, or...spicy.

CITIES ON RIVERS

From the days of the first great civilizations on Earth, people have built cities beside rivers. The Tigris and Euphrates in Mesopotamia, the Indus in India, and the Yellow River in China were just a few rivers that provided ancient peoples with irrigation for crops, transportation for commerce, and defense from enemies by forming a natural boundary. Here are some modern cities and the rivers that help sustain them.

✦ Baghdad, Iraq (Tigris)

✦ Belgrade, Serbia (Danube, Sava)

✦ Bonn, Germany (Rhine)

✦ Budapest, Hungary (Danube)

✦ Buenos Aires (Río de la Plata)

✦ Cairo, Egypt (Nile)

✦ Cincinnati, Ohio (Ohio)

✦ Damascus, Syria (Barada)

✦ Delhi, India (Yamuna)

✦ Dublin, Ireland (Liffey)

✦ El Paso, Texas (Rio Grande)

✦ Fort Yukon, Canada (Yukon)

✦ Hong Kong, China (Pearl)

✦ Lisbon, Portugal (Tagus)

✦ London, England (Thames)

✦ Melbourne, Australia (Yarra)

✦ Moscow, Russia (Moskva)

✦ Mumbai, India (Ulhas)

✦ New York City (Hudson)

✦ New Orleans (Mississippi)

✦ Paris, France (Seine)

✦ Philadelphia, Pennsylvania (Shuylkill)

✦ Portland, Oregon (Columbia)

✦ Quebec City, Canada (St. Lawrence)

✦ Saint Petersburg, Russia (Neva)

✦ Seoul, South Korea (Han)

✦ Shanghai, China (Yangtze)

✦ Tokyo, Japan (Sumida)

✦ Warsaw, Poland (Vistula)

✦ Washington, D.C. (Potomac)

A SPORT ORIGIN

See if you can guess this sport before the end.

✦ Its roots go back at least to the 1400s, and possibly much earlier.

✦ In the original form, the field could be several hundred yards—or several miles—in length, and teams could number from 5 to 1,000 players on each side.

✦ In 1636 French Jesuit missionary Jean de Brebeuf watched Huron Indians in what is now southeastern Canada play it. He said they called it *Baggataway*, meaning "Little Brother of War."

✦ When European colonists first encountered the game, it was popular throughout much of the eastern U.S. and Canada.

✦ In 1834 the Canadian Caughnawaga tribe played a demonstration game for European settlers in Montreal. After stories of the game spread via newspapers, interest grew among nonnatives and leagues began to form.

✦ The sport is played today in more than 20 countries on five continents, with teams in such diverse places as Japan, Germany, Argentina, South Korea, and the Czech Republic.

✦ NFL Hall of Fame running back (and movie star) Jim Brown is considered by many to be the best football player ever to play the game. Many say the same thing about his play in this sport. He was an All-American for Syracuse University in the 1950s and is a member of the sport's Hall of Fame.

✦ The Iroquois Nationals, a multitribe team from New York and Ontario, are the only Native North American sports team of any kind that participates in international competition.

✦ When Brebeuf, the Jesuit missionary, saw it played in 1636, he wrote that the players used curved sticks with pouches on their ends to hurl a ball to each other. The stick reminded Brebeuf of the cross carried by French bishops, called *la crosier*, or "the cross."

✦ That was the first written mention of the game we now know as lacrosse.

WHAT IRONY IS

The word originally came from the Greek *eironia*, meaning "simulated ignorance." It later changed to the Latin form *ironia* and entered the English language in the 16th century. There are different types of irony, but they all share a bond: two meanings—one on the surface, and one underneath that contradicts the surface meaning.

✦ **Situational Irony.** This is when the expected outcome of an action is reversed. Example: A man is caught in a forest fire, so he runs to a lake for safety, but trips on the shore, bonks his head on a rock, and drowns in the one thing that could have saved him.

✦ **Cosmic Irony.** When it almost seems as if a higher power is having a laugh at humanity's expense. Example: Bill Gates enters a contest and his name is drawn randomly out of a hat. His prize: an Apple computer.

✦ **Dramatic Irony.** This is a storytelling device in which the audience knows something that the characters do not (or vice versa), thereby increasing the tension. Example: In Act I of Shakespeare's *Romeo and Juliet*, the title characters share a dance together, unaware of the fact that they are members of rival families. The audience, however, has already been informed of this.

✦ **Verbal Irony.** This can occur when a person says something, but the actual meaning differs from the literal meaning. Example: "As Fred tromped in from that dreadful blizzard, he smiled and said, 'What a beautiful day!'"

WHAT IRONY IS NOT

The term "irony" is used incorrectly so often that its meaning has become somewhat muddled. So to better understand what constitutes actual irony, here are three situations that *aren't* ironic.

✦ **Coincidence.** In 2008, after a five-year police investigation, a mob boss was arrested in his hotel room while he happened to be watching a miniseries that detailed the 1983 arrest of an infamous mob boss. Many news reports incorrectly labeled the story as ironic. It is, in fact, only a coincidence. Now, if the boss had been arrested because he had remained in that room for an extra half hour so he could watch a show about how to *avoid* getting caught, *that* would be ironic.

✦ **Hypocrisy.** If a politician who enacts legislation against illegal immigration is found to have illegal immigrants working in his garden, it's not ironic, it's hypocritical. If the politician had fallen into his pool and was rescued by one of the illegal immigrants he should have been trying to have deported, *that* would be ironic.

✦ **Sarcasm.** The jury's still out on whether sarcasm and irony are the same thing. Many etymologists say that sarcasm is a form of verbal irony, but according to the Sarcasm Society (really), "One main difference between irony and sarcasm is that irony is generally observed and sarcasm is generally created (i.e., spoken, written)."

HOUSEHOLD GENIUS

To clean a coffee grinder and sharpen its blades, grind up some dry, uncooked rice. (Don't overgrind.) Unplug the grinder, empty out the rice, and wipe out the residue with a clean, dry cloth.

ANIMAL SCENTS

✦ During mating season, male Asian elephants secrete a pheromone-laden substance from glands in their temple area that attracts females. In young males it smells like honey—so much so that bees are attracted to it. In adult males the odor is less pleasant, and is commonly described as "pungent."

✦ Dog owners often report that their pet "smells like fish." The source: pea-sized glands near a dog's anus that emit a brown, oily, odorous substance when it urinates and defecates. The fishy-smelling substance is used both to mark territory and to provide vital information concerning the dog's sex and mating status.

✦ The crested auklet, an Alaskan seabird known for a ponytail-like tuft of feathers on top of its head, smells like tangerines. The odor emanates from a substance produced in glands in the bird's neck region. Biologists don't know its exact purpose, but believe it may repel insects. The tangerine odor is so powerful that, even in dense fog or complete darkness, experienced Bering Sea fishermen know when they're approaching islands inhabited by the auklets.

✦ The African civet, a small carnivorous mammal with a cat-like appearance, secretes a musk, also known as "civet," from perineal glands near its anus. In Ethiopia the animals have been domesticated for centuries—just for the musk. At "harvesting" time, the animals are put into cramped cages that don't allow them to turn around; a small door at the rear of the cage allows owners to extract the musk with a small spoon. Civet is still used in perfumes today. Its odor is most commonly described as a mix of urine, feces, and flowers.

BLACK DAYS

Black Monday. The nickname for Monday, October 19, 1987. Several major stock markets around the world crashed, including Hong Kong (which dropped by 46%), Australia (42%), Spain (31%), New Zealand (60%), and the U.S. (23%). At the time, it was the largest one-day worldwide drop in history.

Black Tuesday. October 29, 1929, the date of the crash of the New York Stock Exchange, which precipitated the Great Depression.

Black Wednesday. On September 16, 1992, the British pound was forced out of the European Exchange Rate Mechanism, severely devaluing the currency. Investors (and the British government) lost more than £3.5 billion (about $5 billion), and the event was one of many that led to the creation of the euro, the European-wide currency.

Black Thursday. On February 1, 1996, President Bill Clinton signed the Communications Decency Act into law. It was a far-reaching attempt to regulate content on the Internet, including the amount of indecency and pornography. To call attention to what they felt was a violation of free speech protection, on Thursday, February 8, several major Web sites (including Yahoo!) changed the background color of all their sites to black. (The Communications Decency Act was ruled unconstitutional by the Supreme Court in 1997.)

Black Friday. The nickname for Friday, September 24, 1869, when bankers Jay Gould and James Fisk Jr. tried to corner the gold market, creating a Wall Street Panic.

Black Saturday. September 10, 1547, when Scottish attempts at independence were thwarted by English troops at the Battle of Pinkie, outside Edinburgh.

Black Sunday. Disneyland opened on Sunday, July 17, 1955, in Anaheim, California. The day came to be known as "Black Sunday" in the Disney corporation because the park's freshly poured asphalt hadn't yet dried. Hundreds of visitors' shoes got stuck and were left behind.

COMMON WORD MISTAKES

Further or Farther? When speaking of a measurable distance in physical space, use "farther"; when you want to express an addition to an abstract concept, use "further."

> "The farther down the road we traveled, the further into oblivion we fell."

However, since so many people use "further" to refer to distance as well, it may soon become standard. But "farther" should never be used to express an abstract concept.

More Than or Over? As a general rule, "over" refers to one thing being higher in physical space than something else, whereas "more than" is used to denote that one specific amount is greater than another. However, according to the editors of *The Chicago Manual of Style*, it's just as correct to say "Over 40 people loved my casserole" as it is to say "More than 40 people loved my casserole." The latter example, they explain, is simply more formal. So pick the one that sounds better to you.

Hung or Hanged? "Hung" is the past tense of "hang" in every case save one—the act of putting someone to death by hanging. In that case, the past tense of "hang" is "hanged."

WHO PUT THE "GOOD" IN GOOD FRIDAY?

This Christian holiday marks the day of the crucifixion of Jesus, so why call it good? Historians believe that the name is derived from "God's Friday" (the same way the phrase "good-bye" came from "God be with you"). In other countries, Good Friday is known as Long Friday, Silent Friday, or Holy Friday.

PERMAFROST

Permafrost is the name used for any soil, sediment, or rock that has remained below freezing temperature for more than two years. It is found on land and underwater, and ranges in thickness from about a foot to nearly a mile. In the Northern Hemisphere, it is generally found above 60 degrees north latitude (the latitude of Anchorage, Alaska) in Scandinavia, Russia, Mongolia, China, Greenland, Canada, and Alaska, and also in high mountain ranges such as the Himalayas and the Rockies. It's less prevalent in the Southern Hemisphere due to the fact that there's not as much unglaciated land at comparable latitudes, though it does occur in ice-free areas of Antarctica, and in the Andes Mountains in South America.

Millions of people around the world live in regions where permafrost is prevalent. Buildings, roads, pipelines, and other man-made structures can cause the permafrost to melt—and whatever is constructed on it to sink. As a result, permafrost has been studied extensively, and is classified into different types:

Cold permafrost. Remains below 30°F, and is often much colder. Temporary warm temperatures in the atmosphere do not cause thawing.

Warm permafrost. Remains just below 32°F, so warmer temperatures can cause thawing to occur relatively quickly.

Thaw-stable permafrost. Permafrost with low ice content found in bedrock, well-drained sediments such as gravel, and sand-and-gravel mixtures. Low ice content means thawing causes little settling.

Thaw-unstable permafrost. Found in poorly drained, fine soils, resulting in large amounts of ice. Thawing can cause excessive settling and movement.

✦ Permafrost is also categorized as *continuous* (large areas of uninterrupted permafrost, such as those in northern Russia and northern Alaska), *discontinuous* (permafrost broken up by patches of thaw, found in much of central Alaska), and *sporadic* (small permafrost oases; found in many areas of northern Canada).

✦ Roughly 24% of the land in the Northern Hemisphere is covered in permafrost.

✦ There are areas of permafrost on Earth that have been continuously frozen for more than a million years.

HOW PAPER IS MADE

Wood is made up of tiny strands of cellulose that stick together because of a natural adhesive called *lignin*. The splitting and restructuring of those fibers is how paper is made.

✦ Paper isn't made out of any one kind of wood. It's made by combining hardwoods and softwoods. Hardwoods (oak and maple) have short fibers, which make weak paper but produce a smooth surface that's ideal for writing and printing. Softwoods (pine and spruce) are made up of long fibers that yield strong paper with a rough finish.

✦ Trees are harvested and transported to a paper factory. Dirt and sap is rinsed off in a high-pressure water bath before the logs are ground into small chips of wood.

✦ The pulping stage: The individual wood fibers in the chips are separated in a water bath and then bleached white. The resulting pulp is 99% watery mush, but all the fibers are separate.

✦ The pulp is placed on a long, thin meshed screen called a *wire*. Much of the water drains out; the fibers collect and bind together.

✦ The "fiber mat" that forms is then squeezed through felt rollers to press out more water. At this point, the product is still more than 60% liquid.

✦ Next, metal silos filled with hot steam shoot the steam into dozens of sets of hot rollers, where the 30-foot-wide paper pulp runs through. The heating and drying moves the fibers closer together, gradually forming lumpy rolls of almost-paper.

✦ The rolls then go through a machine called a *calender*, in which iron rollers press the paper into uniform thickness (or thinness).

✦ Next, the paper is coated with a fine clay to make the writing surface smoother.

✦ It's then dried once more and rolled onto spools, where it's cut and shipped.

MISERY INDEX

Economist Arthur Okun devised the misery index in 1948 as an economic indicator to gauge the effect of a sour economy on the average citizen (it's the rate of unemployment added to the rate of inflation). Jimmy Carter introduced the phrase to a wider audience during his 1976 presidential campaign, citing that summer's misery index, which was high—13.45%. He won the election, but the index came back to bite him. The misery index hit at an *all-time* high of 20.76% in 1980, when Carter was running for reelection against Ronald Reagan, and it was one of the factors that cost him the election. Since the misery index has been measured, the lowest rate was in July 1953, at 3.74%.

THE DIFFERENCE BETWEEN...

Elevation and Altitude. Generally, elevation is used to describe how far a point *on land* is above sea level; altitude is used to describe how far a point *in the air* is above sea level.

SUPERMARKET SECRET

Almost everybody buys milk when they shop. To get to that milk, you have to walk through a good chunk of the supermarket, often along the perimeter. That's no accident—it's exactly where the store wants you to go. The more time you spend shopping along the sides and back of the supermarket, the more money the store makes. About half its profits come from these "perimeter items," often bought on an impulse by milk shoppers, including fruits and veggies, other dairy products, and meat, poultry, and fish.

"TAKE ME OUT TO THE BALL GAME"

One of the most iconic American songs, "Take Me Out to the Ball Game," written by Albert von Tilzer and Jack Norworth, was registered for copyright on May 2, 1908. Norworth, a successful vaudeville entertainer, wrote the song on a scrap of paper aboard a subway train to Manhattan and later gave it to Tilzer to compose music for it. By the end of 1908, the song was a hit...even though neither writer had ever been to a baseball game. The verses, rarely sung today, are about a girl whose "beau" wants to take her to a show, but she'd rather go to a ball game. The song has been a regular feature of the seventh-inning stretch at baseball games since the 1970s. Below are the complete lyrics, as originally published. (The term "sou" was slang for a coin of low denomination.)

Katie Casey was base ball mad.
Had the fever and had it bad;
Just to root for the home town crew,
Ev'ry sou Katie blew.
On a Saturday, her young beau
Called to see if she'd like to go,
To see a show but Miss Kate said,
"No, I'll tell you what you can do."

(Chorus) "Take me out to the ball game,
Take me out with the crowd.
Buy me some peanuts and Cracker Jack,
I don't care if I never get back,
Let me root, root, root for the home team,
If they don't win, it's a shame.
For it's one, two, three strikes, you're out,
At the old ball game."

Katie Casey saw all the games,
Knew the players by their first names;
Told the umpire he was wrong,
All along good and strong.
When the score was just two to two,
Katie Casey knew what to do,
Just to cheer up the boys she knew,
She made the gang sing this song:

(Repeat chorus)

THE AGE OF REASON

More than 90% of the scientists who
have ever lived are alive today.

CHAPTER 10

SEX, LIES, AND BAT BUGS

African bat bugs are small, reddish-brown parasites in the
bedbug family that feed off the blood of bats in caves in East
Africa. They have a peculiar and violent form of reproduction.
The females have genitalia, but they are used only for egg-laying,
not for mating. Mating instead consists of the male piercing the
abdomen of the female with his sharp penis and injecting sperm
directly into her bloodstream. Males also sometimes pierce
other males. In both cases, the procedure can severely wound
the victims.

In 2007 evolutionary biologist Klaus Reinhardt of the University of Sheffield in England discovered something even more
bizarre about African bat bugs: At some point in their evolutionary history, females of the species developed orifices on their
abdomens that very closely resembled their actual genitalia.

Inside these "paragenitals" are infection-stopping immune cells. When subjected to a dangerous mating attempt, the female guides the male's sharp penis into this opening—and is thereby protected from injury and infection.

And then it gets even weirder.

As we said before, male bat bugs can also be victims of the amorous attacks, and, Reinhardt discovered, some males of the species had also developed female paragenitals on their abdomens. So they too were offered some protection from the violent mating attempts. Reinhardt describes the African bat bug sexual habits as a "hotbed of deception."

HAT SIZES

Unlike shoes, which are sized in a straightforward manner (whole numbers and half numbers), or clothes, which are sized as small, medium, and large, hats are sized from 6½ to 8, with a different size at each eighth of an inch. For example, a small-headed person might have a hat size of 6⅝, and a larger-headed person would wear a 7⅜. What does the number mean? It's the circumference (in inches) of the sweat band inside the hat, divided by π (roughly 3.14).

EVERYDAY GENIUS

In 1986 in Bakersfield, California, carrot producer Mike Yurosek found that he was wasting up to 400 tons of carrots every day: He had to throw them out because they were too bent, twisted, or broken to sell. Realizing that some of the processors who bought his perfect carrots cut them up into coins and sticks anyway, Yurosek had an idea. He bought an industrial green-bean cutter from a defunct cannery (it cuts anything you put into it into two-inch pieces), and cut the "waste" carrots into shorter chunks. Then he put them in an industrial potato-peeler twice—once for a rough peel, and then again to "polish" the two-inch carrot pieces and round out the edges. Yurosek had invented the "baby carrot."

HOW TO CHANGE A TIRE

1. Put the car in park on level ground and apply the parking brake. To prevent the car from rolling, place a wheel chock or rock in front of the front wheel if you're changing a rear tire, or behind the rear wheel if you're changing a front tire.

2. Using a tire iron, remove the hubcap. Loosen the lug nuts about ⅓ of the way—do *not* remove them.

3. Place your jack under the frame of the car, near the tire that you're changing, as recommended in your owner's manual.

4. Jack up the car just enough to remove the old tire and so there's room to put on the new one.

5. Remove the lug nuts completely, then take off the flat tire.

6. Place the new tire on the wheel studs, with the air valve facing outward.

7. Replace the lug nuts and tighten them slightly.

8. Lower the jack and remove it.

9. Fully tighten the lug nuts and put the hubcap back on.

NATIVE AMERICAN NAMES

Most of the "official" names of Native American tribes were not the names they called themselves—they were given to them by other tribes. Some examples:

Cheyenne. This derived from the Dakota Sioux words for "red talkers," or "those who speak unintelligibly." (The Dakota and Cheyenne speak very different languages.) They call themselves the Tsistsistas, which means "the Like Hearted People."

Winnebago. These Great Lakes Indians got their name from the Chippewa people. It means "Filthy Water People," possibly because the Winnebago lived near algae-rich waters. Their own name: the Horogióthe, or the "People of the Sacred Language."

Gros Ventres. When French fur trappers and traders asked neighboring tribes about the name of these people, they responded—in Native American sign language—by sweeping their hand out from their chest and downward. Researchers believe they were trying to say "the Water Falls People," referring to part of the Saskatchewan River where they lived. The French mistook the gesture and called them the name they are still called today, the Gros Ventres, or, the "Big Bellies." They called themselves the A'aninin, or the "White Clay People."

BURGLE

The verb *burgle*, meaning "to steal," is what's called by etymologists a "back formation": a word that is formed by removing part of an older, longer word (in this case, the noun *burglar*), but has the appearance of being formed first. The English word *burglar* goes back to 1541 and has its root in the Latin word *burgare*, which meant "to break open" or "to commit burglary." The word *burglary* was formed around the same time. The word *burgle* didn't come into use until 1870. (Another example is the verb *edit*, which came after the appearance of the noun *editor*.)

THE MASON-DIXON LINE

By 1763, the two founding families of the colonies of Pennsylvania and Maryland, the Penns and the Calverts, had been embroiled in an eight-decade dispute over the location of their border. They finally hired two British land surveyors, Charles Mason and Jeremiah Dixon, to resolve it. It took four years to complete the task, and in 1767 both sides approved a border at the latitude of 39°43'26.3" north. The 233-mile-long line determined not only the border between Pennsylvania and Maryland, but also the border between Maryland and Virginia (including what is now West Virginia). In 1820, as part of the Missouri Compromise, the line was used as the eastern portion of the border between the North's slave-free states and the South's slave states. That led to the "Mason-Dixon Line," as it became known, becoming the unofficial border between the North and the South during the American Civil War.

4 GREAT MOMENTS IN ART HISTORY

Chauvet Cave painting. About 25,000 years ago, large, graceful depictions of several kinds of animals, primarily lions, mammoths, and rhinoceroses, were painted with natural dyes by primitive human artists in Chauvet Cave in southern France.

First clay pottery. About 12,000 years ago, the ancient Japanese Jomon people made the earliest known clay pottery. They used string to impress intricate patterns in the clay. (*Jomon* means "cord-mark.")

Giant heads. Giant, highly stylized human heads (some more than 9 feet tall) were carved out of solid basalt rock about 2,800 years ago by Olmec sculptors in what's now southern Mexico.

Pompeii's mosaic. About 2,100 years ago, the "Alexander Mosaic" was laid onto a floor at a private residence in the Roman city of Pompeii. It depicts Alexander the Great's victory over Darius, king of Persia, measures roughly 19 by 10 feet, and contains more than a million tiny colored tiles.

LANDLOCKED NATIONS

Of the 194 nations in the world today, 43 are landlocked, meaning they have no coastline and therefore no direct and unfettered access to major seas or oceans. Historically, this has been a great economic disadvantage; many of the nations on the list are among the world's most impoverished.

The largest landlocked country: Kazakhstan, the ninth-largest nation in the world, at just over one million square miles. Two countries, Liechtenstein and Uzbekistan, are *double landlocked*: they are surrounded by other landlocked countries. The 43 landlocked nations, by continent:

Africa	Asia	Europe
Botswana	Afghanistan	Andorra
Burkina Faso	Azerbaijan	Armenia
Burundi	Bhutan	Austria
Central African Republic	Kazakhstan	Belarus
Chad	Kyrgyzstan	Czech Republic
Ethiopia	Laos	Hungary
Lesotho	Mongolia	Liechtenstein
Malawi	Nepal	Luxembourg
Mali	Tajikistan	Macedonia
Niger	Turkmenistan	Moldova
Rwanda	Uzbekistan	San Marino
Swaziland		Serbia
Uganda	**South America**	Slovakia
Zambia	Bolivia	Switzerland
Zimbabwe	Paraguay	Vatican City

GREAT MOMENTS IN CIGARETTE LIGHTER HISTORY

✦ **Circa 1650** "tinder pistols" were recycled flintlock pistols that instead of lighting a gunpowder charge lit a small amount of tinder—easily burnable material, often cloth—creating a flame that could be used to light a pipe. This was the first lighter made strictly for tobacco. Very intricate and elaborate models were made and used until the 1880s. (They're prized antiques today.)

✦ **In 1823** German chemist Johann Wolfgang Döbereiner designed a lighter comprised of a glass jar about the size of a beer mug that utilized chemical reactions between sulfuric acid, zinc, hydrogen gas, and platinum. The user opened a cap on the lid, and a small flame appeared. Close it, and the flame went out. Tens of thousands of "Döbereiner Lamps" were used for many purposes—including lighting pipes and cigars—until the late 1800s. (They can still be found today.)

✦ **In 1903** Austrian scientist Carl Auer von Welsbach invented a metal alloy known as *ferro-cerium* that created sparks when scratched. It's the "flint" that's been used in lighters ever since.

✦ **In the early 1900s,** mass production of prerolled cigarettes skyrocketed, and in 1913 Louis V. Aronson of Newark, New Jersey, introduced the "Ronson Wonderliter." It had a metal body stuffed with naphtha-soaked cotton, with a wick protruding from the top (naphtha is a flammable oil). A flint (ferro-cerium) rod was attached to the cap; striking it on the lighter's top lit the wick. It wasn't very popular, but it was the first pocket cigarette lighter.

✦ **In 1926** Ronson released the first single-motion lighter. Called the Banjo, it used "hammer-action": Pushing down on a lever on the lighter's top pulled a small cap off the wick, simultaneously turning a "flint-wheel" to create sparks that lit the wick. They were hugely popular.

✦ **In 1933** the first Zippo lighter was released, changing the industry forever. It already had the rectangular shape of the "classic" Zippo. A hinge held the lid to the body; the flint-wheel was struck by the thumb; and a metal barrel sur-rounded the flame, making the Zippo "wind proof."

✦ **In 1961** Stockholm's Swedish Match company introduced the first disposable (and plastic) lighter—the Cricket.

✦ **In 1971** the first Bic lighters were released. Like the Cricket, Bics were plastic and disposable. Major innovation: They had adjustable flames.

✦ **Present.** Many kinds of lighter technologies have been invented over the last 50 years—piezoelectric lighters (the ones used to light barbecues) and flameless laser lighters among them. And although tobacco use has declined drastically, more than a billion lighters are still sold every year in the U.S. alone (if only to hold aloft at rock concerts).

CANCER BASICS

Cancer is the name used to describe more than 200 different diseases characterized by mutated (damaged or altered) DNA, which results in the cells dividing uncontrollably, allowing them to infiltrate and damage healthy body tissue.

✦ Cell division is one of the most fundamental processes of life—all life. In humans, life starts as a single fertilized egg cell containing DNA from each of the parents. That cell (along with its DNA) divides; its daughter cells divide again; and eventually become the trillions of cells that make up our bodies. During adulthood, cell division continues, maintaining our bodily functions.

✦ Cancer is a breakdown in the cell division monitoring process. If, during division, a cell's DNA is in some way damaged, protein molecules biochemically react and repair it. If it can't be repaired, other proteins are activated and kill it.

✦ Proteins are made by genes. (Genes and DNA are basically the same thing—genes are short sections of long, chainlike DNA molecules.) In humans, about 20,000 "protein-encoding" genes create about 20,000 proteins that biochemically interact in the cells they inhabit, "telling" the cells how to do their jobs: such as how to grow into organs, bones, and other tissues, or how to transport oxygen from the air to the bloodstream throughout our lives. That is *all* that genes do.

✦ If a gene is damaged in some way, it will make damaged proteins. This is because genes make proteins by essentially making copies of themselves.

✦ If the damaged proteins are meant to regulate cell division, a cell with mutated DNA can be allowed to divide, creating two abnormal cells; then 4, then 8, then 16, with more mutations occurring along the way until there are millions of abnormal cells, and, finally, a tumor. (It must be noted that one mutation alone does not lead to cancer. A series of mutations must take place over several cell generations in order for cancer to occur.)

✦ Another important characteristic of cancerous cells is that they don't die when they're supposed to. All cells have a life span, whether just hours or many years, and are programmed to die at a certain point. That, like everything else cells do, is maintained by genes and proteins. If genes are damaged, then the cells just keep living...and dividing.

✦ Cancers are named for their point of origin (stomach, lung, brain, etc.)

✦ Cancerous cells can travel through the lymph and blood systems from their place of origin and grow into new tumors. This process is called *metastasis*. Primary tumors are ones formed at the place of origin; others are called *metastatic tumors*.

✦ For more cancer basics, go to page 384.

10 -ISMS

1. Accidentalism: the idea that all events are random

2. Malism: the belief that the world is inherently evil

3. Panspermism: the theory that life on Earth is derived from extraterrestrial germs

4. Animism: the belief that all things have souls

5. Psychomorphism: the belief that inanimate objects have thoughts

6. Zootheism: the idea that animals are divine

7. Antidisestablishmentarianism: the opposition to a movement to strip any church of its status as that country's state religion

8. Acosmism: the belief that the entire universe is not real

9. Antinomianism: a rejection of the common moral code

10. Adamitism: the belief in being naked for religious reasons

DOMESTIC CORMORANTS

For more than 1,000 years, traditional fishermen in Japan and China have trained cormorants—birds that dive, catch, and eat fish—to do their fishing for them. The birds are taken on boats onto rivers or lakes, where they're allowed to dive for prey...but a string is tied around the base of their long necks. This allows only the smallest fish to be swallowed. When the birds come back to the boat, the fisherman extracts the larger fish that are still in their mouths and throat. Then the birds go hunt for another batch.

THE DIFFERENCE BETWEEN...

Carat and karat. A *carat* is a unit of weight used for precious gems and is equal to 200 milligrams (about the weight of a small vitamin tablet). A *karat* is a unit of purity for gold; 24-karat gold is 100% (actually 99.9%) pure gold, 20-karat gold is 83.3% pure, 18-karat gold is 75% pure, and so on. Confusion reigns: "karat" can also be spelled as "carat."

GENE AUTRY'S COWBOY CODE

1. The Cowboy must never shoot first, hit a smaller man, or take unfair advantage.

2. He must never go back on his word or a trust confided in him.

3. He must always tell the truth.

4. He must be gentle with children, the elderly, and animals.

5. He must not advocate or possess racially or religiously intolerant ideas.

6. He must help people in distress.

7. He must be a good worker.

8. He must keep himself clean in thought, speech, action, and personal habits.

9. He must respect women, parents, and his nation's laws.

10. A cowboy is a patriot.

WHY IS ICE SLIPPERY?

For more than a century, two related answers were commonly given to this question: 1) The heat caused by the friction of an object moving on ice is enough to cause a thin layer to melt, and the meltwater acts as a lubricant between the object and the ice; and 2) the pressure of an object simply resting on ice causes enough heat to melt a thin layer of water—so you can go from standing on your feet to lying flat on your back in an instant. It wasn't until the mid-1990s that research revealed there was more to it than that. A thin layer of molecules at the surface of ice, it turns out, acts differently than molecules *inside* the ice. The surface layer is only very weakly attached to the molecules beneath it, and therefore acts more like free-moving water than solid ice. This is true about ice even when the air around it is far below freezing—down to –200°F. That means that ice already has a thin, melted layer on it even before something makes contact with it—and that's why it's slippery.

THE 17 PENGUIN SPECIES

Emperor	Adélie	Macaroni
King	Chinstrap	Royal
Little blue (or fairy)	Rockhopper	Galápagos
	Fiordland	African
Yellow-eyed	Snares	Magellanic
Gentoo	Erect-crested	Humboldt

THE AGE OF EXPLORATION TIMELINE

Beginning around the year 1000 C.E.—but especially in the 15th and 16th centuries—exploration of the planet boomed among the seafaring nations of Europe, namely Spain, Portugal, and England. Here's a look at who opened up new sea routes, and who "discovered" what during this time.

982: Eric the Red, a Viking, lands in Greenland. Four years later, he returns with colonists.

1002: Eric the Red's son, Leif Eriksson, finds North America. He explores the east coast of the landmass from as far north as Newfoundland to as far south as Cape Cod in Massachusetts.

1488: Bartholomo Dias of Portugal rounds the Cape of Good Hope, the southern tip of Africa. In the process, he becomes the first European to negotiate more than 1,200 miles of African coastline.

1492: Sailing from Spain, Italian explorer Christopher Columbus begins the first of four voyages, eventually landing in the Bahamas, Jamaica, Cuba, and Central America.

1497: Amerigo Vespucci, an Italian mapmaker, reaches Guyana. In 1499 he crosses the equator and explores the coasts of Guyana and Brazil, as well as the Amazon River.

1498: Vasco de Gama of Portugal rounds the Cape of Good Hope and reaches India, which establishes the first sea route from Europe to Asia.

1500: Pedro Alvares Cabral, a Portuguese navigator, lands on the coast of what is now Brazil. The country still speaks Portuguese and was the only lasting Portuguese colony in the New World.

1513: Vasco Nunez de Balboa of Spain sails to Central America and then crosses the Isthmus of Panama on land, becoming the first European to reach the Pacific from North America.

1519: Ferdinand Magellan of Portugal names the Pacific Ocean and leads an expedition to sail around the world. It takes three years. He's killed along the way, and the trip is completed by Juan Sebastian del Cano.

1542: Hernando de Soto of Spain leads the first expedition through the interior of what is now the United States. Included in this journey: the European discovery of the Mississippi River. (He was actually looking for gold and a western route to China.)

1578: Sir Francis Drake of England sails to the New World, down the coast of South America, and around it to the Pacific Ocean.

SOUND IN SPACE

No matter what you may have seen in science-fiction films, there is no sound in space. Period. Sound needs some kind of material—air, water, hotel room walls, etc.—to travel through. Slam your hand down on your desk and the molecules that make up the desk (as well as your hand, to a lesser degree) are induced to vibrate. The vibrating desk molecules cause the air molecules around them to vibrate, which causes the air molecules next to them to vibrate, and a sound wave travels through the air. Slam your hand on the outside of a spaceship door while it's in space, and the molecules in the door will vibrate—but there are no air molecules in space, so no sound waves can form. (The people *inside* the spaceship would be able to hear it, though, because there's air inside the craft.)

FAIRY TALES

What are the names of the seven dwarfs? The original dwarfs from the German fairy tale, first published by the Brothers Grimm as *Snow White and the Seven Dwarfs* in the book *Children's and Household Tales* in 1812, had no names. For the 1937 animated feature film, Walt Disney gave the dwarfs the names Doc, Grumpy, Happy, Sleepy, Bashful, Sneezy, and Dopey.

SNOWFLAKES

It's true that no two snowflakes are alike. Every snowflake starts out as a simple hexagonal crystal that forms on a particle of dust. As it falls through the clouds, it changes dramatically. Depending on how cold and moist it is inside the cloud, the flake can assume many different shapes: it grows one way, then another, building on itself in an endlessly complex crystalline pattern. If two snowflakes followed the exact same path as they fell through the sky, *then* they'd look exactly alike...but they never do.

YOU AREN'T "YOU"

The average adult human body is made up of more than 100 trillion cells, all of them descendants of the one original *zygote*—the egg cell from your mother that was fertilized by sperm from your father. The average body also contains microbes: organisms that enter from the environment, such as the bacteria that line the intestines and aid in digestion. These beneficial microbes colonize our bodies during and shortly after birth, and they stay with us our entire lives. In fact, the average adult human body contains at least *20 times* as many colonizing microbes as native human cells.

KANGAROO COURT

This phrase refers to a sham legal trial in which the rules of justice are not followed and the guilt of the accused is a fore-gone conclusion. The first written record of the phrase appeared in 1853. Exactly how the phrase was born is disputed, but the strongest case says that it arose from roving judges in the western United States who were paid by the case and "jumped" from town to town to up their earnings. Others believe it had to do with "claim jumping" trials in the Gold Rush days, or that it referred to proceedings that "jumped" quickly from accusation to sentenc-ing, or that it came from where you might think it did—Australia. More than a few Australians made their way to the U.S. for the Gold Rush, and many were subjected to shady legal tactics, which they termed "kangaroo courts."

THE MOON CAME FROM THE PACIFIC

Over the centuries, there have been several theories explaining how the Moon came to be. Three prevailed for more than 100 years, until humans actually traveled to the Moon in the 1960s.

The Co-Accretion Theory (late 1800s). The exact origin of this hypothesis is unknown, but it was a popular one. It proposed that the Moon was formed during the *accretion* process that formed Earth. (See page 260 for more on that.) For this theory to be true, however, the Moon would have to have the same chemi-cal composition as Earth—and lunar samples taken during the Apollo missions showed that this is simply not true.

The Fission Theory (1878). Mathematician and astronomer

George Howard Darwin, son of Charles Darwin, proposed that centrifugal force caused by the spinning of the very early, still molten Earth caused a large piece of it to break off and fly into space, where it was caught in orbit and became the Moon. In 1882 geologist Osmond Fisher added that the Pacific Ocean basin was the scar left behind by this event. Again, lunar composition makes this theory very unlikely.

The Capture Theory (1909). This theory was proposed by American astronomer Thomas Jefferson Jackson See. It says that the Moon was formed far away from Earth and later passed close enough to be captured in its gravitational field. That would explain why the composition of the Moon is different from Earth, but this theory is largely discounted due to the extreme unlikeliness that a passing object would be moving at the correct speed and direction to be pulled into a perfect orbit.

The Giant Impact Theory (1975). Not long after humans finally walked on the Moon and samples were brought back and studied, astronomers W. K. Hartmann and D. R. Davis proposed a new theory: When Earth was just 50 million years old—some 4.5 billion years ago—a planetary object the size of Mars slammed into it (a slightly off-center hit, they said). The enormous impact resulted in a huge amount of debris—both from the object and from Earth's mantle—being thrown into space. Much of it was affected by Earth's gravity and fell into orbit. This material eventually coalesced into the Moon. This would explain not only the different makeup of the Moon but also its lack of a large iron core, since the Earth's mantle was by this time largely free of iron (because the iron was in the core). Today, the Giant Impact Theory is the most widely accepted.

IDIOSYNCRASIES OF GENIUS

Beethoven counted out exactly 60 beans for each cup of coffee.

CHAPTER 11

CREDIT SCORES

Your credit score is officially called a FICO score, created by the Fair Isaac Corporation (FICO), which distills a credit report into a three-digit number that represents a person's credit "worthiness." The FICO score is used by all three major credit bureaus: Experian, TransUnion, and Equifax, which keep track of every lending and credit action in the United States. Ranging from a 300 (low) to 850 (high), the score is used by FICO to determine interest rates on cars and homes, insurance rates, and down-payment amounts. It's even used by employers to judge the risk of a potential new hire. Here's a look at what determines your FICO score:

✦ 35% of the score is determined by your payment history, including the timeliness with which you've paid every bill or loan payment.

✦ Another 30% is based on your current number of debts, such as student loans or an outstanding (unpaid) credit card balance, and how much credit you have available.

✦ 15% of the score is based on the length of your credit history. A lot of activity is usually better than no activity. Lenders tend to be suspicious if you've never charged anything or borrowed any money—you haven't established a pattern of borrowing and repaying, or borrowing and repaying on time. Activity shows that you've had credit and can use it responsibly. And the longer you've had a particular credit card or account, the better.

✦ Another 10% is determined by recent applications for credit. Too many suggest financial desperation, unreliability, or fraud.

✦ The final 10% is based on the different types of overall credit in your history. Once again, this establishes your credit patterns and reliability. If all of your credit history comes from credit cards, you appear as more of a risk. But if you have a varied history (credit cards, mortgage payments, student loans), it gives the appearance of a responsible person.

LESSER-KNOWN GREEK GODS AND GODDESSES

Bia: the goddess of violence

Ate: the goddess of foolish acts

Alastor: the god (or demon) of family feuds

Hypnos: the god of sleep

Anthenia: the goddess of flowers and wreaths

Iris: the goddess of the rainbow

Momus: the god of criticism

Nyx: the goddess of darkness

Adephagia: the goddess of gluttony

Caerus: the god of luck

Peitho: the goddess of persuasion

Ceto: the goddess of sea monsters

Eileithyia: the goddess of childbirth

Aeolus: the god of the winds

Hygieia: the goddess of cleanliness

Priapus: the god of male virility

THE TEAPOT DOME SCANDAL

It was one of the biggest scandals in American political history, and you've probably heard the name, but do you know what happened in the Teapot Dome affair? In 1921 President Warren Harding issued an executive order to shift control of oil reserves in Teapot Dome, Wyoming, from the Navy to the Department of the Interior. The following year, Interior secretary Albert Fall leased the Teapot Dome fields (and the right to the oil) to an oilman named Harry Sinclair. That's legal, but Sinclair secured the contract without bidding. This launched an investigation by the U.S. Senate, which revealed that in 1921, Sinclair had given Fall an interest-free loan of as much as $100,000—essentially a bribe for drilling rights to the Teapot Dome oil fields. Fall was indicted on charges of conspiracy and accepting bribes, and was convicted for the latter; he was sentenced to a year in prison and fined $100,000. (Fall was the first sitting cabinet member ever sentenced to a jail term.) Sinclair was acquitted of the bribery charge, but was imprisoned for contempt of Senate. In the 1922 Congressional elections, Republicans—the party of Harding and Fall—lost 77 seats, a quarter of their delegation.

101 ACCEPTABLE TWO-LETTER SCRABBLE WORDS

These actual words are taken from the Official Tournament Word List, the "official word authority" for tournament Scrabble games played in the United States, Canada, and Thailand:

AA	AM	BA	EF	EX	HO	KI	MO	OE	OS	RE	UM	XU
AB	AN	BE	EH	FA	ID	LA	MU	OF	OW	SH	UN	YA
AD	AR	BI	EL	FE	IF	LI	MY	OH	OX	SI	UP	YE
AE	AS	BO	EM	GO	IN	LO	NA	OI	OY	SO	US	YO
AG	AT	BY	EN	HA	IS	MA	NE	OM	PA	TA	UT	ZA
AH	AW	DE	ER	HE	IT	ME	NO	ON	PE	TI	WE	
AI	AX	DO	ES	HI	JO	MI	NU	OP	PI	TO	WO	
AL	AY	ED	ET	HM	KA	MM	OD	OR	QI	UH	XI	

CORE, MANTLE, CRUST

Geologists divide the Earth into three main sections: the core, which makes up about 15% of the planet's volume; the mantle, about 84%; and the crust, which makes up less than 1%. Nobody has ever observed the mantle or core; data collected by geologists, seismologists, and metallurgists has been used to identify their characteristics.

The core is Earth's innermost section. It was formed, geologists believe, soon after the planet's formation roughly 4.57 billion years ago. As the molten planet cooled, it compacted, and the heavier elements sank to the center. That's why the core is made up primarily of iron and nickel. It's divided into the inner and outer core: The inner core is about 1,500 miles in diameter (the entire planet's diameter is about 7,900 miles). Although the core's temperature is over 9,000°F, it's still solid—the pressure is so great and its density so high that it can't melt. The outer core is about 1,400 miles thick; its temperature ranges from 7,200°F to 9,032°F; and though it's also very dense, it is always molten.

The mantle is made primarily of lighter elements, mostly oxygen, silicon, and magnesium. It's about 1,800 miles thick, with temperatures between 1,800°F at the boundary with the crust to more than 7,200°F at the boundary with the core.

The crust is made up primarily of igneous, metamorphic, and sedimentary rocks (see page 336) and is broken up into tectonic plates that "ride" on top of the liquid magma at the surface of the mantle. The *continental* crust, the crust under the continents, ranges from 15 to 20 miles thick, and is less dense than the *oceanic* crust—which is why it has risen higher than the oceanic crust. The temperature increases with depth, reaching about 1,650°F at the boundary with the mantle.

SPEAK LIKE A GENIUS

Fewer or Less? "Fewer" denotes a specific amount of something countable; "less" denotes a general amount of something not countable.

> "Fewer mimes are performing on the boardwalk, so there's less of a chance you'll get to see one, Timmy."

7 TYPES OF "VEGETARIANS"

People who don't eat meat—and even many who eat a very meat-limited diet—often refer to themselves as "vegetarians," but there are many different varieties:

✦ *Ovo-vegetarians* eat eggs but no meat or dairy products.

✦ *Lacto-vegetarians* eat dairy products, but no meat or eggs.

✦ *Lacto-ovo-vegetarians* eat both eggs and dairy products—but no meat.

✦ *Vegans* don't eat any land or sea animals, nor do they eat eggs, dairy products, or anything that contains animal products, such as gelatin (which is made from the bones, tendons, and other assorted parts of cattle and horses). Vegans also avoid white cane sugar because it's often filtered through bone char, which is charcoal…made from animal bone. (Beet sugar is okay.)

✦ *Raw food vegans* are just like vegans, only colder. They don't eat any food heated above 115°F.

✦ *Macrobiotic* dieters are often thought of as vegetarians, but they do eat meat and fish, just not a lot of it. Grains, vegetables, and beans are the major components of this diet.

✦ *Fruitarians* eat fruit…and only fruit. This includes foods not typically considered fruits but which actually are, such as tomatoes, bell peppers, and avocados.

FIRST CATTLE

Can you picture the typical cave painting depicting early man hunting a large ox-like animal? That animal is called the *aurochs*. The ancestor of all modern European cattle, the aurochs is an extinct species of wild *ungulates*, or hoofed mammals. The name is taken from the German *Auerochs*, or "primeval ox." Fossil remains, some remarkably intact, reveal that they were very large animals, standing more than six feet at the shoulders and weighing up to 2,200 pounds. Written accounts say that, unlike most modern cattle, the aurochs was fiercely aggressive and would attack anything that entered its territory. Yet even with its two massive, forward-sweeping horns (often three feet long), the aurochs was no match for human hunters. The last known member of the species died in the Jaktorów Forest in Poland in 1627.

FLOWER MEANINGS

Since ancient times, people all over the world attached symbolic meanings to flowers. It became especially popular in Victorian-era England: You didn't just "send flowers" on an important occasion—the flowers you sent had a certain meaning. Here are a few of those.

Tulips: Sent to indicate passionate, romantic love

Carnations: To express platonic admiration

Sunflowers: To express loyalty or devotion

Zinnias: "Thinking of you," to someone who's very far away

Laurels: To express congratulations on a victory

Cherry blossoms: Sent to call out duplicitous behavior

Marigolds: To offer sympathy in times of sorrow

Iris: "Have faith—things will get better"

Peonies: "Get well soon"

HOW TO MAKE BONE CHAR

Some cane sugar producers use bone char to refine white sugar. Here's how they make it:

✦ Get bones from dead cows. Most U.S. sugar refineries that use it (reports indicate that about 25% of the major producers do) buy them from "bone merchants" who extract them from cows that have died in Third World countries.

✦ Heat the bones at a high temperature until they're black and have a granular, charcoal-like consistency. They have now undergone a chemical transformation and consist of calcium phosphate and carbon. Your bone char is now ready for sugar filtering use.

✦ Place the char in a filter (the larger sugar refineries have "filter columns" up to 40 feet high that can hold more than 70,000 pounds of char) and pass liquid cane sugar through the filter.

✦ Bone char naturally attracts the impurities that discolor

sugar; when the liquid sugar crystallizes, it becomes much whiter, the way consumers like it.

✦ Bone char is also used in water filters, for drinking water, and in aquariums.

✦ Beet sugar, which is made from beets, not sugarcane, doesn't require bone char as it is naturally white when processed.

ALLERGIC TO BOYS

A 2003 European study found that mothers whose first babies are male are much more likely to have miscarriages in subsequent pregnancies than mothers whose first babies are female. And the difference was stark: Among those whose first babies were girls, 73% successfully bore another child; among those with boys, the number dropped to just 53%. Subsequent studies have reported similar results. The explanation is believed to be that male and female humans are different enough—we produce different hormones, for example—that a pregnant woman's immune system can sometimes react to a male fetus as a "foreign" object—as it would a virus or bacteria. Having this happen in a first pregnancy, researchers say, might "sensitize" women, just as vaccines sensitize us to certain diseases. That results in an even stronger immune system reaction when a later pregnancy occurs—whether with a male or female fetus—and therefore results in a higher likelihood of miscarriage.

ORIGIN OF THE NICOTINE PATCH

Nicotine is the most addictive ingredient in tobacco, and its health risks are further exacerbated by the tars and carbon monoxide ingested during smoking. In 1979 Dr. Frank Etscorn, a psychology professor studying addictive substances, was experimenting with liquid nicotine when he accidentally spilled some on his arm. A little while later, he felt the telltale effects of a nicotine "buzz." That gave him the idea that it might help people attempting to quit smoking if they were given, through the skin, gradually decreasing doses of nicotine. Etscorn was right. The first nicotine patches hit drugstore shelves in 1992. Under brand names such as NicoDerm and Habitrol, patches have been used by more than 20 million smokers in the United States.

WORD SEARCH: *BAZOOKA*

1940s radio comedian Bob Burns often played a homemade horn consisting of a few feet of metal piping with a funnel on the end. He called it the "bazooka." The popularity of his radio show at the onset of World War II brought the word to the battlefield, where it took on the name of a powerful, shoulder-fired antitank gun, and has come to represent such weapons ever since.

FROM FOSSIL TO FUEL

How prehistoric flora and fauna end up in your gas tank, furnace, and kitchen stove.

✦ When tiny marine plants and animals die, they settle on the ocean floor. Trillions of these dead organisms accumulate over the eons, mixing with sand and sediment to form layers of carbon-rich material—carbon being the main ingredient in all life—on the sea floor. These layers can grow to be many miles thick.

✦ As additional layers build up, the pressure on those below rises to immense proportions, which in turn causes the temperature to rise dramatically. The pressure and heat cause the sand and sediment to harden into rock and the organic material to be transformed into hydrogen and carbon compounds—*hydrocarbons*.

✦ Hydrocarbons come in many forms, from gases to very thick sludge. Because they're lighter than rock, they're pushed upward through cracks and through permeable rock and, if able, are eventually emitted on the ocean floor or on land. If these traveling hydrocarbons encounter impermeable rock, they become trapped in underground reservoirs.

✦ After tens of millions of years, the hydrocarbon reservoirs—found mostly beneath oceans (though the process can occur in rivers and lakes)—are pumped or drilled out as natural gases or liquids.

✦ All hydrocarbons are made of the same things—carbon and hydrogen—but they come in hundreds of forms. These differences revolve around their molecular makeup (which is what gives each its unique properties). Methane molecules consist of one carbon and four hydrogen atoms, CH_4, a lighter-than-air gas (like helium) at room temperature. Propane has three carbons and eight hydrogens, C_3H_8, and is also a gas. Octane, with 8 carbons and 18 hydrogens, C_8H_{18}, is a clear, odorless liquid.

✦ Gas and liquid hydrocarbons are often found together. If there is more gas, the location is called a *natural gas field*; if there is more liquid, it's called an *oil field*. The liquid form is called *crude oil*, also called *petroleum*. Neither form is pure: They are always a mix of different hydrocarbons, as well as other compounds, and must be refined to extract usable forms.

✦ In the case of crude oil, the oil is pumped (or shipped) from the well to a refinery, where the impurities are removed. Then the oil is processed to separate the different hydrocarbons. The process: Each hydrocarbon, from very light gases to thick, sludgy oils, has its own boiling point. This is due to their unique molecular makeups, and because of this they can be easily distilled.

✦ In a refinery, crude oil is boiled in the bottom of a distillation tower about 120 feet high. The gases travel up and pass through specially made collecting plates at different heights that cool off the gases. When gas from a specific hydrocarbon rises to a height in the tower where the temperature is the same as its melting point, it condenses back into liquid and is collected in a tray and then piped out of the tower.

✦ The heaviest hydrocarbons, such as asphalt, have the highest melting points (over 1,000°F) and are collected very low in the tower. Lighter ones, such as gasoline (melting point around 100°F), make it pretty far up in the tower. Gases like methane, which has a melting point of –297°F, go all the way to the top of the tank and are piped to another tank for further distillation. Average percent of gasoline distilled from a barrel of crude oil: 46%.

✦ Other products that come from crude oil refining: LPG (liquefied petroleum gas), naphtha, jet fuel, kerosene, diesel fuel, and lubricating oil.

✦ Natural-gas processing is largely the same. Straight out of the ground, it's primarily methane, along with varying amounts of other gases such as ethane, butane, carbon dioxide, and water vapor. It's piped to a processing plant for "sweetening," where contaminants are removed. Different gases are then separated via distillation.

✦ In the U.S., the gas is then pumped out of the refinery and into a network of pipes that take it to one of the more than 1,400 compressor stations in the country. These regulate and maintain the pressure in the pipes. (The toxic leakage depicted in the film *Erin Brockovich* was from a natural-gas-compressor station.)

✦ From there, the natural gas is piped to the more than 60 million American homes and hundreds of thousands of businesses that use it for heating and cooking purposes.

APRIL FOOL'S

In the 16th century, many Europeans began the new year with an eight-day springtime celebration that culminated in a huge party on April 1. But the calendar was different then, and various regions held holidays (such as Christmas) on different days. So in 1564, 14-year-old French King Charles IX issued the Edict of Roussillon, placing France on the 365-day Gregorian calendar (the one we use today). The edict also established the first day of the calendar year as New Year's Day—January 1. But back then, news traveled much slower, especially in rural areas. It took decades for the calendar to be universally adopted, resulting in many French still celebrating the new year in the spring. According to some accounts, those people came to be called "fools," to the extent that those in the know of the new calendar sent them on "fool's errands," also known as practical jokes.

HORSEPOWER

Horsepower is a measure of power, most often associated with internal combustion engines (as in cars). The concept was first theorized by English inventor Thomas Savery in 1702 but was developed by Scottish inventor James Watt in the late 1700s. In promoting a new steam engine design he'd developed, Watt determined that a horse could lift 150 pounds and move it 220 feet in one minute. A unit of horsepower became (150 x 220) divided by 1 minute, or 33,000 "foot-pounds" of work per minute.

MEASUREMENT MEANINGS

Fathom. In the 19th century, it was used to measure depth of water, stemming from the length of rope held between the hands of outstretched arms. In other words, it was the arm span of an average sailor. Today, a fathom is officially six feet.

Furlong. Coined in England around the year 1300, it meant the distance a team of oxen could pull a plow in one session. Officially, it's since been set at 660 feet, or ⅛ of a mile.

Nautical mile. One-sixtieth of one degree of latitude. That works out to about 1.15 miles.

League. On land, it's three miles. At sea, it's three nautical miles.

Light-year. Light travels at, well, the speed of light, which is about 186,000 miles per second. A light-year is how far light travels in one year: 5,874,601,678,800 miles (that's about 5.9 *trillion* miles).

Acre. It's 1/640 of a square mile, or 43,560 square feet.

Astronomical Unit (AU). Used to measure the distances between celestial objects in a way the layman can understand. One AU is equal to the average distance from Earth to the Sun, or 93 million miles.

International Unit (IU). A near-universal way of measuring pharmaceutical products, vitamins, and hormones. However, one IU of one substance is not the same as one IU of another; it's relative to each individual substance being measured. For instance, 1 IU of insulin is about 45.5 grams, and 1 IU of Vitamin E is about 0.667 milligrams.

THE SCIENTIFIC METHOD

In 1021 C.E. Islamic scholar Ibn al-Haytham of Basra, Iraq (though he spent most of his life in Cairo), wrote *Optics*, a treatise on the nature of light, just one of his more than 200 writings on the sciences. In it he outlined the seven steps he used in his experiments.

1. observation

2. statement of a problem or question

3. formulation of a hypothesis, or a possible answer to the problem or question

4. testing of the hypothesis with an experiment

5. analysis of the experiment's results

6. interpretation of the data and formulation of a conclusion

7. publication of the findings

The work made its way slowly through Europe as it emerged from the Dark Ages, being read by such scientific giants as Roger Bacon (in the 13th century) and Leonardo da Vinci (in the 15th and 16th centuries). His experimentation system is known today as the "Scientific Method" and is seen as the foundation of the modern scientific era. Al-Haytham is widely regarded as the world's "first scientist."

THE POLITICAL SPECTRUM

The French Legislative Assembly met for the first time during the French Revolution on October 1, 1791. Like legislative bodies today, the group of 745 lawmakers and representatives grouped themselves according to their political affiliation. For no reason in particular, the more liberal members sat to the left of the speaker and the conservatives sat to the right. Today, "left wing" and "right wing" are still used to denote those same political affiliations.

THE TYPESETTER'S DESK

In the early days of printing, typesetters had to place each letter on the press individually. Capital letters were stored in an "upper case," literally a case, or drawer, located above the typesetter's desk. The rest of the letters were kept in a "lower case"—hence the common terms for what are technically called *majuscule* and *minuscule* letters.

SURVIVING A PLANE CRASH

✦ Listen to the flight attendant's preflight safety instructions, especially concerning emergency exits. You may think you've heard it all before, but different planes have different escape procedures. Studies have shown that those who made it out alive did so because they knew where to go after surviving the initial impact.

✦ During any flight, keep your seat belt fastened; move through the cabin only when absolutely necessary. Many plane crashes begin with a sudden movement that can propel unfastened passengers out of their seats like projectiles.

✦ Many who survive the initial crash are killed by fire or fumes from burning upholstery because they hesitate or try to collect their belongings first. Leave your carry-on items behind and use the escape plan you memorized to get off the plane immediately.

✦ Once you've escaped from the plane, get a safe distance away to protect yourself from an explosion, but stay close enough for rescuers to find you.

✦ If the plane crashes in water, don't inflate your life vest until you are safely out of the plane. An inflated life vest may get stuck in an exit or otherwise hamper your escape.

✦ Finally, think twice before you grumble because you can only afford to fly coach—sitting in the rear of the cabin can improve your odds of survival.

IDIOSYNCRASIES OF GENIUS

Looking through his telescope one evening, Galileo could no longer find the rings of Saturn. They were gone...and didn't reappear again until a few years later, causing the astronomer to question his own sanity. (We now know that due to Saturn's tilt, every 14 years or so, the rings seem to disappear because they face Earth edge-on.)

THE DIFFERENCE BETWEEN...

Stalactites and Stalagmites. Both are *speleothems*, mineral deposits that form inside caves. Stalactites resemble icicles and extend down from a ceiling or overhang; stalagmites extend up from the floor. An easy way to remember which is which: Stala**c**tite, with a **c**, comes from the **c**eiling.

CHAPTER 12

FINE YOUNG CANNIBALS

While sand tiger shark pups are still inside their mother's body, they develop sharp teeth. The larger pups use those teeth to eat their smaller womb-mates. Only one, maybe two, will make it out alive.

THE ORIGIN OF THE RESTAURANT

The oldest direct ancestor of the restaurant is the tavern, which dates back to the Middle Ages. Typically, taverns served a single meal at a fixed hour each day, usually consisting of only one dish. According to many food historians, it wasn't until 1765 that someone first came up with the idea of giving diners a choice of fare. A Parisian soup vendor known as Monsieur Boulanger is said to have offered his customers poultry, eggs, and other dishes, but it was his soups, which he called *restaurants* because they "restored" strength, that gave this new type of eatery its name.

EAU DE MONKEY

Mexican spider monkeys have been observed picking the leaves of three different plants—the Alamos pea tree, the flowering trumpet tree, and wild celery—each of which is pleasantly aromatic. The monkeys chew the leaves, one at a time, mix them into a mush, and then rub it onto their armpits and breastbones. Biologists aren't sure why the monkeys do this. It could be that wild celery has insect repellent properties, but the other two plants do not. The monkeys may use the musky mush simply because they like the way it smells.

12 MENSA MEMBERS

Mensa International is the world-famous organization of "smart people." Membership is open to anyone who has "attained a score within the upper 2% of the general population on an approved intelligence test that has been properly administered and supervised." There are about 100,000 members worldwide. Twelve current members:

Scott Adams (creator of the comic strip *Dilbert*)

Jean Auel (*The Clan of the Cave Bear* author)

Bobby Czyz (two-time World Boxing Association Champion, 1990s)

Geena Davis (Academy Award-winning actress)

Maurice Kanbar (creator of Skyy Vodka)

Julie Peterson (*Playboy* Playmate of the Month, February 1987)

Norman Schwarzkopf (retired U.S. Army general)

James Woods (Emmy Award-winning actor)

Bob Specta (triathlete and professional "domino toppler")

Mell Lazarus (creator of *Momma* and *Miss Peach* cartoons)

Derek Keith Barbosa (better known as rapper Chino XL)

Asia Carrera (adult film star)

You (if you take the test…and pass)

LAKES: EXORHEIC AND ENDORHEIC

An *exorheic* (ex-oh-REE-ik) lake is a body of water that receives its water from rivers and streams and loses that water via rivers and streams, too, as well as through underground seepage. An *endorheic* (en-duh-REE-ik) lake, on the other hand, has no natural outlets, above or underground. Water can flow into it, but losing that water occurs only through evaporation. Endorheic lakes always, and to different degrees, have higher salinity levels, because water coming into lakes always carries minerals such as salts. In exorheic lakes, they're carried out again, but in endorheic lakes the water is trapped and evaporates, and the salt is left behind. Some endorheic lakes: the Caspian Sea in western Asia, Lake Chad in North Africa, the Dead Sea in Israel, and the Great Salt Lake in Utah. (The word "endorheic" comes from the Greek *endo*—"inside," and *rhein*—"to flow.")

LAKE BONNEVILLE

The Great Salt Lake is one of several lakes left behind by the disappearance of Lake Bonneville, a massive body of water that once covered most of what is now Utah, along with parts of Nevada and Idaho. Geologists believe climate changes caused its formation about 32,000 years ago, and at its peak it was more than 1,000 feet deep. How did it lose its water? About 16,000 years ago, lava flows in Idaho diverted the waters of the Bear River into

Lake Bonneville. That caused the lake to overflow at a mountain ridge near what is now Downey, Idaho. The ridge collapsed, causing the lake to drain in a catastrophic event that geologists call the Bonneville Flood. Most of the water ended up flowing into the Snake River, and finally into the Pacific Ocean. The remnant of the collapsed ridge still exists in southeastern Idaho: It's called Red Rock Pass.

STORMWATER RUNOFF

The Hydrologic Cycle. When it rains, where does the water go? Some of it seeps into the earth and collects far underground in layers of permeable rock called *aquifers*. The rain that falls on trees and plants either gets absorbed into the plant or evaporates back into the air; the rain that falls on oceans, rivers, lakes, and streams recharges those bodies of water. But in a storm, rain can fall too fast to be absorbed by the ground, vegetation, or bodies of water. The excess water produced by the storm is known as *runoff*.

Stormwater Runoff. Once people began paving open land with asphalt, building homes in the flood plain, and putting slate roofs on houses and schools, they created surfaces that promote additional stormwater runoff. This causes stream erosion, flooding, and ironically, drought. (More runoff means that less water evaporates back into the air, which means less overall rainfall.) But the most destructive effect of stormwater runoff comes from the pollution it picks up on land and then carries into waterways. Stormwater runoff picks up pesticides and fertilizers from our lawns; car exhaust and oil leaks from our roads; pet waste; refuse from sewer systems; dirt from construction sites that clogs waterways with sediment; plus a variety of chemicals from agriculture, construction, and industry. According to the U.S. Environmental Protection Agency, stormwater runoff is now the greatest source of water pollution in American waterways.

FOOD FOR THOUGHT. You might think that stormwater runoff goes to a sewage treatment plant; it doesn't. Anything that goes down a storm drain goes directly into area waterways, unfiltered and untreated.

Tips to keep pollution out of stormwater runoff

1. Don't hose off your driveway—sweep it. Same for sidewalks and gutters.

2. Use little or no chemical pesticides or fertilizer on your lawn or garden.

3. Clean up after your dog.

4. Use a rain barrel to collect stormwater.

5. Don't litter. Stormwater can wash plastic bags, food scraps, cigarette butts, and other litter down the storm drain—and into local waterways.

6. Recycle used motor oil and other hazardous household wastes.

7. Use a bucket and sponge instead of a hose to wash your car.

HOW A NEW POPE IS ELECTED

Between 15 and 20 days after the death of a pope, as many as 120 high-ranking cardinals and archbishops—the College of Cardinals—are sequestered inside the Sistine Chapel in the Vatican. After a few hours of deliberation, they begin a very ritualized voting process that dates back to the year 1274 C.E. Each cardinal is given a rectangular piece of paper. At the top is written "*Eligo in Summum Pontificem*" (Latin for "I elect as supreme pontiff"), and he writes in the name of his candidate, who is nearly always one of the other cardinals present, though this is not an official requirement. The paper is folded twice, held in the air, and then carried to the chapel's altar. The voter must then announce (in Latin), "I call as my witness Christ the

Lord who will be my judge, that my vote is given to the one who before God I think should be elected." The ballot is placed on a plate atop a ballot box, and the cardinal uses the plate to drop the ballot into the ballot box. Three *scrutineers*, selected from among the College of Cardinals, count the ballots individually. A two-thirds plus one majority is required. If a consensus has not been reached, they vote again. If, after six rounds of voting, a new pope is not elected, a simple majority vote suffices. After each vote, the ballots are burned. The smoke goes out over the Vatican, visible to the public. If no pope has been selected, chemicals are added to create black smoke, advising election-watchers that the process will continue. White smoke means there's a new pope.

HOW TO STAY YOUNG

Wisdom from Satchel Paige (1906–82), Hall of Fame baseball pitcher:

1. "Avoid fried meats, which angry up the blood."

2. "If your stomach disputes you, lay down and pacify it with cool thoughts."

3. "Keep the juices flowing by jangling around gently as you move."

4. "Go very light on the vices, such as carrying on in society. The social ramble ain't restful."

5. "Avoid running at all times."

6. "Don't look back. Something might be gaining on you."

FLOUR

The word "flour" generally refers to finely milled plant parts. The most common source is wheat, but it's also made from rye, barley, corn, as well as nongrains like buckwheat and quinoa. (True grains are members of the grass family; buckwheat, quinoa, and other "pseudograins" are from different plant families.) The name comes from the French word *flur*, for "flower," and actually referred to the fact that flour products were thought of as the best part, or "flower," of a meal. It was even spelled "flower" in English until the 1800s, when it acquired its modern spelling simply to quell confusion. Common flour types:

Gluten flour. After wheat flour is soaked in cold water and stirred, the water dissolves the starch, leaving a gummy brown substance. That's gluten, the protein found in grain seeds that gives dough its elasticity and aids in the rising process. Mill it and it's gluten flour. It's very low in carbohydrates (since the starch is dissolved away) and much higher in protein than other flours. It's commonly used for special diets (e.g., diabetic) and is often mixed with other kinds of flour to give foods certain characteristics, such as the chewiness of bagels.

All-purpose flour. Different wheat species have different gluten content: "Hard" flour is made from high-gluten wheat and is commonly used in breads and pastas; "soft" flour from lower-gluten wheat is used in cakes and pastries. All-purpose mixes the two roughly half and half, resulting in very versatile flour. It's sold both bleached (chemically treated for whiteness) and unbleached.

Self-rising flour. All-purpose flour with baking powder and salt added.

Whole wheat flour. "Whole" refers to the fact that the entire wheat kernels are ground, including the *bran* (the hard outer layer), the *endosperm* (the inside of the kernel), and the *germ* (the "heart" or embryo of the grain). This is different from white flour, which uses only the endosperm. Whole wheat flours are also higher in fiber and nutrients such as protein, calcium, and iron.

Bread flour. This is unbleached, high-gluten wheat flour mixed with less than 1% malted barley flour (which increases yeast activity). It results in larger, lighter bread loaves, and is the flour most often used in the commercial bread-making industry.

Cake or pastry flour. Very finely milled and bleached soft wheat flour (low gluten) used for lighter foods like cakes, pastries, and muffins.

Semolina flour. Coarsely ground flour made from the very high-gluten *durum* wheat species. Often used in pastas.

Durum flour. This flour is the very fine by-product of semolina milling. Used for pasta, couscous, and some breads.

THE THREE PARTS OF THE PSYCHE

According to 19th-century psychoanalyst Sigmund Freud, the human psyche, or conception of the "self," is made up of three elements.

Id. A person's instinctive impulses, such as the desires for food, sex, and to strike out violently at others when threatened.

Superego. The system of censors and personal restraints, such as morals, that have been deeply embedded in the brain since childhood.

Ego. The part of the psyche that experiences and reacts to the outside world. It acts as a middleman between the primal urges of the id and the social constructs of the superego.

HALLOWEEN TRADITIONS

Halloween customs began in Ireland in the fifth century B.C.E. The Celts who lived there believed that on October 31 and November 1 (the end of the year on their calendar), spirits of people who'd died the previous year returned to possess the body of an animal or person for the next twelve months. The festival was called *Samhain*, named for the lord of the underworld. The Celts protected themselves by wearing scary costumes to frighten away the wandering spirits, as well as leaving them offerings of food. Christianity dominated Europe by the Middle Ages, and the Church adopted some older folk and pagan traditions to help attract converts. In 835 C.E., Pope Gregory IV moved a religious holiday called All Hallows Day, in which the spirits of the dead are remembered and honored, from mid-May to November 1. The pagan revelry of October 31 continued and came to be known as All Hallows Eve, of which "Halloween" is a corruption. The two main elements of Samhain—dressing up in scary costumes and offering food (in this case, candy)—are still part of the modern Halloween celebration.

INSTANT SHAKESPEARE: *KING LEAR*

King Lear (1603) is among Shakespeare's most famous and most-produced tragedies.

The plot: King Lear of Britain decides to retire and divide his kingdom among his three daughters. Before he does, he tests their loyalty by asking each daughter how much she loves him. The conniving Goneril and Regan flatter him, but Cordelia balks. She means that she can't put such a deep love into words, but Lear misunderstands her to mean that she doesn't really love him. He becomes enraged and disowns her. Cordelia leaves for France, where she accepts the marriage proposal of the French king.

Shortly thereafter, Lear realizes he made the wrong decision—Goneril and Regan try to force him off the throne even sooner than he'd intended. Lear flees, wandering around the wilderness in the middle of a storm, accompanied by Kent, a nobleman. Meanwhile, back in the kingdom, the nobleman Gloucester has been tricked by Edmund, his illegitimate son, into thinking that Edgar, his legitimate son, is planning to kill

Gloucester. Gloucester sends police to arrest Edgar, so he flees, disguised as a beggar named Poor Tom. He too ends up wandering the wilderness in a storm. Gloucester hears of Goneril and Regan's conspiracy against Lear and decides to help the king regain his throne. Regan finds out about Gloucester's plan and has him blinded, then forces him into the wilderness, where Poor Tom leads him around. (Gloucester, blind, doesn't realize that Poor Tom is actually his son, Edgar.)

The French army arrives in Dover, near Lear's kingdom. It's part of a plan by Cordelia to thwart her sisters and save her father. An army led by Edmund defeats the French; Lear and Cordelia are captured; Cordelia is executed for treason. Edgar kills Edmund in a duel, Gloucester dies (just after learning that Poor Tom is really his innocent son, Edgar). Goneril's actions are exposed and she kills herself. Lear dies of grief over the loss of his one good daughter.

Memorable line: "How sharper than a serpent's tooth it is to have a thankless child!" (Lear, Act I, Scene 4)

GOOSEBUMPS

Human beings used to be covered in hair. When it was cold, tiny muscles at the base of each of those hairs would constrict, causing the hairs to stand up. Air would become trapped between the hairs, creating a layer of insulation for the body. We don't have as much hair as we used to, but we still have that reaction to cold weather—and that's what causes goosebumps.

CHIRPING EXPLAINED

✦ The sounds made by animals that involves rubbing body parts together is called *stridulation*. The best-known music makers are crickets, the males of which use their stiff, leathery forewings to produce sound (as opposed to their lacy rear wings, which they use to fly).

✦ Cricket forewings overlap slightly, making chirping possible. The underside of the base of the top wing has a raised ridge with 50 to 300 "teeth" on it (it's actually a specially adapted vein). The top of the lower forewing has a "scraper." To produce sound, the wings are lifted up from the back, and the top wing is moved back and forth over the bottom, making the teeth slide over the scraper with an effect similar to rubbing a comb over the edge of a hard object. The wings move very quickly, with up to thousands of teeth being played per second. The sound is amplified via the structure of the wings, allowing the tiny creatures to produce sounds as loud as 100 decibels.

✦ Crickets have at least three different songs: one to attract distant females, one to attract a particular female after he gets her attention, and one to warn off other males.

✦ Each cricket species has its own particular chirp.

✦ Cooler weather slows down a cricket's chirping rate. Cricket chirp temperature formula, according to the *Old Farmer's Almanac*: Count how many chirps you hear in 14 seconds, add 40, and that's the temperature in degrees Fahrenheit.

✦ Recent studies have found that when a cricket's wings move to begin chirping, its auditory nerves stop working. Just how this happens isn't certain, but it explains why crickets don't go deaf when they chirp.

✦ Other animals that use some form of stridulation: grasshoppers, katydids, cicadas, some ants, and some beetles.

✦ Some tarantula species use stridulation, producing a hissing sound by rubbing the hairs on their legs together.

✦ Some species of snakes use it when threatened. One, the saw-scales viper—found in Pakistan and one of the most venomous snakes in the world—makes several folds in its body and rubs its skin together, producing what is described as a "sizzling" sound.

FLAK AND FAHRVERGNÜGEN

Two modern words that made their way from German to English:

Flak. From the German words *FLieger Abwehr Kanone*, meaning "plane defense cannon" (or "anti-aircraft gun"). "Flak" became the name for anti-aircraft fire, and in 1938 led to the use of "flak jackets"—basically bulletproof vests—by American airmen. In 1963 its use evolved to mean abuse, e.g., "Don't give me any flak."

Fahrvergnügen. This word was made famous in the English-speaking world after it started appearing in Volkswagen commercials in 1989. It means "driving enjoyment" and is a combination of two German words, the verb *fahren*, "to drive," and the noun *Vergnügen*, "enjoyment" or "delight."

THE DIFFERENCE BETWEEN...

Weather and Climate. "Weather" is used to describe atmospheric conditions in a specific region over a short period of time; "climate" describes how a region's—or the entire planet's—atmosphere behaves over many years.

BEER

There are essentially just two kinds of beer: ale and lager. Both are characterized by the behavior of the yeast used in the fermentation process. Ale is brewed with top-fermenting yeast (it ferments at the surface) at temperatures between 60 and 75°F, then stored and aged only briefly. Lager is brewed with bottom-fermenting yeast (it ferments closer to the bottom of brewing vats) at 46 to 55°F, then stored and aged at 32 to 40°F (*Lager* is German for "storehouse") for a longer period of time than ale. All beers are either a type of ale, or a type of lager. For example, porter is a dark-colored lager with a strong flavor and higher alcohol content, both of which are the result of toasting the malt before brewing. Stout, which is similar to porter in taste and color, also uses toasted malt, except it's an ale because it's made with top-fermenting yeast.

HONORARY CITIZENS

Only six nonnative people have been named Honorary Citizens of the United States. They are:

✦ British Prime Minister Winston Churchill (1963).

✦ Raoul Wallenberg, a Swedish diplomat who aided the escape of Jewish people from the Nazis during World War II (1981).

✦ William and Hannah Callowhill Penn, British citizens who founded the Pennsylvania colony in the 17th century (1984)

✦ Mother Theresa, the Albanian-born Catholic nun who ministered to and cared for the sick (mostly lepers) in India from the 1950s to the 1990s (1996).

✦ The Marquis de Lafayette, a French noble who fought in the American Revolutionary War (2002).

NUMEROLOGY

Numerology is the name of many different systems developed since ancient times in which numbers are deemed to have a "mystical" power. According to popular systems used today, the numbers 1 through 9 can be used to "divine" meanings from everyday experiences or things. An example is the "birthpath number," believed to describe one's natural abilities and character traits.

To calculate your birthpath number, write down your date of birth and add up all the digits. Then add together the digits of the resulting number, and so on, until you arrive at a single number between 1 and 9. Example: If your birthday is August 28, 1953, add: $8 + 2 + 8 + 1 + 9 + 5 + 3 = 36$; $3 + 6 = 9$. In this case, 9 is your birthpath number. What do you do with the birthpath number? If you believe in that sort of thing, you can use the following list of numbers and character traits to help "interpret" its meaning.

1. A self-sufficient, ambitious leader who is also stubborn.

2. An understanding, insightful, loving person who is also shy and may be lonely.

3. Someone outgoing, social, and enthusiastic, but who may exaggerate.

4. A solid, traditional, even dull person who is practical and productive.

5. A bold, influential, sensual person, but self-indulgent and restless.

6. A responsible, balanced caregiver, but prone to anxiety and feelings of guilt.

7. Someone spiritual or mystic, maybe eccentric, but distant or narrow-minded.

8. A decisive, successful, wealthy person who can be ruthless.

9. An intelligent, intuitive philosopher who is also absent-minded or detached.

BLONDES HAVE MORE BLOOD

Andrew Spielman, a professor of tropical health in the Department of Immunology and Infectious Diseases at the Harvard School of Public Health, wrote in 2001 that studies proved mosquitoes are drawn to people with lighter rather than darker hair. Mosquitoes can sense the breath of animals from as far as 100 feet away, but once they get close, vision comes into play. They notice contrast above all else, so lighter-haired people stand out in an area full of both light- and dark-haired people, making them more likely to get bitten.

NAMES OF THINGS YOU PROBABLY DIDN'T KNOW HAD NAMES

✦ *Rowel:* the spinning star on the back of a cowboy's spur

✦ *Columella:* the little piece of skin on the bottom of the nose between the nostrils

✦ *Ophyron:* the space between the eyebrows

✦ *Rasceta:* the creases that form on your wrist when you bend your hand inward

✦ *Purlicue:* the tight skin fold between the index finger and extended thumb

✦ *Ferrule:* the metal band on a pencil where the eraser sits

✦ *Obdormition:* technical term for a limb "going to sleep"

✦ *Armsaye:* an armhole on a shirt

✦ *Chanking:* unedible things you spit out of food, like pits or rinds

✦ *Minimus:* the pinky finger or "baby" toe

✦ *Solidus:* technical name for a slash (as in "3/4" or "either/or")

THE TRUTH ABOUT QUICKSAND

It's a common scene in old movies: An explorer gets lost in a jungle and then steps into a patch of quicksand, where he slowly sinks to his death. It's pure Hollywood myth. Quicksand is just sand that has mixed with groundwater under the surface. The sand might appear normal on the surface if it has formed a crust, dried by air and sunlight, that hides the pool below. If you do get stuck in quicksand, it's actually not that difficult to escape; depending on how dense it is, you may be able to wade out of it, as long as you're not in up to your waist. Beyond that, it will be harder, but it's too thick to actually sink into; your body is less dense than the quicksand, so you will float to the top if you move slowly and work your way onto your back. Avoid panicking—it is possible to drown in quicksand if you work your way too deep into it by flailing your arms and legs.

IMPEACHMENT

When an elected official is impeached, that doesn't mean that they have been removed from office, although the term is commonly used that way. Impeachment refers to the process by which the elected official is tried for their offenses. Two U.S. presidents have been impeached: Andrew Johnson in 1868 (for suspending Secretary of War Edward Stanton against the Senate's wishes) and Bill Clinton in 1998 (for perjury and obstruction of justice). Both were acquitted of all charges.

ON GENIUS

"Next to possessing genius oneself is the power of appreciating it in others."

—Mark Twain

THE THREE REICHS

During the period of Nazi rule over Germany, Adolf Hitler referred to his regime as the "Third Reich." *Reich* is the German word for "empire," an open admission that he was after world domination by Germany. But Nazi Germany was the *third* reich. What were the first two reichs of German dominance? The First Reich was the Holy Roman Empire, which lasted from about 800 to 1806 C.E. It included what later became German states, and in the late 15th century the empire was called the Holy Roman Empire of the German Nation. The Second Reich began with the unification of German states into one empire in 1871 under Chancellor Otto von Bismarck. It lasted until 1918. Following World War I, Germany briefly adopted a democratic form of government and called itself the Weimar Republic. That ended with the rise of Hitler's Third Reich in the 1930s.

CHAPTER 13

WHAT'S IN YOUR HOT DOG?

Manufacturers are required by law to list a food's ingredients on the label. If you see the words "beef," "pork," "chicken," or "turkey," it means that your hot dog contains meat that came from the muscle tissue of that animal. If it also says "meat byproducts," this indicates that there are things like snouts, stomachs, hearts, tongues, lips, and spleens present. All of the meat and meat byproducts are then ground with water, seasonings, sweeteners, preservatives, lots of salt, and chemicals that bind it all together. Next, the mixture is stuffed into casings, which are usually made from sterilized sheep intestines.

HOW A THERMOS WORKS

The *theory of exchanges*, proposed by Pierre Prévost in 1791, states that two adjacent bodies will eventually become the same temperature because the colder of the two absorbs heat waves from the other. A thermos counteracts this effect by reducing the ways that heat waves can travel. Inside the thermos is another container made of two layers of glass, with the lips of each layer melted together. Glass doesn't conduct heat well, and the space between the glass creates a near vacuum, slowing down heat transfer even more. To prevent heat transfer from radiation, the surfaces of the glass are coated with aluminum, which reflects heat waves and doesn't absorb them. The glass bottle is held in place by a stopper and pads usually made of cork, which also conducts heat poorly.

BODILY FLUIDS

Everybody is familiar with blood—but it's only one of our precious bodily fluids. Here are a few more:

Amniotic fluid: Nourishing fluid in the *amnion*, the sac surrounding a developing fetus

Aqueous humor: Thick, watery fluid between the cornea and the lens of the eyeball. *Vitreous humor* fills the area between the lens and the retina; both provide the eyes with necessary lubrication.

Cerebrospinal fluid: Surrounds the spinal cord and brain; the brain essentially "floats" in this fluid.

Cerumen: Commonly called "earwax," this substance is secreted into the ear canals. It aids in cleaning as well as providing protection from infection.

Colostrum: Super-nutritious breast milk produced at the end of pregnancy and for a few days after birth; also called "immune milk" for its anti-infection properties.

Cowper's fluid: Prepares the urethra for sperm by removing leftover acidity from urine; produced in the *Cowper's glands*.

Mucus: Thick, slippery secretion of the body's mucous membranes that lines body cavities such as the eyes and mouth as well as the organs; includes phlegm and snot.

Pleural fluid: Just 10 to 15 milliliters of this slippery fluid is contained between the *pleura*, which are thin membranes; one surrounds the lungs, one lines the chest wall. Pleural fluid allows the membranes to slide over each other during breathing.

Pus: A thick, white/yellow substance present in areas of inflammation caused by bacteria; consists mostly of dead and living immune cells.

Sebum: Secreted by *sebaceous* glands found throughout the skin (except on the palms of the hands and soles of the feet), it consists of oily fats and dead cells. It moisturizes and waterproofs skin.

Vernix caseosa: It's the white, "cheesy" substance you often see on newborns and infants. This highly antibiotic substance is produced by the baby's sebaceous glands to protect its skin from becoming waterlogged by amniotic fluid.

HOUSEHOLD GENIUS

Ever wonder if you're supposed to replace the cotton in a pill bottle once you've opened it? According to pharmacists, you're not. The cotton stops the pills from breaking during transport, but once a bottle is opened the cotton can attract moisture that can damage the pills. (And it's often not cotton—it's rayon.)

TRIALS OF THE CENTURY

Harry Orchard trial (1907). In December 1905, Idaho governor (and antiunion advocate) Frank Steuenberg was killed by a bomb strapped to the front gate of his home in Caldwell, Idaho. James McParland, an agent for the Pinkerton Agency (well known for busting union activity) conducted an investigation and arrested miner and union member Harry Orchard. Orchard entered a plea bargain in which he implicated as conspirators Western Federation of Miners general secretary Bill Haywood and president Charles Moyer, and labor organizer George Pettibone. The trio were arrested in Colorado in 1906 and tried in Boise, Idaho, in 1907. The only evidence in the case came from Orchard's testimony. The plea backfired; Pettibone and Haywood were acquitted, charges against Moyer were dropped, and Orchard got life in prison, where he died in 1954.

Sacco and Vanzetti (1921). Ferdinando Sacco and Bartolomeo Vanzetti were Italian immigrants and anarchists accused of the murders of a paymaster and security guard as well as the theft of $16,000 from a safe at the shoe company in Massachusetts where they worked. Because of anti-immigrant sentiment at the time and the political views of the defendants, the trial was highly publicized and less than fair. Despite a lack of evidence, both were found guilty and were executed in 1927. In the decades since, weapons testing, a confession by a known bank robber, and other evidence has largely exonerated Sacco and Vanzetti.

Chicago Seven (1969). Seven people (initially eight) were charged with conspiracy for inciting a riot at the 1968 Democratic National Convention in Chicago. The defendants were antiwar activists Abbie Hoffman, Jerry Rubin, David Dellinger, Tom Hayden, Rennie Davis, John Froines, Lee Weiner, and Bobby Seale. Seale, a founding member of the Black Panther Party, was ultimately tried separately and convicted of contempt of court after calling the original trial's judge a "racist pig." Hoffman and Rubin were consistently disruptive, showing up in court wearing judicial robes and blowing kisses at the jury. The trial became a critical examination of the 1960s counterculture, with figures such as Jesse Jackson, Timothy Leary, and Arlo Guthrie testifying. After five months, all seven were found innocent of conspiracy, Froines and Weiner were acquitted completely, and the other five were convicted of the intent to riot and sentenced to five years in prison and fined $5,000. (The convictions were reversed on appeal due to the original judge's refusal to screen jurors for political and racial prejudices.)

WHAT'S A GHOTI?

As British publisher Charles Ollier pointed out in an 1855 letter to one of his writers, it's a fish.

> My son William has hit upon a new method of spelling Fish. As thus: G.h.o.t.i., Ghoti, fish. Nonsense! say you. By no means, say I. It is perfectly vindicable orthography. You give it up? Well then, here is the proof. Gh is f, as in tough, rough, enough; o is i as in women; and ti is sh, as in nation. So that ghoti is fish.

In the 20th century, the ghoti concept was falsely attributed to George Bernard Shaw. It was understandable, though, as Shaw often championed reforming the many confusing aspects of the English language.

FOOD FOR THOUGHT. Theodor Geisel, also known as Dr. Seuss, pointed out the absurdities of our language in one of his most famous sentences: "The tough coughs as he ploughs through the dough." That's five different pronunciations of the same four letters: "ough."

COLOR BLINDNESS

Why are some people said to be "color-blind," and what exactly does it mean? It has to do with the *cones* in our eyes, which allow us to see color in the first place. Here's how color vision works:

✦ *Seeing* means seeing light that is reflected off objects. That light enters our eyeballs, goes through the lenses, and hits the retinas. There it affects specialized cells called *photoreceptors*, which send neural signals to the brain's visual center.

✦ There are two main types of photoreceptors in the retina: *rods* and *cones* (so-called because of their shape). Rods detect different *amounts* of light (bright to dark), and cones detect different *wavelengths* of light—meaning different colors.

✦ Humans have three types of cone cells, which give us *trichromatic* (three-color) vision. One type of cone cell responds to short-wavelength light (the blue part of the spectrum), another to medium-wavelength light (the green part), and the third to long-wavelength light (the reds). Color blindness is simply the condition of having defective or missing cone cells. It is most commonly inherited but can also be caused by injury, illness, and aging. The five types:

Protanopia. This is the lack of long-wavelength (red) cones, the effect being that reds look more like beiges and appear darker than they are; colors like violet and purple are seen as shades of blue because the red in them can't be seen. (The name comes from the Greek *protos* for "first," as red is considered the first primary color, and an *opia* for "blindness," literally "without eye"; plus *ia*, denoting a condition or disease.)

Deuteranopia. "Second blindness," or "red-green blindness," is the most common form and is the lack of the medium-wavelength, green-detecting cones. Its effect: Green and red appear identical. This condition is also known as *Daltonism*, after English chemist John Dalton, who in 1794 wrote the first scientific paper about color blindness (which he suffered from). DNA analysis of Dalton's preserved eyeballs was performed in 1995, 150 years after his death, and confirmed his diagnosis of deuteranopia.

Tritanopia. "Third blindness" is the lack of short-wavelength cones (the blues). It makes blues and greens difficult to distinguish, and yellows can appear as shades of red.

Blue cone monochromacy. Also called "one color," only one type of cone, the blues, functions properly. A *cone monochromat* can see next to no color but otherwise has good vision in normal daylight.

Rod monochromacy. This is the condition of having only rods—and no functioning cones at all. It's the only condition for which the term "color-blindness" is completely accurate—red monochromats can't see any color at all.

FOOD FOR THOUGHT. The eyes of the mantis shrimp, which lives among ocean reefs, have at least 12 different cone cell types. It's not known how many colors they can see.

AN HISTORY OF "A" AND "AN"

The word "an" has its origin in the 12th century Old English word *an*, which meant "one." "An brick" meant "one brick." By the 1300s it had stopped meaning "one" and had become an indefinite article. ("An" answer means any answer; "the" answer means a particular answer. Hence "a" and "an" are indefinite articles, and "the" is a definite article.)

✦ Somewhere along the line, the "n" in "an" began to be dropped when preceding a word that began with a consonant, creating today's well-known rule—"*a* before a consonant" and "*an* before a vowel," i.e., a banana, an apple, a car, an airplane.

✦ There are exceptions. When a word begins with a vowel that is sounded as a consonant, "a" is used, e.g., a eulogy; a one-time offer.

✦ It is has become increasingly common in American English to use "an" before words beginning with the letter "h," such as "an historical document," "an hotel," or "an hour." Others use one or the other depending on the word: "an" is used with words that have a silent "h," and "a" is used before words with a hard "h." Examples: an hour, a hotel, an honorable fellow, a hot dog.

✦ Some etymologists believe this confusion stems from differing influences on Old English through its history. In 1066 the Norman invasion brought speakers of Old French to power in

Britain, and with them an enormous influence on the language. One change in particular: Old French (like modern French) always dropped the "h" beginning a word—"hotel" was pronounced "otel." That made "an hotel" common in English after 1066, and the use spread to using "an" before all h-words.

✦ Beginning in 1714, a line of German kings—the Hanovers—ruled England, further influencing the English language. Germans always pronounce the "h" at the beginning of a word. After 1714 it became a rule of sorts to use "an" before h-words if they had a French origin, and "a" with h-words of German origin—regardless of how they were pronounced.

REAL UNICORNS

In the Middle Ages, many explorers actually reported seeing unicorns during their travels to Asia. But while the modern image is one of a white horse with a horn jutting out of its head, these explorers reported that unicorns had the head and body of a horse, the hindquarters of an antelope, a lion's tail, and a goat's beard. What about the horn? It was black, similar in consistency to a tooth, and magical—supposedly imbued with the power to detect or even neutralize poison.

THE FAT EARTH

Distance from sea level to the center of Earth: about 3,963 miles—but it depends where you are.

✦ The Earth is not a perfect sphere: it's "fatter" than it is tall, so to speak, since it has an equatorial bulge. That means the distance to the planet's center is 3,963.189 miles at the equator—and just 3,949.901 miles at the poles.

✦ The equatorial bulge has been growing since 1998. Prior to that year, and for thousands of years, Earth, in a geological process called *post-glacial rebound*, was becoming more round. In other words, it was getting taller at the poles and slimmer at the equator. That's because it was very slowly recovering from being squashed at the poles by the weight of the enormous amounts of ice during the last ice age. In 1998 satellite tracking devices recorded that the process had stopped, and the planet was getting fatter at the equator and flatter at the poles once again.

THE DEVIL'S HOOF

One legend about why the horseshoe is considered good luck: A very long time ago, the Devil went to an English blacksmith named Dunstan and asked that his horse be shod. Dunstan instead grabbed one of the Devil's feet, held it between his legs, and nailed a shoe to it. The Devil howled in pain and begged the blacksmith to remove it. Dunstan said he would—but not until the Devil promised to never enter a home where a horseshoe hung over the door. The Devil agreed. Dunstan the blacksmith went on to become the archbishop of Canterbury in 959, and in 1029 he was canonized, becoming Saint Dunstan—and horseshoes have been good luck ever since.

✦ Another version says the tradition is Celtic in origin and had to do with fairies. They're afraid of iron—which was deemed a "magical" substance—and horseshoes were the most common iron objects, so people hung them on their doors to keep fairies away. In time the horseshoe, rather than the iron, become the charm.

✦ In some cultures the horseshoe is hung points down, in others points up (so the luck doesn't spill out).

ANAPHORA...ANAPHORA...ANAPHORA

An *anaphora* is a tool used in rhetoric, the art of verbal oration and argument, first developed by the ancient Greeks and used by writers, speakers, singers, and politicians ever since.

An anaphora is simply a word or phrase repeated at the beginning of several sentences or clauses. An anaphora you may be familiar with—and one of the most famous in U.S. history—was employed by Reverend Martin Luther King Jr., speaking from the steps of the Lincoln Memorial on August 28, 1963. That anaphora: "I have a dream." (A word or phrase repeated at the end of sentences or clauses, on the other hand, is called an *epiphora*.)

BEAUJOLAIS DAY

Beaujolais Nouveau is a light red wine made in the Beaujolais region of France. It's harvested in the fall and, after a short fermentation period (only about six weeks), is bottled in November. Beaujolais Nouveau is supposed to be drunk young; vintners recommend drinking it no later than the following June. If you ever want a taste of the very first Beaujolais from a given harvest: Every year on the third Wednesday of November, wine lovers gather in cafés and bars all over the world and wait for midnight to strike. When it does, it's officially "Beaujolais Day"—and the first Beaujolais Nouveau of the year is uncorked and the party begins.

INFAMOUS LANDSLIDES

The Frank Slide. On April 29, 1903, in the Canadian Rocky Mountain coal-mining town of Frank, Alberta, a 90-million-ton section of limestone broke off the side of 7,251-foot Turtle Mountain. In less than two minutes, the slide demolished seven miners' cottages, a dairy farm, a ranch, a shoe store, a livery stable, a mile and a half of a road, and two miles of the Frank and Grassy Mountain Railway. Of the 600 people who lived in the town, 70 were killed.

The Gansu Landslide. On December 16, 1920, a 7.8-magnitude earthquake caused slides, falls, and avalanches in Gansu Province in north-central China. Some of those slides are estimated to have been more than a mile wide and several miles in length. Dozens of villages disappeared in the deluge, and more than 200,000 people were killed in the quake and ensuing slides.

The Sacred Falls Rockfall. At about 2:30 p.m. on May 9, 1999, scores of people were visiting one of Oahu's most picturesque spots, Sacred Falls. The 90-foot waterfall sits at the end of a narrow canyon with sheer cliffs rising up hundreds of feet on either side. That day, a slab of rock about 3 feet thick, 10 feet tall, and 20 feet across suddenly broke off the side of the canyon wall about 500 feet above the base of the waterfall. It bounced down a 70° slope for about 350 feet, then free-fell for the final 150 feet. Researchers believe the massive rock was traveling about 100 miles per hour when it hit the ground. Eight people were killed and 50 more were wounded. Sacred Falls Park has still not reopened.

FOOD FOR THOUGHT. Landslides can happen underwater, too. About 8,100 years ago, the largest known landslide in history occurred off the northwest coast of what is now Norway. An underwater coastal shelf roughly the size of Iceland slid hundreds of feet deeper into the ocean, triggering tsunamis that inundated every coast around the North Sea. Studies indicate that more than 840 cubic miles of sediment slid more than 50 miles out to sea, leaving a scar about 190 miles across.

FASCINATING FLORA

If you came across this plant, you might think it was nothing more than a yard-high pile of dead seaweed. But the *Welwitschia mirabilis* is one of the world's rarest, oddest, and most primitive plants. It grows naturally only on a strip of coastal desert about 500 miles long and 50 miles deep in the African countries of Namibia and Angola, some of the driest and harshest land on Earth. Mature plants have a deep taproot; a woody "trunk" from one to four feet high; and two strap-shaped, leathery, blue-green leaves that can be more than three feet wide at the base. Those two leaves are all they'll ever have; they keep growing throughout the plant's life, which can last more than *1,500 years*. The leaves grow from the trunk outward and are continually shredded and split in the desert wind over the centuries.

The plant's ability to survive in such a harsh environment is the result of another oddity: Most plants absorb water from the soil through their roots and circulate it to the rest of the plant. The Welwitschia plant does the opposite. It absorbs water from nightly fog through millions of *stomata* (pores) on the leaves' surfaces and stores it in its root. The first part of its scientific name, *Welwitschia*, comes from Austrian botanist and explorer Friedrich Welwitsch, who wrote about the plant in 1859. *Mirabilis* means "marvelous" or "wonderful" in Latin.

WORD SEARCH: *DROMEDARY*

Dromedaries are one-humped camels found in the Middle East and North Africa. Their name entered the English language in the 13th century and goes back to the Greek *dromas kamelos*— "running camel"—so named because they were used for racing (and still are). Another variant of the name that arose in the late 1500s and has since disappeared: *drumbledairy*.

HOW TO MAKE HAGGIS

It's been called one of the world's most disgusting foods. But if you're up to it, here's how to prepare the national dish of Scotland.

Ingredients: A pound of sheep liver, a large chopped onion, two pounds of dry oatmeal, a scraped and cleaned sheep stomach, a pound of chopped suet (beef fat), three cups of beef stock, and a half teaspoon each of black pepper, cayenne pepper, and salt

Preparation: Boil the liver and onion until the liver is cooked. Mince them together. Lightly brown the oatmeal in a skillet, stirring constantly to prevent burning. Mix all the ingredients together and fill the sheep's stomach with it. Press down as you fill to remove the air. Sew the stomach up and prick it with a needle a few times so it won't burst while cooking. Slowly boil for four hours.

TRES QUESOS DE MEXICO

Some cheeses from South of the Border.

Queso asadero is also known as "queso Oaxaca" for the state of its origin, and as "queso quesadilla" because it's the cheese most often used in quesadillas and similar hot dishes (*asadero* means "roaster" or "broiler" in Spanish). It's a stretched curd cheese made from cow's milk, is semisoft, white, and it comes in braids or balls.

Queso cotija is named after a town in the southwestern state of Michoacán. It's an uncooked, pressed cheese that is salted and aged for 3 to 12 months, and has a hard texture like parmesan. In 2006 cotija was voted "Cheese of the Year" at the prestigious Festival Internacional de Cremona in Italy.

Queso panela is a soft, fresh, mild white cheese often called "queso de canasta," or "basket cheese," because the impression of the baskets they are molded in can be seen on their surfaces.

PICA

Pica is a nutritional disorder characterized by an insatiable craving for things that aren't food, such as dirt, sand, paint, or paper. It can also mean a craving for raw ingredients of food, such as cornstarch or flour. The condition is most common in pregnant women and developmentally disabled children. The name of the condition comes from the Latin name for the magpie, a bird that will eat almost anything. Pica can cause a very specific craving, including one for wood, soil, clay, glass, hair, or even feces.

TONS OF TONS

A ton is not necessarily 2,000 pounds. In the United States and Canada, a ton is 2,000 pounds, but in the United Kingdom a ton is 2,240 pounds. To differentiate between the two, the 2,000-pound measure is sometimes called a "short ton," and the 2,240-pound figure is a "long ton." But there are also other tons:

Shipping ton: a British measure of 42 cubic feet

Freight ton: an American measure of 40 cubic feet

Metric ton: 1,000 kilograms

Assay ton: It's not a unit of measurement like the others. It's a ratio used to measure precious metals. The number of milligrams of the metal in one assay ton of ore should roughly equal the same number as ounces of the metal in 2,000 pounds (a ton) of ore.

WHITE CHOCOLATE?

According to Food and Drug Administration standards, chocolate must contain no fat besides that found in cocoa butter and up to 5% dairy butter (allowed for the emulsification process). That means that white chocolate isn't really chocolate at all. It shares a consistency with chocolate, but its main flavoring agent is vanilla, not cocoa or cocoa butter. In addition to 10% vanilla, white chocolate is about 30% sugar, 30% milk solids, and 30% vegetable fats, which means it has way too much fat to technically be called chocolate anyway.

PRINCIPAL OR PRINCIPLE?

Principal is an adjective meaning "main" or "most important," or a noun meaning the "main or most important thing or person." *Principle* is always a noun, and means "a law or doctrine." An easy way to remember the difference: Because the term "principal" is often used to describe a person, remember that the princi*pal* of your high school is your *pal*, and he has good princi*ple*s.

HOW MUCH GRASS DID DINOSAURS EAT?

Very little, and maybe none at all. At least that's what paleontologists theorize. Dinosaurs existed until about 65 million years ago, when conifer trees and shrubs dominated the landscape. Grasses, fossil records indicate, didn't show up until shortly after the dinosaurs were gone.

INSTANT KNOWLEDGE

The world's most sparsely populated country is Mongolia, with an average of 4.7 people per square mile.

DON'T SMELL...LIVE LONGER

It's long been known that restricting the amount of calories an animal eats can increase its lifespan. It was first reported by researchers Clive McCay and Mary Crowell of Cornell University in 1934. In their experiments, they fed rats a very low-calorie diet while providing enough essential nutrients (vitamins and proteins) for survival—and the very skinny rats lived an average of twice the normal rat life span. Why this is true still isn't known, but tests are ongoing.

In 2007 a team of researchers in Texas and New Mexico found that even exposure to the *odor* of food can affect life span. Like the rats in the earlier experiments, fruit flies were subjected to a very low-calorie diet, but some of the flies were kept in the presence of the odor of live yeast, which fruit flies eat, and some weren't. The ones in the odor-free environment lived 6% to 18% longer. Again, nobody knows why.

CHAPTER 14

THE WOW! SIGNAL

On August 15, 1977, astronomer Dr. Jerry Ehman proved that there is intelligent life on other planets in the universe. Well, not really, but that's what a lot of people believe happened. Ehman was working on a SETI (Search for Extra-Terrestrial Intelligence) project at the "Big Ear" radio telescope at Ohio State University. SETI, formed in 1960, has been funding projects such as the Big Ear—a radio telescope searching for radio signals that appear to be more than randomly occurring—ever since. That night in 1977, Ehman made a note on a computer printout record of what the Big Ear "heard." The note: Ehman circled a particular section of a radio signal and wrote "Wow!" next to it. The "Wow! signal," as it's known, is now famous among astronomers. Simply put, it was a very strong signal—the strongest in the telescope's 35 years in operation (it was dismantled in 1998)—and had what were deemed signatures of being artificially produced. And it definitely wasn't from Earth. No explanation for the signal, either for or against it being of extraterrestrial origin, has ever been found.

WOODSTOCK: THE FIRST 8 SONGS

The first performer on the first day of the legendary rock concert on Max Yasgur's farm outside of Woodstock, New York, on August 15, 1969, was folksinger Richie Havens. He played these eight songs:

"High Flyin' Bird"

"I Can't Make It Anymore"

"With a Little Help from My Friends"

"Strawberry Fields Forever"

"Hey Jude"

"I Had a Woman"

"Handsome Johnny"

"Freedom"

MARRIAGE BY PROXY

Can you legally marry someone who's not, at the moment of marriage, in the same room with you? How about someone who's not even in the same country? The answer to both is yes, but not everywhere.

✦ A *proxy marriage* is one in which one of the parties is not present. It's been around for centuries, used both for nefarious reasons, such as human trafficking, as well as compassionate ones, such as allowing couples separated by war to marry. One of the most famous examples is the marriage of French emperor Napoléon to the archduchess Marie Louise of Austria in 1810. Napoléon was in Paris, Marie Louise in Vienna—and the archduke Charles stood in for Napoleon.

✦ The practice became popular in the United States with "picture brides" in the early 1900s, which saw mostly Japanese and Korean immigrants marrying girls from back home—by proxy—after selecting them from photographs. It rose again during World War I, with women in the U.S. marrying absent soldiers. Today it's legal in just four U.S. states—Montana, California, Colorado, and Texas. In Montana, *double-proxy* marriages are even legal, in which both participants are absent. These usually involve couples serving in the military.

PROXY MARRIAGE EXTRAS

✦ Double-proxy "mail-in" marriages are legal in Mexico and Paraguay for $500 to $1,000—and those two countries are the official marriage "locations" of thousands of people around the world whose home countries' laws restrict them from marrying in the way they choose. In Israel, for example, in order for marriages to be officially recognized they must be performed by orthodox rabbis. Orthodox wedding rites allow women very little role in the marriage, so many Israeli couples get married—by mail—in Paraguay or Mexico.

✦ On December 2, 1959, the Malpasset Dam broke and almost completely destroyed the French town of Fréjus. More than 400 people were killed, including a young man named André Capra. His fiancée, Irène Jodart, survived. She appealed to then-President Charles de Gaulle and then directly to the French people via the press. The French government quickly passed a law—and a month later Irène was legally married to the dead André. It's still legal to do this in France today.

✦ On August 10, 2003, Ekaterina Dmitriev was in Texas when she married Yuri Malenchenko. Where was he? He was traveling about 17,000 miles an hour aboard the International

Space Station. It was the first by-proxy space wedding in history.

ANCIENT YEASTY SECRET

How did ancient peoples discover how to make bread that rises? One theory says that people may have made the kneading of large quantities of dough easier by using their feet…and the yeasts commonly found in toe fungus made it rise.

HOOVES AND PAWS

Why do some mammals have hooves and others have paws? Good question. To answer it, we must travel back about 65 million years to the end of the age of dinosaurs. They'd been Earth's dominant land animals for more than 150 million years, but with their extinction, the mammals, who had been around for nearly as long, were able to take over.

✦ There weren't a lot of mammal species at the time, and they were all quite small, with the largest believed to be only opossum-sized. They were also primarily *insectivores*, meaning insects were their main food source. Other important characteristics: they all had paws; five digits on each paw; short, stumpy legs; and they used *plantigrade locomotion*—they were flat-footed. But changes were…afoot.

✦ With the dinosaurs gone, vast amounts of territory and extremely plentiful food supplies became open to the mammals. Over the next several million years, some mammals acquired adaptations that allowed them to become herbivores (plant eaters)—and they became the dominant animals throughout the enormous expanses of vegetation no longer inhabited by the dinosaurs. Other mammals became carnivores (meat eaters)—and some of the meat they ate was the new herbivores.

✦ These two new types of animals eventually developed into

the hoofed herbivores, such as antelope, sheep, and cows, and the pawed carnivores, such as lions and wolves. The two had an "arms race" of sorts over the millennia, and it was all about speed: The herbivores had to become faster to escape the carnivores, and the carnivores had to become faster so they could catch the herbivores.

✦ As we said, all mammals once used plantigrade locomotion: the entire sole of the foot, right back to the heel, contacts the ground while walking. Fossil records show that by about 55 million years ago, this had already started to change.

✦ Many carnivore species developed *digitigrade* locomotion: The balls of the feet and the digits contact the ground while walking or running, but not the heels. Over millions of years, the bones of the heels shifted up and became part of the length of the leg. Those longer legs resulted in much faster running ability. They also resulted in the shape of the carnivore paw, which you can see on a cat or dog. They have four padded toes on the ground, and small *dewclaws*—remnants of their innermost toes—slightly higher on their legs.

✦ Similar adaptations developed in herbivore mammals, but they did their predators one better: They went from plantigrade to digitgrade to *unguligrade* locomotion. This means, basically, that they run on the very tips of their toes; even the ball of the foot lifted off the ground and became part of the leg. Over the millennia, herbivore legs became much longer, and what was once their claws became much larger and flattened out on the bottom, i.e., their claws became hooves. (All hoofed creatures are known as the *ungulates*, from the Latin *unguis*, for "nail," "claw," or "hoof." (Some, like whales, no longer have hooves. Go to page 141 for more on that.)

6 AUTOANTONYMS

Autoantonyms are words that can have two opposite or contradictory meanings.

Game: ready or willing; crippled

✦ "Are you game?"

✦ "I would be if I didn't have this game leg."

Fast: speedy or quick; tied down or immovable

✦ "Is that a fast boat?"

✦ "Yeah, but it's tied fast to the pier, so it's not going anywhere."

Blunt: dull; pointed

✦ "He acts as if he was hit over the head with a blunt object."

✦ "That was a pretty blunt comment."

Bill: paper money; a list of charges owed

✦ "Your bill comes to $20 exactly."

✦ "I'll pay it with this $20 bill."

Fix: a problem; a solution

✦ "We're in quite a fix here."

✦ "No problem—I have a quick fix."

Either: one or the other; both

✦ "Well, she either lives on the right side or the left side."

✦ "There are houses on either side of the street."

ANIMAL ODDITIES: SEA CUCUMBERS

If you're swimming in the ocean and you happen to frighten a sea cucumber, get ready for a really odd show. Sea cucumbers have internal organs called *Cuvierian tubules*, and when scared they expel them out their anuses, where they expand to entangle and "slime" an enemy.

✦ The Cuvierian tubes are "respiratory trees": A sea cucumber breathes by drawing water into its *cloaca* (or anus) and into the tree, acquiring oxygen from the water much like a fish's gills do.

✦ A species of fish called pearl fish have evolved alongside sea cucumbers and have adapted to their unique anatomical equipment: They swim into the sea cucumber's cloacas, break through the membranes of the respiratory trees, and make themselves at home. Every night they leave to hunt for food, and every morning they smell their way back to the sea cucumber, wait for it to breathe, and swim back inside its cloaca.

EINSTEIN ON GENIUS

"Any fool can make things bigger, more complex, and more violent. It takes a touch of genius—and a lot of courage—to move in the opposite direction."

GIRL…GIRL…BOY

Are you male? Did you know that you were once female? Well, sort of…

✦ The sex of a child is determined at the moment of conception and relates to how mammals produce sex cells (eggs and sperm).

✦ Each egg cell produced in a female mammal's ovaries contains one sex chromosome, and it's always the female X chromosome. Each sperm cell produced in a male mammal's testes also carries one sex chromosome, but it can be either an X chromosome or the male Y chromosome.

✦ When an egg is fertilized by a sperm cell carrying an X chromosome, giving it an XX chromosome pair, it becomes a girl. When an egg is fertilized by a sperm cell with a Y chromosome, giving it an XY combination, it becomes a boy— eventually.

✦ Because eggs start out with just the female chromosome, they are, basically, programmed to develop into females. If an egg is fertilized by a sperm cell with a female X chromosome, it simply develops in that "X" way, eventually developing female sexual organs and so on.

✦ Here's the kicker: If an egg is fertilized by a sperm cell carrying a male Y chromosome—for more than a month it develops just as it would if it were going to become a girl. Even though it has already been determined that it will be male, it's not until about six weeks that genes on that Y chromosome are activated and the development process is altered—and *male*, rather than female, sexual organs begin to develop. What would have become ovaries instead become testes. Because of this, some biologists refer to female development as the "default" development of mammals, with male development being a later augmentation of that…and therefore maintain that every one of us, for a brief time, was female.

FOOD FOR THOUGHT. Why do women produce only X chromosomes, while men produce both X and Y? Because women don't have any Y chromosomes. Having two X chromosomes defines what a female mammal is, in a manner of speaking. They can't, therefore, produce eggs with Y chromosomes. Men, being defined by their XY chromosome combination, can naturally produce sperm with either chromosome.

HIGH PRIEST

In 423 C.E. a Christian monk in Syria climbed to a small platform at the top of a pillar about 13 feet high. He stayed there for four years. For three years after that, his followers built higher and higher pillars, the final one about 50 feet high, topped by a 12-foot-square platform. The monk remained there, without leaving once, exposed to the desert weather, until he died…30 years later.

Saint Simeon Stylites (*stylites* means "pillar-dweller") was known throughout western Asia and Europe. Thousands of people came to him for advice, including many emperors, who would sit with him on the raised platform. In 473 a church was built at the site; the well-preserved ruins can still be seen, along with the foundation of the pillar, near the town of Aleppo in the desert in northwestern Syria.

DEAD SPACE

No, it's not the latest Stephen King novel; it's something inside you right now. With breathing, the object is *gas exchange*: When we inhale oxygen-rich air into our lungs, the oxygen is absorbed by structures that line our lungs called *alveoli*. The alveoli then expel carbon dioxide, which the air carries away as we exhale. But every time we exhale, a significant amount of the air that we breathed in—as much as a third of it—leaves exactly the way it was inhaled, with its oxygen still intact and with no carbon dioxide present. Part of the reason for this is simply because that air didn't come into contact with the alveoli; it remained in our mouth and *trachea* (the tube extending from the throat to the lungs) after a full inhale. That's known as "dead space." Another way it happens is deemed *aveolar dead space*, and is a result of not enough blood flowing in the alveoli for efficient exchange to occur.

Lung Fact: The average amount of air taken in one breath by a 150-pound adult human is about five liters. The average dead space: about 1.5 liters. (The amount of air inhaled in one breath is known scientifically as the *tidal volume*.)

MUSHROOMS AND ALCOHOL

There are many types of toxins found in the many species of poisonous mushrooms. One in particular isn't poisonous itself... except if it's taken in combination with alcohol. The toxin is the amino acid *coprine*. (It's chemically similar to *disulfiram*, the active ingredient in *Antabuse*, the drug used to treat alcoholics.) Though rarely fatal, if consumed with alcohol, within two hours the unlucky imbiber will experience an increased pulse rate, hot flashes, a metallic taste in the mouth, numbness in the hands, a violent headache, nausea, and vomiting. The mushrooms known to contain coprine include popular and commonly eaten varieties in North America known as "inky caps," defined by having gills on the underside of the caps that when mature liquefy into a dark, inky substance. And the mushrooms and alcohol don't have to be ingested at the same time for the ill effects to appear: Cases involving sickness where alcohol was consumed as long as several days after the mushrooms have been reported.

STAR BRIGHTNESS: APPARENT

The brightest star in the sky, aside from the Sun, is Sirius, the "Dog Star." How bright is it? It's -1.47m. Or 1.4M, depending on how you measure it. Astronomers measure the brightness of celestial bodies in two ways: *apparent* and *absolute* brightness. Apparent brightness is just what it sounds like—how bright objects appear compared to each other from our perspective on Earth. This has its roots in an ancient Greek system that classified stars in six different *magnitudes* of brightness, 1 being the brightest and 6 being the weakest.

✦ In the 19th century, astronomers decided to keep that system, with a few adaptations. There were many more factors added—telescopes made that necessary—and it was decided that 5 steps up in orders of magnitude would equal 100 times in intensity of brightness. For example, if a star is given a rank of 5 on the apparent brightness scale, it is 100 times brighter than a star with a rank of 10. (Notice that the smaller the number, the brighter the celestial object.)

✦ The star Vega, a consistently bright star, was chosen to be the "baseline star," and was given a rank of 0. Every other object in the sky was given a magnitude ranking based on how many times brighter or weaker it was than Vega. (This has changed in modern times, and Vega is now measured at 0.03.)

✦ The brightest celestial object, for example, is the Sun, and it has an apparent brightness of -26.73m (a small "m" is used for apparent brightness). Do the math and we find the Sun is about 60 billion times brighter than Vega.

✦ More examples: The Moon has an apparent brightness of -12.6m; the brightest planet, Venus, is at -3.7m, and the brightest star (other than the Sun), Sirius, ranks at -1.47m.

✦ The faintest stars that can be seen with the naked eye under the best conditions have apparent brightnesses of about +6.5m, and the faintest objects detected by the Hubble Space Telescope are about +35m. (For Absolute Brightness, go to page 347.)

THE HEISMAN TROPHY

The Heisman Trophy is awarded each year to the country's best college football player, as voted by sports reporters. It's named for John Heisman, a coach at Clemson and Georgia Tech during the sport's early days in the 1890s and 1900s. Heisman worked tirelessly to streamline football's rules. His greatest contribution: the forward pass. In the 1930s, he worked as the athletic director at the Downtown Athletic Club in New York City. Since 1935, the club has issued the Heisman Trophy in honor of his contributions to the sport.

ANIMAL GROUP NAMES

You probably know that a group of fish is called a "school" and a bunch of lions is a "pride." But there are dozens more:

A murder of crows	A scurry of squirrels
A volery of birds	A cry of hounds
A pod of dolphins	A leash of foxes

A pod of seals

A pack of wolves

A flock of sheep

A sleuth of bears

A tribe of goats

A kettle of hawks

A troop of kangaroos

A nide of pheasants

A charm of finches

A knot of toads

An army of caterpillars

A smack of jellyfish

A flange of baboons

A bevy of swans

A gam of whales

A skein of geese

A swarm of bees

A sedge of cranes

A labor of moles

A team of horses

A crash of rhinoceroses

A herd of elephants

A covey of quail

A sounder of boars

A rhumba of rattlesnakes

A cete of badgers

KNOW YOUR AGES

The Three-Age System refers to a 19th-century European classification system used to date ancient artifacts used by humans, based on the materials that were used to make them. The three ages are the Stone Age, Bronze Age, and Iron Age. A brief explanation:

The Stone Age. For more than two million years, humans used stones to make their hardest and most lasting tools.

The Copper Age. Around 4000 B.C.E., people began melting ores (metals mixed with other minerals) to extract the metal in a process known as *smelting*. Metals had been used to make jewelry for thousands of years by this time, but smelting allowed for greater production of copper tools and weapons. Copper was the first to be used because it has the lowest melting point (1,984°F) of the prominent naturally occurring metals. (The Copper Age, because of its relatively short span, is considered a transitional phase between the Stone and Bronze Ages.)

The Bronze Age. Around 3500 B.C.E., it was discovered that mixing a small amount of tin with copper during smelting produced a much harder and more durable metal—bronze. (Mixes of a metal and other substances to make another metal are called alloys.) This marked the beginning of the Bronze Age. An added bonus was the fact that bronze actually has a lower melting point than copper (1,742°F), because the melting point of tin is so low—just 449°F. (Tin wasn't widely used by itself because it is very rare, and much softer than copper.)

The Iron Age. By about 1200 B.C.E., smelting technology had improved to the point that the commonly occurring and much harder element iron—with its melting point of 2,795°F—was regularly used for toolmaking in several places around the world (including western Africa, India, and Turkey)—and so began what is called the Iron Age.

✦ People soon began making iron alloys by adding carbon and other ingredients to the iron. Some common iron alloys include wrought iron, pig iron, cast iron, and different types of steel.

MORE ALLOYS

Steel is a simple iron alloy consisting of iron and between 0.5% and 1.5% carbon, along with trace amounts of other elements, and is generally much harder and more durable than iron. *Tool steel* is roughly the same but has a different heating process that results in an even harder steel. *Stainless steel* has about 11% of the metal element chromium added.

Pig iron is an iron alloy with a higher carbon content than steel, between 2% and 4%, and usually small amounts of silicon, resulting in a very hard but brittle metal.

Gunmetal is a type of bronze, generally with about 88% copper, 10% tin, and 2% zinc. It's also called "red brass." As the name implies, gunmetal was originally used for making guns, but was subsequently replaced by steel, which is much harder.

Brass is a copper alloy made with zinc. There are many different kinds, with between 5% and more than 50% zinc in the mix. Many are known for their yellow, goldlike appearance.

Solder (pronounced "SAH-der") is an alloy of either lead or tin, depending on which one is higher in content. Common solder used for joining metals together (with a soldering gun) is a tin alloy and has about a 40% lead content, resulting in a very soft metal with a relatively low melting point.

Sterling silver is about 93% silver along with 7% of an alloying agent, often copper. This makes it much harder than pure silver, which too soft for many applications.

ANATOMY OF AN ORCHESTRA

A full orchestra can exceed 100 members (as opposed to a chamber orchestra, which has 50 members or less). It is composed of four main sections: woodwinds, brass, strings, and percussion.

Woodwinds. These are instruments made out of wood, metal, bone, or plastic. Sound is created when the player blows air through a mouthpiece, causing a *reed* (made of cane), or *resonator*, to vibrate. Pitch is changed by the covering and uncovering of holes on the instruments. The woodwind section is usually composed of two flutes, clarinets, oboes, and bassoons, plus a bass clarinet, contrabassoon, and English horn.

Brass. Here, the player's lips do the vibrating instead of a reed or resonator. After air is blown through a mouthpiece into the long, usually curved tube (which can be made of brass, other metals, or even wood), pitch is controlled either by valves, which the player opens and closes with the fingers, or by a slide that changes the length of the tube. The brass section consists of the French horn, tuba, flugelhorn, trumpet or cornet, and the trombone. (Although it's made of brass, the saxophone is considered a woodwind because it has a reed.)

Strings. As the name implies, these instruments produce sound via vibrating strings. The largest of the orchestral sections, strings are divided up into the first and second violins, violas, cellos, and double basses, with six to twelve of each. Many orchestras also have a harp.

Percussion. These instruments—which are struck, shaken, or scraped to make sound—fall into two categories, *tuned* and *untuned*. The timpani, or kettle drum, is the oldest, having been a part of orchestras for more than 300 years. Other common percussion instruments are the snare drum, tenor drum, bass drum, cymbals, triangle, wood block, tambourine, marimba, vibraphone, xylophone, glockenspiel, gong, and tubular bells.

FOOD FOR THOUGHT. Where does the piano fit into all of this? It could be considered a string instrument because felt hammers hit different combinations of its 242 steel strings. But because the player must strike the piano keys first, it is classified as a tuned percussive instrument.

HOUSEHOLD GENIUS

To peel the skins off of fresh tomatoes easily, first plunge them into boiling water for one minute, then rinse under cold water (to stop them from cooking). The skins will slip off easily.

11 U.S. STATES NAMED AFTER PEOPLE

1. Delaware: Named in honor of Lord De La Warr (1577–1618), the first governor of the Virginia colony.

2. Georgia: Named for King George II of England (1683–1760), who granted the charter that allowed the colony of Georgia to be founded in 1733.

3. Louisiana: Named for King Louis XIV of France (1638–1715).

4. Maryland: Named for Queen Henrietta Maria (1609–69), the wife of King Charles I of England.

5. New York: Named for James, Duke of York (1633–1701), who ruled England as King James II from 1685–88.

6 and 7. North and South Carolina: Named for Charles I of England (1600–49).

8. Pennsylvania: Named for William Penn (1644–1718), who founded the colony.

9 and 10. Virginia and West Virginia: Named for the "virgin queen," Elizabeth I (1533–1603).

11. Washington: Named in honor of George Washington (1732–99).

LEARNING TO NOT LIKE YOU

In 1981 Terry F. Pettijohn, Professor of Psychology at Ohio State University, Marion, carried out a series of experiments with pairs of Mongolian gerbils. He allowed two gerbils to meet and "introduce themselves" for about five minutes—then injected one of them with lithium chloride, which gave it "gastrointestinal distress," or a stomachache. When a gerbil that had been injected was placed with other gerbils 48 hours later, it acted normally—running up to them and sniffing them. But when it met the gerbil it had met just before the injection, it showed a marked aversion to the animal, "often moving away from it and spending time in the corner of the open field." The experiment proved, Dr. Pettijohn claimed, that not only are Mongolian gerbils very good at recognizing other individual gerbils (most likely by smell), but that they can learn social aversion to other gerbils by recalling unpleasant memories that had nothing to do with the other gerbils.

LATIN PROVERB

Absentem laedit cum ebrio qui litigat. "To quarrel with a drunk is to wrong a man who is not even there."

CHAPTER 15

THE NUCLEAR BOY SCOUT

In 1994 David Hahn, a 17-year-old from Detroit, Michigan, learned that it was possible to find small amounts of radioactive material in common store-bought items. *Americium-241*, for example, is found in most smoke detectors. The science-minded Boy Scout set his sights on earning the "Atomic Energy Badge"… by building a nuclear reactor in his mother's backyard shed.

First, he had to create a "neutron gun" (the nuclear reactions that power most nuclear plants are set off by bombarding a radioactive element, usually uranium, with neutrons). Hahn collected americium-241 from hundreds of smoke detectors and packed them into a hollow piece of lead with a tiny opening. Radiation can't pass through lead, so the radiation from the americium-241 could now only escape through that pinhole—as a focused beam. Hahn covered the hole with a thin strip of aluminum, which reacts to radiation by ejecting neutrons. He now had his "neutron gun."

Over the next several months, Hahn attempted to create a nuclear reaction by shooting different radioactive substances with his neutron gun. That included thorium-232, which can be found in gas camping lanterns, and beryllium, which he stole from a chemistry lab. After that, he acquired some pitchblende, a type of rock that contains small amounts of uranium.

Hahn never succeeded in creating a nuclear reaction... but he did create extremely high and very dangerous levels of radiation—more than 1,000 times normal levels. The fiasco finally ended when police stopped Hahn one night in August 1994, and he told them he had radioactive substances in his car. The FBI and the Nuclear Regulatory Commission were immediately called, a Federal Radiological Emergency Response Plan was initiated, and Hahn's mother's property was designated a hazardous materials site. The shed, along with all of its contents, was buried at a radioactive waste disposal site in Utah. Hahn refused medical evaluation against the advice of experts, despite having been told that he had been exposed to more radiation than a person can safely endure...in an entire lifetime.

Postscript: In August 2007, the 30-year-old Hahn was arrested in Detroit for larceny. He pled guilty...to stealing several smoke detectors. He was sentenced to 90 days in jail.

PAKISTAN: THE NAME

On August 14, 1947, Pakistan became an independent nation, gaining independence from the United Kingdom, which had ruled the Indian subcontinent since 1858. (India became an independent nation the following day.) The name chosen for the new country was coined 14 years earlier by Muslim nationalist leader Choudhary Rahmat Ali. It was a rough acronym of the names of the traditional homelands of Muslims in the region: *P* for Punjab, *A* for Afghania, *K* for Kashmir, *S* for Sindh,

T for Turkestan, and the *AN* from Baluchistan. It was originally "Pakstan"—the I was later added to make it easier to pronounce.

THE ORDER OF PRESDENTIAL SUCCESSION

Any potential successor to the presidency must satisfy the requirements for office as described in the U.S. Constitution: natural-born citizen, age 35 or older, a resident of the U.S. for 14 years. If he or she does not meet these qualifications, the presidency passes to the next eligible person in the order of succession:

1. Vice President
2. Speaker of the House of Representatives
3. President Pro Tempore of the Senate
4. Secretary of State
5. Secretary of the Treasury
6. Secretary of Defense
7. Attorney General
8. Secretary of the Interior
9. Secretary of Agriculture
10. Secretary of Commerce
11. Secretary of Labor
12. Secretary of Health and Human Services
13. Secretary of Housing and Urban Development
14. Secretary of Transportation
15. Secretary of Energy
16. Secretary of Education
17. Secretary of Veterans Affairs

U.S. POSTAL SERVICE ABBREVIATIONS FOR AMERICAN TERRITORIES AND DEPENDENCIES

American Samoa: AS

Federated States of Micronesia: FM. (These islands were once part of the "Trust Territory of the Pacific Islands," administered by the United States from 1947 until 1994, when Palau, the last remaining member of the territory, became completely self-governing. The Federated States of Micronesia gained independence in 1986 but it remains a U.S. protectorate.)

Guam: GU

Marshall Islands: MH (another former member of the Trust Territory of the Pacific Islands)

Northern Mariana Islands: MP

Palau: PW

Puerto Rico: PR

Virgin Islands: VI

ESCAPE FROM AMERICA: THE REVOLUTION

We're used to the idea of fleeing refugees being a part of war. But did you know that the American Revolution produced waves of refugees who left the United States?

Loyalists. Historians estimate that as many as 20% of the people living in the 13 Colonies during the Revolutionary War remained loyal to Great Britain, and when the war ended, 10% to 15% of these "Loyalists"—as many as 70,000 people—left the United States to escape open hostility, persecution, and the confiscation of property. Of these, 7,000 returned to Great Britain, and 17,000 went to the various British colonies in the Caribbean.

But the overwhelming majority, more than 46,000 in all, went to British North America—modern-day Canada. Rather than assimilate into existing French communities that dated back to Canada's days as a French possession, the Loyalists petitioned the British government to give them their own settlements, and the government acceded, carving the province of New Brunswick out of Nova Scotia in 1784 and dividing Quebec into Upper Canada (in modern-day Ontario) and Lower Canada (in parts of modern-day Quebec as well as Newfoundland and Labrador) in 1791.

Black Loyalists. There were also 8,000 former slaves who left the United States after the war, many of whom fought in a special black corps of the British army in exchange for their freedom. (One former slave, Henry Washington, escaped from the service of General George Washington.) As many as 1,000 black Loyalists moved to London to join the community of 10,000 free blacks that was already established there. Several thousand went to the Bahamas, and another 4,000 went to Canada with the hope, if not the expectation, that they would be treated similarly to white Loyalists. When this turned out not to be the case, about half set sail for Freetown, Sierra Leone, in west Africa, which was founded as a settlement for freed slaves in 1787 by British philanthropists. Modern-day Sierra Leone's creole minority is descended from freed slaves.

GENIUS IS...

"Genius is always allowed some leeway, once the hammer has been pried from its hands and the blood has been cleaned up."

—science fiction author Terry Pratchett

A TRUFFLE TIP

Truffles are a kind of mushroom found in Asia, Europe, North Africa, and North America. They grow underground, are irregularly shaped, can be walnut- to grapefruit-sized, have a pungent odor—and they've been considered a delicacy for thousands of years. If you can afford some (they can cost as much as $2,500 per pound), here's a simple and tasty way to enjoy them:

✦ Place two or three truffles in an egg carton with as many eggs as you'll need for the meal.

✦ Close the carton, seal it in a plastic bag, and put it in the fridge for about two days.

✦ Truffles are so powerfully pungent that the smell will be absorbed by the eggs—right through the shells.

✦ Cook the eggs however you like them—scrambled, in an omelet (with the truffles), deviled—and they'll have the great flavors of both eggs and truffles. Enjoy!

25 ENGLISH-LANGUAGE NOVELS PUBLISHED SINCE 1900 THAT SOLD AT LEAST 10 MILLION COPIES

✦ *The Lord of the Rings* trilogy, J. R. R. Tolkien (150 million)

✦ *Harry Potter and the Philosopher's Stone*, J. K. Rowling (120 million)

✦ *And Then There Were None*, Agatha Christie (100 million)

✦ *The Hobbit*, J. R. R. Tolkien (100 million)

✦ *The Catcher in the Rye*, J.D. Salinger (65 million)

✦ *The Da Vinci Code*, Dan Brown (57 million)

✦ *Anne of Green Gables*, Lucy Maud Montgomery (50 million)

✦ *Charlotte's Web*, E. B. White (45 million)

✦ *To Kill a Mockingbird*, Harper Lee (30 million)

✦ *Valley of the Dolls*, Jacqueline Susann (30 million)

✦ *Gone with the Wind*, Margaret Mitchell (30 million)

✦ *The Godfather*, Mario Puzo (21 million)

✦ *Jaws*, Peter Benchley (20 million)

✦ *Fear of Flying*, Erica Jong (18 million)

✦ *Shogun*, James Clavell (15 million)

- *The Pillars of the Earth*, Ken Follett (15 million)
- *The Horse Whisperer*, Nicholas Evans (15 million)
- *God's Little Acre*, Erskine Caldwell (14 million)
- *Peyton Place*, Grace Metalious (12 million)
- *Dune*, Frank Herbert (12 million)
- *The Bridges of Madison County*, Robert James Waller (12 million)
- *The Exorcist*, William Peter Blatty (11 million)
- *Catch-22*, Joseph Heller (10 million)
- *The Lovely Bones*, Alice Sebold (10 million)
- *The Kite Runner*, Khaled Hosseini (10 million)

EVEREST DOWNSIZED

It's fairly common, uncommon knowledge that Mt. Everest, at 29,017 feet, is not the tallest mountain in the world. That distinction goes to Hawaii's Mauna Kea—although its peak rises 13,796 feet above sea level, half of the volcano is underwater. In all, Mauna Kea measures 33,476 feet from base to tip. While Everest is not nearly as tall, at least its peak is the highest point on Earth, right? Not exactly. Technically, it is the highest point above sea level. But if one thinks of the highest point as being the farthest from the center of Earth, then that title goes to Chimborazo, a volcano in Ecuador. Because our planet bulges at the equator due to centrifugal force, Chimborazo, at 20,703 feet above sea level, is actually 7,217 feet *farther* from Earth's center than Mr. Everest. In other words, Chimborazo's peak, when compared to Everest's, is about a mile and a half closer to outer space.

QUIPU: THE KNOT LANGUAGE

When Spanish explorers conquered the Incan Empire in 1532, the Incas had no written language—but they did have a *tied* language. They used a recording system in which knots were tied in strings hanging from a length of thick cord. The number of strings could range from a few to 2,000 on a cord. They were dyed different colors and could have many different types of knots tied in them. The Incas called this writing system "Quipu," and the knots, as well as the colors of the strings, represented numbers that could be "read" by people. Quipu was used extensively throughout the empire in many ways, including census recording, figuring tax amounts, keeping track of the contents of warehouses, and for performing simple mathematics.

✦ Some anthropologists believe that Quipu was also used to record either sounds or words found in the Incan language, Quecha. Unfortunately, it's impossible to prove. The Spanish brutally suppressed the Incan people, and use of Quipu was forbidden. It faded into obscurity, but in recent times interest has renewed, so perhaps someday somebody will break the Quipu code.

THE BLOOMSBERRIES

The Bloomsbury Group was a tightly knit and highly influential group of intellectuals, writers, and artists that met in Bloomsbury Square in London from the early 1900s to the 1930s. The group included novelists E.M. Forster and Virginia Woolf, historian Lytton Strachey, art critic Clive Bell, art historian Roger Fry, economist John Maynard Keynes, painters Vanessa Bell and Duncan Grant, as well as socialite Vita Sackville-West. Though there was no single intellectual or aesthetic idea that united them, many of the "Bloomsberries" held some key ideas in common: They followed philosopher G.E. Moore's "Principia Ethica," which argued that "human intercourse and the enjoyment of beautiful objects" were "good in themselves"; they venerated honest speech, freedom of information, and experimentation in their work; they rejected nationalism, and were conscientious objectors to World War I; they embraced post-Impressionist painting (Gauguin, Van Gogh, Matisse), and the decorative arts; they rejected Victorian notions, especially of gender roles (many of them were feminists) and sexuality. Historians say they helped paved the way for the "Lost Generation" of artists and writers in post-World War I Europe, including Pablo Picasso, Ernest Hemingway, and F. Scott Fitzgerald.

SURVIVING A DOG ATTACK

✦ If a dog is charging at you, running away may make you more vulnerable. Run only if you're sure you can get to a fence, tree, or doorway well before the dog gets to you.

✦ If there's no escape, prepare yourself for the attack. Two defense plans: 1) Hit the dog hard, directly on its nose; 2) hold your forearm out in front of you. When the dog lunges for it, quickly jam it into the dog's mouth and keep pushing. Use your other arm to flip the dog onto its back, which will temporarily incapacitate it.

✦ If there is more than one dog, crouch into the smallest ball you possibly can, shielding your head and throat.

✦ After the attack, go to a hospital immediately to be vaccinated for rabies and tetanus.

WORD SEARCH: *NERD*

Most etymologists agree that the word "nerd" was invented by Dr. Seuss in his 1950 book *If I Ran the Zoo*. (Seuss's Nerd is a strange humanoid with disheveled hair and a grumpy expression.) Within a year, the word showed up in *Newsweek*: "In Detroit, someone who once would be called a drip or a square is now, regrettably, a nerd."

Two other theories of the word's origin have circulated for many years, but both have been proven to be myths. One comes from Ottawa, Ontario, where the Northern Electric Research and Development Laboratories invented pocket protectors in 1947. In the 1950s, company workers supposedly wore these pocket protectors on their lab coats...directly underneath their company patch, which featured the acronym "NERD." The other says that the word comes from "knurd"...or "drunk" spelled backward.

MADAME VICE PRESIDENT

You've heard of Sarah Palin, and if you're 35 or older you probably remember Geraldine Ferraro, the 1984 Democratic nominee for vice president. It turns out they're not the only women ever to run for that position. There have been many minor-party candidates over the years, including these women:

✦ **Marie Caroline Brehm (Prohibition Party, 1924).** The ratification of the 19th Amendment to the Constitution in 1920, which gave women the right to vote and, by extension, to run for public office, made Brehm the first female nominee for vice president who would actually have been legally eligible to take office, had she won the election.

✦ **Theodora Nathalia Nathan (Libertarian Party, 1972).** Nathan was the first woman to receive an electoral college vote in a presidential election, when Roger MacBride, an elector from Virginia, cast his vote for her instead of for the candidate who carried Virginia, Richard Nixon.

✦ **La Donna Harris (Citizens Party, 1980).** When the administration of Democratic President Jimmy Carter turned out to be too moderate for many environmental and liberal advocacy groups, they banded together to found the Citizens Party in 1979. Barry Commoner was the nominee for president; Harris was the pick for vice president. They won only 233,000 votes and played almost no role in Carter's loss to Ronald Reagan. The party disintegrated following the 1986 mid-term elections.

✦ **Marilyn Chambers (Personal Choice Party, 2004).** The party, whose logo is a smiley face, believes the role of government should be limited to preventing people from hurting each other. Beyond that, it's anything goes! True to its principles, the party nominated adult film star Marilyn Chambers, famous for her role in the 1972 film *Behind the Green Door*, for vice president. The ticket qualified for the ballot in only one state—Utah.

WORLD LAKES

✦ **Highest navigable lake:** Lake Titicaca, which extends across Peru and Bolivia, was the center of the Inca empire. It sits at 12,500 feet above sea level.

✦ **Deepest lake:** Lake Baikal, in Siberia, is 5,524 feet deep and contains 20 percent of the world's freshwater.

✦ **Saltiest lake:** Lake Assal, in the African nation of Djibouti.

✦ **Longest lake:** Lake Tanganyika, in Tanzania, has 420 miles of lake coast. The lake covers a total of 12,700 square miles.

✦ **Largest lake:** The overall biggest freshwater lake is Lake Superior, in the United States. It covers 31,698 square miles. It's roughly the size of South Carolina.

SPIDER SILK

✦ Spiders produce silk by secreting a liquid known as *dope* from glands located in their abdomens. There are seven known types of gland, each producing a different type of silk. No single spider species has all seven gland types; each has different combinations, usually only three to four types.

✦ The dope is secreted through *spinnerets*—nozzles on the abdomen's underside that can be controlled and moved. Two to eight spinnerets are found on spiders depending on species. Upon contact with the air the dope hardens into silk.

✦ The seven different types of silk:

Swathing silk for wrapping and immobilizing prey.

Sticky silk for catching prey in webs.

Draglines are the strongest type of silk and are used to attach the spider to the web in case it is knocked off.

Ballooning silk is used primarily for spider flight: young spiders of some species climb to the top of grasses, emit strands of silk into the air, the strands are eventually caught by the wind and the spiders are taken to a new area with a new food source.

Shelter silk is used to build nests or line burrows.

Egg-sac silk is very fine and used to encapsulate eggs.

Mating silk is made by males: They weave webs on which they deposit sperm, and transfer it to their front *palps*, a pair of arm-like sensory organs on the front of their heads. The palps are later used to insert the web into females.

✦ Only about one third of spider species spin webs to catch prey. Some species hold silk "nets" in their forelegs and cast them over passing insects. Spitting Spiders have a unique web use: they have poison-producing glands in their heads. When they spy prey they spit a mix of poison from their heads and silk from their spinnerets at it, immobilizing and poisoning the prey at once.

THE QUIET MOON

Why does the Moon appear to be more pock-marked and cratered than Earth? Because its small size allowed it to cool quickly and thoroughly, making it a geologically "quiet" planetary body. Earth, on the other hand, is an active planet, with a very large, hot core, shifting tectonic plates, and earthquakes and volcanoes that constantly change the surface and erase old scars. Earth also has weather that erodes the surface, whereas the Moon has virtually no weather. Result: The surface of the

Moon still shows its many meteor-impact craters, several of which are billions of years old.

BEAVER DAMNED

In the 17th century, beavers were a regular part of the diet of French fur trappers in what was to become Canada. That presented a problem: Most of the trappers were Catholics, and eating meat was forbidden during the fasting period of Lent, comprising the 40 days leading up to Easter. Eating fish, however, was allowed. That prompted François de Laval, the first bishop of New France, as it was called then, to make a request of the pope—a request that was granted. It decreed that beavers were fish…and allowed the trappers to eat them during Lent.

4 DELUSIONS

In psychiatric terms, "delusions" are medical symptoms in which a person has one or more persistent false beliefs even when the person has evidence that these beliefs are not true. They can have a number of causes, including drug intoxication and psychosis. Four of the many types:

Capgras delusion. The belief that a person known to an individual has been replaced by an identical double. A common symptom of the mental illness schizophrenia, it was named after French psychiatrist Joseph Capgras, who described it in 1923.

Delusional perception. In this condition, false significance is given to a familiar perception without any logical reason, e.g., the belief that a broken lightbulb means that something terrible is about to happen.

Fregoli delusion. A symptom of the very rare *Fregoli syndrome* in which a person holds a delusional belief that different people are in fact one single person who changes appearance either through disguise or magic. It was first described in 1927 and was named after Italian actor Leopoldo Fregoli, renowned for his very quick costume changes during his stage act.

Somatoparaphrenia. This is a type of delusion in which a person believes that a part of his body—often a limb or part of a limb—does not belong to him.

ISOTOPES AND IONS EXPLAINED

On page 147 you read that all the atoms of a given element (such as hydrogen or oxygen) have roughly equal numbers of atomic particles: protons, neutrons, and electrons. "Roughly" because the numbers of neutrons and electrons can actually vary. Here's the basic explanation:

✦ Atoms of any given element all have the same number of protons—always. That's why the proton number is used to determine an element's *atomic number*.

✦ For example: atoms of the element *carbon*, atomic number 6, have 6 protons in their nuclei. But there are three different *isotopes* of carbon, having either 6, 7, or 8 neutrons along with those 6 protons.

✦ All elements have different isotopes. Some elements have only a few, some have many. (Xenon and cesium, for example, each have 36.)

✦ Isotope names are constructed by listing the name of the element (or just its initial) and its atomic weight—the number of protons and neutrons combined. That means that the three isotopes of carbon are Carbon-12 (6 protons and 6 neutrons), Carbon-13 (6 protons and 7 neutrons), and Carbon-14 (6 protons and 8 neutrons).

✦ *Ions* are atoms of a given element that have a different number of *electrons*, the negatively-charged particles inside atoms.

✦ Atoms become ions by gaining or losing electrons during a chemical reaction with other atoms.

CHAPTER 16

7 THINGS YOU COULDN'T DO IN THE YEAR 2000

✦ Find colors other than green on U.S. money

✦ Visit a nation called East Timor

✦ Watch *American Idol*

✦ Access Wikipedia

✦ Listen to an iPod

✦ Wear Crocs

✦ Watch YouTube

NEUTRALITY IN LIECHTENSTEIN

In 1868 the European nation of Liechtenstein disbanded its

80-man army, deeming it too costly, and declared permanent neutrality. The army retired its weapons to the Vaduz Castle in the capital city of Vaduz—where many of them remain to this day. Since then, Liechtenstein has not had an army, nor has it been invaded, not even by the neighboring Nazis during World War II. The country has, however, had some odd border troubles: In 1985 neighboring Switzerland, also a neutral state (although it still has a standing army), had to pay Liechtenstein several million dollars for starting a large forest fire after accidentally firing rockets across the border. And in 2007 a 171-man Swiss infantry company marched a full two miles into Liechtenstein...after getting lost.

CAN ONE BAD APPLE REALLY SPOIL THE BARREL?

Yes. When an apple starts to rot, it releases a chemical called *ethylene* that causes decay. If a rotten apple is being stored in a crate, the other apples can sense this chemical reaction, and when they do, they start producing their own ethylene, causing all the apples in the barrel to spoil.

A FORMAL TABLE SETTING

✦ **Charger:** An oversized dinner plate on which the dishes containing the actual food are placed. The charger is there so a table never appears to be "empty."

✦ **Butter plate:** Placed to the left of the place setting

✦ **Napkin:** Folded on the center of the charger

✦ **Salt and pepper:** Both placed just "above" the charger (meaning closer to the center of the table)

✦ **Crystal:** Although glasses don't have to be made of crystal, this is the umbrella term for wine glasses and water goblets. Usually three glasses, they are placed above the knives on the right-hand side of the setting. Left to right are the water goblet, then the red wine glass, then the white wine glass. A champagne flute, if necessary, is set behind the water goblet.

✦ **Forks** are set on the left-hand side of the setting. From farthest from the plate inward: salad fork, fish fork, meat fork.

✦ **Knives** are placed on the right-hand side of the setting (with the cutting side faced inward). From outside in: salad knife, meat knife, butter knife.

✦ **Soup spoons** and **fruit spoons** are set just to the right of the knives.

BONE MATRIX

Bone is part of the body's connective tissue, just as tendons and cartilage are. Connective tissue is characterized by having an *extracellular matrix*: the tissue's defining cells—bone cells in this case—don't make up all of the tissue; rather, they are separated by a matrix of other cells. In the case of bone, the matrix is comprised chiefly of very hard mineral (mostly calcium), which gives bones their hardness and strength, and the protein *collagen*, which gives them their elasticity. Bone cells, therefore, actually make up very little of the mass of bones. Here are the four main kinds of bone cells:

Osteogenic cells respond to trauma by activating bone-forming cells.

Osteoblasts are bone-forming cells that produce and secrete *osteoid*, which becomes the extracellular matrix.

Osteocytes secrete enzymes that help maintain the mineral content of bones.

Osteoclasts help maintain bone content by breaking down and *resorbing* old bone tissue. (Overactive osteoclasts are responsible for the disease known as osteoporosis, in which bone tissue is broken down faster than it can be replaced.)

BONE TYPES

There are four categories of bones in the human body: long, short, flat, and irregular.

Long bones include the femur, tibia, and bones that make up the fingers. They're defined by being much longer than they are wide, and are made mostly of compact, rather than spongy, bone.

Short bones are roughly cube-shaped and include the carpal bones of the hands and wrists, as well as the carpal bones of the feet and ankles. They consist primarily of spongy bone with a thin compact bone exterior.

Flat bones are thin, and most are curved. They include most of the bones of the skull, the sternum, and ribs, and are made up of thin layers of compact bone surrounding a layer of spongy bone.

Irregular bones have no definite shape and include the vertebrae, the hips, and the coccyx (the tailbone). They consist primarily of spongy bone with thin, compact exteriors.

ENDANGERED WEIRDNESS

Everybody hears about "famous" endangered animal species—pandas, tigers, polar bears, and the like—but we don't hear a lot about the thousands of others. With the goal of garnering some attention for less well known but equally endangered animals, a London-based group, Evolutionarily Distinct and Globally Endangered (EDGE), published a list in 2008 of 100 endangered—and unique—amphibians. Why amphibians? Because they're highly sensitive to pollution and climate changes, which makes them an "indicator species," i.e., when they're in danger, it's often a sign that an entire ecosystem is in danger. In addition, amphibians are by far the most endangered class of animal, with almost half of all species facing extinction. Here are six of the more unusual species chosen by EDGE:

Sagalla caecilian. This is a limbless amphibian that deserves its nickname the "naked snake," looking like a brownish snake/worm with no pattern on its body. Little is known about it, as it was only discovered in 2005. It was named after Sagalla Hill, an isolated mountain in Southern Kenya—the only spot it is known to inhabit.

Purple frog. A small, rotund, purple-pigmented frog from western India that was discovered in 2003. Why so hard to find? The purple frog spends most of the year buried up to 12 feet underground.

Ghost frogs. Just six species of this one- to two-inch-long frog genus exist and are found only near fast-moving streams in South Africa's Drakensberg Mountains. They get their ghostly name from one of the species found solely in the traditional human burial grounds of Skeleton Gorge in South Africa's Table Mountain.

Olm. Native to Eastern Europe, this is an entirely aquatic blind, white salamander. Individuals can live for nearly 60 years—and can go for up to 10 years without food.

Chinese giant salamander. How giant? They can grow to about the thickness of an adult human's thigh, can reach six feet in length, and can weigh up to 25 pounds. They live in streams and lakes in southwestern China, and they're descendants of a family of amphibians that goes back 170 million years.

Chile Darwin's frog. Native to Chile, this small frog species has the odd characteristic of having young tadpoles spend part of their development in their father's mouth. These frogs haven't been seen since the early 1980s. They may already be extinct.

THE FOUR ESTATES

During the feudal era of Europe, society was divided into three "estates." The First Estate was the clergy; the Second Estate was soldiers, nobility, and royalty; and the Third Estate was peasant farmers (pretty much everybody else). This formed the basis of the two houses of England's Parliament: Members of the House of Lords were from the First and Second Estates and members of the House of Commons were from the Third Estate. The term "fourth estate" was coined in 1828 by Parliament member Thomas Babington Macaulay, referring to newspaper reporters who detailed the activities of the other pillars of society. It's still used today as a nickname for the media.

HANDY MNEMONIC DEVICES

Mnemonic devices are used to help remember hard-to-remember lists, usually by assigning the first letter of the things to be remembered to a word in a phrase that shares the same first letter. (Sometimes just initials are used to form a word.)

Super Man helps every one: The five Great Lakes—Superior, Michigan, Huron, Erie, Ontario.

Mary's violet eyes make Jack sit up nights pining: The planets of the solar system, in order of their distance from the Sun—Mercury, Venus, Earth, Mars, Jupiter, Saturn, Uranus, Neptune, and Pluto (if you still consider it a planet).

How I want a drink, alcoholic of course, after the heavy lectures involving quantum mechanics: The number of letters in each word corresponds to each of the first 15 digits in π (pi). Those digits are 3.14159265358979.

Easter bunnies get drunk at Easter: The strings on a guitar (E, B, G, D, A, E), from the highest pitch to the lowest.

Every good boy deserves fudge: The notes on a treble clef scale—E, G, B, D, F.

Mr. (and) Mrs. Lamb: An old law school trick for recalling what were once the nine major felonies—murder, rape, manslaughter, robbery, sodomy, larceny, arson, mayhem, and burglary.

The ancient society of weird foreign scientists seized neither leisure nor the sheik's heifers at these heights: Except for the shorter words, every word in the sentence gives an exception to the "i before e, except after c" rule of spelling.

Richard of York gave battle in vain (or "Roy G. Biv" for short): The colors in the spectrum of visible light—red, orange, yellow, green, blue, indigo, violet.

HOW OUR SOLAR SYSTEM FORMED

The prevailing theory on the formation of the Sun and the planets (and of solar systems in general) goes as follows:

✦ After a star dies, all that remains is an immense and diffuse cloud of cold gas and cosmic dust. Its contents adhere to each other due to the natural forces of attraction.

✦ These interstellar clouds are called *nebulae* and come in many sizes. Only extremely large ones can create stars and planets. They are believed to rotate slowly. (You may have seen images of nebulae taken by the Hubble telescope, and many can be seen through a backyard telescope.)

✦ The gas, primarily hydrogen, along with some helium, has been around since the Big Bang. Cosmic dust consists of tiny crystal structures formed by the clumping of negatively and positively charged atoms shot out of novas and supernovas (dying stars).

✦ After many millions of years, a nebula collapses into itself. This can be caused by a number of things: It is believed that nebulae have a small amount of gravitational force when they are created, and that force naturally causes the loosely gathered material in the cloud to move toward its center, making it denser and increasing its gravity until it finally has enough to cause a chain reaction and completely collapse.

✦ According to the laws of physics, as the nebula collapses, its rate of spin increases. (Think of a spinning ice skater bringing her arms in.) Another effect: an increase in contact between atoms in the nebula, which causes it to heat up.

✦ At the core of the swirling, burning mass is an increasingly dense collection of hydrogen and helium gas. (Our Sun is composed of about 74% hydrogen and 25% helium.)

✦ The gases outside the core, along with the cosmic dust, begin to orbit the collapsed nebula. The spinning motion causes the material to flatten out, like spun pizza dough, and it becomes what is known as a *protoplanetary disk*. (The disk theory explains, among many other things, why all the planets in our solar system orbit the Sun on the same plane.)

✦ As the disk gets thinner and thinner, more and more dust and gas molecules come into contact with each other and clump together. They grow from pebble size to boulder size and eventually to miles in diameter, colliding with each other numerous times along the way. After tens of millions of years, they form meteors, comets, dwarf planets, planets, and other celestial bodies in a solar system.

✦ The planets that form far from the star accumulate a vast amount of ice. Ones closer to the star, such as Earth, are rocky. (The four inner planets of our solar system, Mercury, Venus, Earth, and Mars, are all considered *rocky planets*. The next four, Jupiter, Saturn, Uranus, and Neptune, are *ice* or *gas giants*. Pluto, now considered a *dwarf planet*, is composed primarily of rock and ice.)

✦ After many millions of years of becoming denser and hotter, the core of the spinning mass has attained enough heat and pressure to cause nuclear fusion of hydrogen. It now has its own source of energy, creating an outgoing force that counters the incoming gravitational force, allowing it to attain a state of equilibrium. It is now a star.

✦ Young stars create tremendous solar winds that blow the

remaining gases and dust in the disk into interstellar space...
and a solar system is born.

PIPERINE

Pepper makes you sneeze because it contains the chemical
piperine. (That's what creates pepper's biting sensation when
you taste it.) When you eat something with pepper on it, piperine molecules enter your nose and irritate your nasal passages.
Your body tries to get rid of them as it would any other foreign
particles...by sneezing.

THE (OBSCURE) PATRON SAINT OF...

Accountants: St. Matthew

Gun dealers: St. Adrian Nicomedia

Beekeepers: St. Bernard of Clairvaux

Advertisers: St. Bernardino of Siena

Flight attendants: St. Bona

Butchers: St. Luke

Comedians: St. Vitus

Librarians: St. Jerome

Postal workers: St. Gabriel

Unhappy marriages: St. Gengulf

Hairdressers: St. Martin de Porres

I, ME, OR MYSELF?

Which is correct—"Jane and I went spelunking" or "Jane and me
went spelunking"? The easy way to remember is to take out all

references to the other person. You would say, "I went spelunk-ing," not "Me went spelunking," so "Jane and I went spelunking" is correct.

✦ Similarly, is it "John went spelunking with Jane and me" or "John went spelunking with Jane and I"? Again, take Jane out of the sentence. You'd say, "John went spelunking with me," not "John went spelunking with I." (You should also say "between you and me," not "between you and I.")

✦ Another don't: "John went spelunking with Jane and myself" is incorrect. "Myself" is a reflexive pronoun that should be used only after the pronoun "I" when you need to mention yourself again. "I taught myself how to spelunk" or "I saved the best ropes for myself." And even though it may sound natural to say "I saved the best ropes for me," it is technically not grammatically correct.

✦ The same holds true with "himself," "herself," "yourself," and "ourselves." All are reflexive pronouns and should be used only if they specifically refer back to the subject.

A JIFFY

A *jiffy* is a slang term for a very brief amount of time. Its earli-est known use dates to the 1780s, though its exact origin is unknown. It's commonly used loosely, as in, "I'll be back in a jiffy," but can also be a term for quite specific amounts of time.

✦ In electronics, a jiffy is sometimes used as the name for the time required for one alternating current power cycle, $\frac{1}{60}$ of a second.

✦ In computer science, it's sometimes used to describe a micro-processor's "clock cycle," which isn't an absolute interval of time—it decreases as the microprocessor's speed increases. With modern computers, a jiffy used this way could be mea-sured as parts of nanoseconds (billionths of a second).

✦ In physics (particularly in quantum physics and often in

chemistry), a jiffy is the time taken for light to travel the radius of an electron. It's also used in physics as the name for the amount of time it takes light to travel the width of one *nucleon* (a proton or neutron), which would make it by far the jiffiest of all jiffies.

TURTLE RULES

The term "turtle" is correctly used to describe all turtle-like animals, including common turtles, tortoises, and terrapins. Specifically, tortoises are terrestrial turtles that generally have much more-rounded backs than the others, as well as columnar, elephantlike legs. Terrapins are aquatic turtles that live in fresh or brackish water, as opposed to sea turtles, which live in salt water.

SEDIMENTARY ROCK SIZES

Traditional rock sizes, as denoted by geologists:

Boulder: minimum diameter of 256 mm

Cobble: 64 mm to 256 mm

Pebble: between 4 mm and 64 mm

Gravel: between 2 mm and 4 mm

Sand: between $\frac{1}{16}$ mm and 2 mm

Silt: between $\frac{1}{256}$ and $\frac{1}{16}$ mm

Clay: anything less than $\frac{1}{256}$ mm

TRIANGLES

A triangle is a geometric figure that has three sides, and in which the sum of the measurements of all three interior angles equals 180 degrees. There are five kinds:

✦ **Right triangle:** One of the three angles is a right, or 90-degree, angle.

✦ **Obtuse:** One of the angles is greater than 90 degrees.

✦ **Equilateral:** All three sides are equal in length, and all three angles are 60 degrees.

✦ **Isosceles:** Two of the three sides, and two of the three angles, are equal.

✦ **Scalene:** None of the sides and none of the angles are equal.

MOTH-CONCEPTION

You may be like the majority of people who believe that caterpillars spin cocoons, from which they later emerge in their butterfly or moth state. It's only half true. Many moth caterpillars do spin cocoons, but butterfly caterpillars do not. When the time arrives for them to go into their *pupal* stage, most butterfly caterpillars hang (usually from a leaf) by their hind legs. They don't cover themselves as cocoon-formers do—they shed their exoskeletons and reveal the new form they have become: a *chrysalis*, named by the Greeks from their word for gold. These are the soft, often very shiny *pupae* of butterflies. (They harden when exposed to air.) At the end of this pupal stage, which can last from days to more than a year, the butterfly sheds the exoskeleton once again, emerging from the chrysalis as a butterfly.

FOOD FOR THOUGHT. While hanging as chrysalises, some butterfly species have the ability to move and make noise to ward off predators.

A WALK IN THE ARTS

Part one of a timeline of the major movements of Modern Art is on page 36.

✦ **Expressionism** (1905–1925). This was a broad cultural movement affecting many different art forms, including literature, theater, film, and visual arts, primarily in Europe and North America. In regards to painting, the basic explanation of the movement is that artists wanted to express their feelings rather than simply paint what they saw. Exaggeration, distortion, blurring, misshapen subjects, unconventional use of space, wildly clashing colors, and often disturbing imagery were just some of the characteristics of the movement. The best known of the Expressionists: Edvard Munch, Egon Schiele, Franz Von Stuck, Wassily Kandinsky, Paul Klee, Max Weber, and Max Pechstein.

✦ **Abstract Expressionism** (1930s–1950s). This primarily European and American movement grew out of the Expressionist and Surrealist movements, but the earliest roots of the movement said to be in the early work of Wassily Kandinsky. It is often divided into two groups: "Action Painting" saw painters working very quickly and spontaneously, often without brushes but simply dripping or flinging paint onto very large canvasses in very complex patterns. There was little or no attempt to represent objects, but rather feeling and emotion, with the physical act of painting seen as important as the finished product. The other, often called the "Color Field Painting" school, is characterized chiefly by large blocks of solid colors. The most well known of the Action Painters include Willem De Kooning, Franz Kline, Jackson Pollock, and of the second group—Mark Rothko, Helen Frankenthaler, and Clifford Still. (For still more information on Modern Art movements, go to page 355.)

SIDEREAL TIME

✦ From the Latin *sidereus*, meaning "starry" or "astral," *sidereal time* is a system of time measurement based on distant stars rather than *solar time*, which is based on the Sun.

✦ Solar time is the time we use in our daily lives: the Sun

appears to revolve around us as Earth rotates. One full rotation—24 hours—is what we call a day. But it turns out that we're wrong about that full rotation.

✦ If Earth were simply sitting in one spot in space, the Sun would return to exactly the same spot in the sky the moment Earth made exactly one full rotation. But we're not sitting still—we're orbiting the Sun. That means Earth actually has to rotate a little more than one full rotation for the Sun to appear to come back to the exact same spot, and that rotation—plus a little more—is what takes 24 hours.

✦ So how much time does it actually take for Earth to make a full rotation? To find out, we use very distant stars rather than the Sun, since they are negligibly affected by the movement of this tiny planet. Precisely measuring how they appear to move, astronomers have found that it takes 23 hours, 56 minutes, and 4.09 seconds to make one full rotation. This is the basis of sidereal time: 23 hours, 56 minutes, and 4.09 seconds is the length of one *sidereal day*.

✦ For a sidereal year, it's the opposite: It's longer than a solar year. The amount of time it takes for the Sun to appear to return to the exact same spot in the sky is actually less than the amount of time it takes for Earth to make one complete orbit of the Sun—20 minutes and 24 seconds less. To be more precise, a solar year is 365.242190402 days. A sidereal year is 365.25636042 days.

✦ Because it's a more accurate means of measuring the movement of celestial objects, sidereal time is used at astronomical observatories.

THE DIFFERENCE BETWEEN...

Rabbits and hares. Both are small mammals with long ears in the family *Leporidae*, and though their names are often used interchangeably, they are quite different. The main difference: Rabbits (with the exception of cottontails; see below) dig burrows and bear their young underground; and all rabbits' young are born blind and hairless. Hares, on the other hand, build nests on the ground. While this results in the young being vulnerable to predators, hares are born fully furred and with open eyes, and are therefore much more able than newborn rabbits to fend for themselves. Also, hares are generally larger and have longer ears.

✦ The largest hare species is the Arctic hare, whose habitat runs from Alaska, across northern Canada, and into Greenland. They can reach up to 12 pounds and measure as long as 28 inches from nose to tail.

✦ Hares are often called "jackrabbits" in the United States. Coined in the mid-1800s, the word was originally "jackass-rabbit," because of the similarity of its ears to a donkey's.

FOOD FOR THOUGHT. Cottontails make up their own genus of rabbits, and all 13 of their species are found only in North and South America. Their young are born hairless and with eyes closed, like other rabbits, but they nest on the ground, like hares. Cottontails develop much faster than rabbits, though, and are ready to live on their own in just four weeks.

HOBA HOBA

On the Hoba West Farm near Grootfontein in the East African nation of Namibia sits a hunk of metal, mostly iron and nickel, about 9' by 9' square and 3' thick. It is the remains of a meteorite that struck Earth some 80,000 years ago, the largest meteorite ever discovered. It is remarkably intact, and some experts posit that this is due to its disklike shape, which could have caused it to skip like a stone on Earth's atmosphere, slowing it down and causing a relatively soft impact when it finally hit. The extraterrestrial boulder was discovered in the 1910s by the farmer who owned the land (his plow struck it). The earth around it has been dug away, but the Hoba West meteorite remains where it landed.

It is a national historic monument today, and is visited (and sat upon) by thousands of people each year.

ROSETTA STONE

In 1798 French general Napoléon Bonaparte conquered Egypt. The next year, the French army was building Fort Julien near the Mediterranean port city of Rosetta (now Rashid), and army engineer Pierre-Francois Bouchard discovered a blue-gray *granodiorite* stone, 45" high, 29" wide, and 11" thick, covered in three kinds of printing. At the top were Egyptian hieroglyphics, in the middle was conversational Egyptian (Demotic), and at the bottom was classical Greek. The army sent the stone to the Institut de l'Egypte in Cairo, and it took a team of scholars 23 years to fully decipher it. They deciphered the Greek first and found that it was a decree written in 196 B.C.E. honoring the Egyptian ruler Ptolemy V. Then they worked backward, translating the Demotic and, ultimately, the hieroglyphics. The discovery—and decoding—of the Rosetta stone was the first key to understanding Egyptian hieroglyphics. The Rosetta stone has been on display at the British Museum in London since 1802.

BRAIN-EATING AMOEBAS

A species of amoeba known as *Naegleria fowleri* is found in fresh, warm waters (above 80°F) all over the world. On rare occasions, they enter the noses of swimmers and then travel up the olfactory nerve to the brain, where they multiply rapidly and cause a disease known as *primary amoebic meningoencephalitis*. Symptoms include lack of ability to smell, headache, fever, vomiting, coma, and in most cases, death within six days. Luckily, there have been only a few hundred cases ever reported.

CHAPTER 17

THERE'S A FULL EARTH OUT TONIGHT

When viewed from the Moon, Earth appears to go through phases, just as the Moon does to us. It appears as a crescent Earth, a half Earth, a full Earth, and so on.

CARPAL TUNNEL SYNDROME

The *carpal tunnel* is a small, cylindrical structure—about the diameter of your index finger—inside the human wrist through which nine tendons and the median nerve, move. In a healthy wrist, all these parts fit in the tunnel snugly but comfortably; they glide over each other easily as they move in different ways and directions so we can move our hands and fingers. When the wrist is injured or used for long periods of time in a repetitive way, however, one or more of the tendons in the tunnel can become inflamed. This causes the tendons to rub against each other with more pressure, causing friction and more inflammation, as well as putting pressure on the median nerve. Result: tingling, numb sensation in the hand, and/or mild to severe pain in the wrist and forearm.

The condition was first medically diagnosed in the early 1900s and became more common in the booming post-World War II years when the number of assembly, packing, and typing jobs exploded. The term "carpal tunnel syndrome" (CTS) was coined in the 1960s by George S. Phalen, Chief of Hand Surgery at the Cleveland Clinic in Ohio. A test commonly administered for the condition was named after him: "Phalen's maneuver" involves pressing the backs of the hands together close to your chest (fingers pointing down), forcing the wrists into strongly flexed positions, for 60 seconds (or until it hurts too much). The test is positive if the symptoms of CTS are reproduced.

AFFECT OR EFFECT?

✦ **Affect**, with the emphasis on the second syllable, is a verb that means "to have an influence upon" or "to assume or cultivate," as an attitude.

"I didn't think the fire sauce would affect you so negatively."

✦ **Affect** is also a verb often used by psychiatrists to denote the emotions that someone *appears* to be feeling.

"Even though the patient knows he is safe, he will affect an air of fear to get attention."

✦ **Effect** is most commonly used as a noun to describe the consequences of some action, as in "cause and effect."

"The rain is having a negative effect on the festivities."

✦ **Effect**, as a noun, can also mean "the condition of being operative."

"The new rules won't take effect until January."

✦ **Effect** can be a verb as well, usually used by politicians, meaning "to bring about."

"I promise, as your president, to effect change."

✦ **Effects.** The plural can be used to denote possessions.

"Among her personal effects were several strands of pearls."

HOW AN X-RAY MACHINE WORKS

If you've ever wondered just what's going on inside an X-ray machine at the dentist's office or (hopefully not too often) at the hospital, here you go:

X-Ray basics. X-rays are a form of *electromagnetic energy*, commonly called "radiation." (So is the light from a lightbulb, the heat from the Sun, and the radio waves that bring you your favorite radio station.) All electromagnetic energy travels in particles known as photons. An X-ray machine is basically a camera—but instead of using either sunlight or electric lights, it creates its own "light" in the form of X-rays.

Making light. Plug in an X-ray machine and power is sent to the glass or ceramic vacuum tube that houses a *cathode* at one end and an *anode* at the other.

✦ The cathode is a filament, like in lightbulbs. When electric current passes through it, it heats up and emits electrons—negatively charged atomic particles—into the vacuum tube. The anode is positively charged, so it acts as a magnet and pulls those negatively charged electrons toward it.

✦ Embedded in the anode is a metal disk, usually made of tungsten. When one of those incoming electrons collides with a tungsten atom, that atom loses one of its own electrons. The place it held cannot remain empty—it's the law of physics—so another electron in the atom jumps in to fill it.

✦ This is the important part: The electron that jumps in comes from a higher orbital in the atom—meaning it's farther away from the atom's nucleus—and has much more energy than the one that got knocked out. When it jumps down to fill the empty spot, it has to release its surplus energy—which it releases as a *photon*. This happens billions and billions of times in one simple X-ray procedure.

Directing the photons. A lead container surrounds the vacuum tube. (Lead absorbs X-rays.) A small opening in the container allows the escape of photons, which first pass through a series of filters that stop all but a pure beam of X-ray photons.

Imaging. Now we take the picture. On one side of whatever it is being X-rayed—say your hand—is the window through which the beam is emitted; on the other side of your hand is the film. As the X-ray photons meet the atoms in your hand, they will either pass through or be absorbed by them. The softer tissue in your body—your skin, organs, blood, and muscles—are made up of relatively small atoms. The X-ray photons pass right through them and leave their mark as the lighter areas on the film, just like light hitting a camera's film. The atoms in your bones—primarily calcium—are much larger, and they absorb the X-rays and stop them from reaching the film. Result: The film has captured an image of your bones...and your quick course on X-ray machines is complete.

3 DUTIES OF THE VICE PRESIDENT OF THE UNITED STATES

1. Become president if the actual president dies, resigns, or is convicted following an impeachment.

2. As president of the Senate, cast tie-breaking votes. (If there is no tie, the vice president is not allowed to vote.)

3. Also as president of the Senate, preside over and certify the Electoral College vote count.

WINNING WORDS

Every summer since 1925, kids (in eighth grade or younger) from all over the United States have gathered in Washington, D.C., for the Scripps National Spelling Bee. Here are the winning words from the last 50 years.

1959: catamaran

1960: eudaemonic

1961: smaragdine

1962: esquamulose

1963: equipage

1964: sycophant

1965: eczema

1966: ratoon

1967: chihuahua

1968: abalone

1969: interlocutory

1970: croissant

1971: shalloon

1972: macerate

1973: vouchsafe

1974: hydrophyte

1975: incisor

1976: narcolepsy

1977: cambist

1978: deification

1979: maculature

1980: elucubrate

1981: sarcophagus

1982: psoriasis

1983: Purim

1984: luge

1985: milieu

1986: odontalgia

1987: staphylococci

1988: elegiacal

1989: spoliator

1990: fibranne

1991: antipyretic

1992: lyceum

1993: kamikaze

1994: antediluvian

1995: xanthosis

1996: vivisepulture

1997: euonym

1998: chiaroscurist

1999: logorrhea

2000: demarche

2001: succedaneum

2002: prospicience

2003: pococurante

2004: autochthonous

2005: appoggiatura

2006: Ursprache

2007: serrefine

2008: guerdon

FISH MIGRATIONS

Many species of fish migrate at some stage of their lives, either to breed or to feed. Fish migrations are classified into five types:

Anadromous (Greek for "running up") fish are born in freshwater, spend most of their lives in the sea, and return to freshwater (swimming upstream) to spawn. Anadromous fish make up about half of all migrating fishes. Some examples: salmon, steelhead, most sturgeons, bass, and lampreys.

Catadromous ("running down") fish are born in salt water, spend most of their lives in freshwater, and swim back to the sea to spawn. The only catadromous species in the Americas: the American eel.

Amphidromous (*amphi* means "both") fish move between freshwater and salt water for feeding reasons and can spawn in either. Examples include gobies, jollytails, and bull sharks. (Yes, bull sharks, which can grow to more than 11 feet in length and are very aggressive, are known to attack humans. Some may be swimming in a shallow river or lake near you right now.)

Potamodromous ("river running") fish migrate significant distances in fresh water. These include some carps and catfish, northern pikes, and walleyes, which migrate hundreds of miles from lake to lake via rivers and streams throughout the Great Lakes region.

Oceanodromous fish migrate within salt water only and include herring, orange roughy, cod, and tuna, all of which migrate thousands of miles throughout the year to regular feeding and breeding grounds.

EGGS

The USDA regulates egg sizes as labeled on packages of eggs. The sizes below are the minimum net weight of how much, in ounces, a dozen eggs of that classification would weigh.

Jumbo: 30 ounces

Extra Large: 27 ounces

Large: 24 ounces

Medium: 21 ounces

Small: 18 ounces

Peewee: 15 ounces

HOW ELECTRICITY IS GENERATED

Power plants create electricity by converting *mechanical energy* into *electrical energy*.

✦ Most plants use petroleum, coal, or nuclear fuel to boil water. Highly pressurized steam is released from the boiler (like from a tea pot) onto the blades of a turbine, causing it to rotate. That rotating turbine has *mechanical energy*—and is attached to the rotor of a generator.

✦ The rotor is lined with magnets, and it spins inside a cylinder lined with coils of copper wire. Through the phenomenon of *electromagnetic induction*, this causes electrical current to be generated in the wire. The mechanical energy has now been converted into electrical energy.

✦ The current is transmitted from the plant to the *transmission grid*, then to the *distribution grid*, and finally makes it to the power lines on your street and to your home, where it is used to power your TV, your lights, and your George Foreman Grill.

ELECTRICITY FOR THOUGHT. Other ways a turbine can be driven: Some solar power stations use the Sun's energy to boil water and generate steam; geothermal plants use steam created by heat from underground sources; hydroelectric plants in dams use moving water to turn turbines; and wind power plants use wind-driven turbines.

REJECTED AMENDMENTS

In creating the U.S. Constitution and the foundation for the new American government, James Madison proposed 15 amendments to the Constitution. Congress accepted 12 of them, which it sent for ratification by the individual state legislatures. By December 1791, three-fourths of the states had approved 10 of the 12 amendments, which became the Bill of Rights. Here are the two that weren't up to snuff.

Rejected amendment #1 dealt with the size of the House of Representatives and the size of each member of Congress's district. It would have allowed for one representative for every 30,000 people. Today, Congressional constituencies are based on census figures, and each member of Congress represents about 650,000 people. If this rejected amendment had been included in the Constitution—and had never been updated—the House would have more than 10,000 members today. (Instead, there are 435.)

Rejected amendment #2 provided that Congress couldn't change the salaries of its members until after the latest election of representatives had been held. That one actually did make it in, eventually. It's the 27th Amendment (the most recent addition), ratified in 1992.

WORD SEARCH: *FLEA MARKET*

The term comes from a 19th-century French bazaar that had the nickname *marché aux puces*, or "market with fleas." This outdoor market, located in a lower-class section of Paris, was considered lowbrow and dirty; many of the booths (and much of the merchandise) were actually infested with fleas. The first known mention of such a market in the United States came in 1891, when the *Janesville* (Wisconsin) *Gazette* ran a story about a woman in Paris who "bought a dilapidated old mattress and, cutting it open, found 14,000 francs in gold."

THE ORIGIN OF VALENTINE'S DAY

Many stories exist regarding the origin of this holiday. One version: Every February in ancient Rome, teenage boys and girls gathered in the name of Lupercus, god of the flocks, to celebrate fertility and choose a "mate." Toward the end of the 5th century, though, when Christianity became the state religion of the Roman Empire, the ribald holiday was abolished. Pope Gelasius

I replaced Lupercus with St. Valentine, a bishop who reputedly had been executed in 270 C.E. by Emperor Claudius II for performing marriages. The holiday evolved over the centuries and by the 1300s had become Valentine's Day, the romantic holiday celebrated each year on February 14.

WORD SEARCH: *BANDANNA*

A triangle-shaped piece of cloth worn around the head above the eyes has been a common practice around the world for centuries. We know them as "bandannas" after the Hindi word *bandahna*, meaning "to tie." It entered the English as "bandanna" in the 1740s. (They are also known as "kerchiefs," from the French *couvre-chef*—"cover the head.")

KASHMIR AND CASHMERE

Kashmir has been the name of a large valley in northwestern India for at least 2,000 years. The ancient Kashmiri text the *Nila-mata Purana* says the name means "land desiccated of water" (*ka* meaning "water" and *shimir* meaning "to desiccate" or "to dry out"). Another story goes that the name is derived from the Hindu saint Kashyapamar, who according to legend diverted a river and thereby emptied a great lake in the valley. Today the name informally describes the entire region; officially, it appears in the name of the Indian state called Jammu and Kashmir. It has been an area of dispute between India and Pakistan since the founding of the two nations in 1947.

Cashmere is the name commonly used for wool (and from fabrics made from the wool) from the *changthangi*, also known as the pashmina or cashmere goat, native to the mountainous Ladakh region of Jammu and Kashmir. The spelling was changed after the introduction of the wool to Europe in the 1600s. Cashmere goats are medium sized, have long twisting horns, and are known for their very fine and soft wool. The wool actually comes from the underhair—the hair beneath the goats' thick coats. Today cashmere goats are bred and raised all over the world, and most of the raw wool comes from China, Mongolia, and Tibet… not from Kashmir.

CAN RATS VOMIT?

No, and they can't burp or get heartburn, either. The main reason for this is that they have a powerful barrier between the stomach and esophagus, and they don't have muscles strong enough to open it. To make up for the fact that they lack the ability to expel ingested toxins from their stomachs, rats are equipped with keen noses that can alert them if something is toxic. They're also very careful when eating, taking just tiny amounts and waiting to see if anything bad happens. If so, they simply avoid that food in the future. (Other *nonemetic*, or non-vomiting, animals include horses and rabbits.)

CALLUS AND CORN

The clinical name for the development of a *callus*—a hardened area of skin that forms due to repeated contact or pressure on that area—is *hyperkeratosis*. This refers to the fact that the affected area has developed high amounts of protective keratin, the same stuff in hair, fingernails, horns, and hooves.

Corns are technically known as *heloma*, from the Greek *helo*, for "nail," and *oma*, for "tumor." The name is usually used for thick, localized calluses that form on the sides of toes due to regular contact with other toes or shoes. They are distinguished from other calluses by having a cone-shaped keratin core that results in inflammation and soreness. A hard corn is called a *heloma durum*, while a soft corn, which can occur in sweaty areas between the toes, is called a *heloma molle*. (The name "corn" comes from the Old French word *corn*—which meant "horn.") Some other common calluses:

✦ *Prayer callus:* A callosity on the forehead common on Muslim men due to repeated touching of the forehead to the ground during daily prayers.

✦ *Cigarette lighter's thumb:* A bump caused by the excessive use of a cigarette lighter.

✦ *Russell's sign:* The calluses on the back of the hand due to contact with incisors, caused by self-induced vomiting in bulimics.

✦ *Spine bumps:* The calluses caused by spinning on the ground while break dancing.

✦ *Vamp disease:* An inflammation of the big toe caused by wearing high-heeled shoes.

PICK A PICKLE

Pickles are made by fermenting cucumbers in a brining solution of vinegar (usually), salt, water, and various seasonings. It's those seasonings that differentiate between the pickle types. Here are a few:

Dill. The herb dill or dill oil is added to the brine during processing. "Genuine" dills are brined for weeks and have a strong lactic acid flavor, making them the sourest of the dills; "kosher" dills have garlic added; and "overnight" dills are fresh cucumber pieces brined for only a day or two, under refrigeration, giving them more of a cucumber flavor.

Sour. Fresh cucumbers brined without vinegar under refrigeration. "Half-sours" aren't brined as long. (Longer brining makes them sour.)

Sweet. Sweet pickles are brined in vinegar with sugar and spices. Variations include thinly sliced "bread and butter" pickles, in which onions and red or green peppers are added to the mix, and "candied" pickles, which are packed in sweet, syrupy liquid.

Gherkins. These can be either dill, sour, or sweet—they're simply miniature versions made with young cucumbers.

FOOD FOR THOUGHT. "Gherkin" entered the English language as "gerkin" in around 1660 and was derived from the Dutch *gurken*, plural of *gurk*, for "cucumber." The *h* was added in the 1800s—to emphasize the hard *g* pronunciation. (The word "pickle" comes from the Middle Dutch word *peeckel*, for "brine.")

THE EARTH'S FOUR SPHERES

Lithosphere. The solid outer shell of the planet (comprised of the crust and upper mantle)

Hydrosphere. All surface water, including the oceans, lakes, rivers, and airborne moisture

Atmosphere. The envelope of gas that surrounds the surface

Biosphere. Earth's network of ecosystems; in other words, all life on the planet

RAMADAN

Ramadan is the name of the ninth month in the Muslim calendar and is also the name of a religious holiday observed throughout the entire month. The Muslim calendar is a lunar calendar, so when the month falls with respect to the Western calendar varies. (In 2009 it begins in August; in 2015 it begins in June.) The holiday commemorates the Muslim belief that during this month, in the year 610, the angel Gabriel first visited the Prophet Muhammad, reciting to him what became the first verses of the Muslim holy book, the Koran. The holiday is observed by fasting between sunrise and sunset on every day of the month. The commemoration ends with a three-day festival known as Eid al-Fitr, the "breaking of the fast," which is celebrated with prayers, feasts, and the exchanging of gifts.

TAXONOMY

Most people are familiar with scientific names: *Homo sapiens* for humans; *Canis lupus* for wolves; *Tyrannosaurus rex* for, well, Tyrannosaurus rexes. These are used in the organizing system known as *taxonomy*, or scientific classification. A brief explanation:

✦ In 1735 Swedish botanist Carl von Linné published an 11-page pamphlet titled *Systema Naturae*, introducing a classification system that grouped life-forms according to appearance, reproduction habits, habitat, and so on. Just as importantly, the pamphlet introduced the two-name system. Although it's been modified over the years to keep up with new discoveries, Linne's system is still used all over the world today.

✦ Modern taxonomy divides every living thing into seven categories called *taxa*, or divisions. The seven, from most general to most specific are *kingdom, phylum, class, order, family, genus*, and *species*. If you look at it as a "tree of life," with life itself as the trunk, the kingdoms are the six largest branches growing off the trunk, the phyla are branches growing from the kingdoms, and so on. (A mnemonic device to help memorize the order of the taxa: "**K**ing **P**hilip **C**ame **O**ver **F**or **G**ood **S**oup.")

Kingdom. There are only six kingdoms of life: *Bacteria, Archaea, Protista, Fungi, Animalia*, and *Plantae*. The first two are comprised of only single-celled organisms, such as bacteria; the next two hold both single-celled and multicellular organisms, including mushrooms; the last two have only multicellular life and comprise all animals and plants.

Phylum. Kingdoms divide into phyla, with all organisms in a phylum sharing basic physical traits. For example, humans and chickens are both in the phylum Chordata—like every animal in the phylum, both have a *notochord*, or a structure similar to a backbone, at some stage of their development.

Class. Phyla divide into classes: All animals in the class Mammalia, for example, have hair, mammary glands, and three middle-ear bones; all in the class Reptilia are cold-blooded.

Order. Classes break down into orders. There are 19 mammal orders, the two major ones being Primata, the primates, and Rodentia, the rodents.

Family. Members of a family are even more similar: dogs and cats are in the same order, Carnivora, but are separated into their own families: Canidae and Felidae.

Genus. Families branch into genera: Orcas (killer whales) and dolphins are both in the family Delphinidae, but their differences, like color, range, and diet, find them in different genera— orcas in Orcinus, common dolphins in Delphinus.

Species. All members of a species are very much alike physically. Beyond that, biologists argue over an exact definition of "species." For animals, however, the longstanding rule is that members of the same species must be able to breed and have offspring that are able to breed. Example: Horses and donkeys, which are in the same genus (Equus), can breed and have offspring, but those offspring—mules and hinnies—cannot. Horses and donkeys are therefore classified as different species.

Binomial nomenclature. Latin was already being used for scientific classification before Linné introduced his system. As a "dead" language (meaning it no longer has any native speakers), Latin is not evolving and changing as modern languages do—which is perfect for the consistency needed for scientific use. Before Linné, many words could be used to describe a species, complicating efforts for the names to be universally recognized. Linné solved this with his introduction of *binomial* (two-name) labels for species, using just the genus and species names. Rules: The genus is always capitalized and italicized; the species is always lowercased and italicized. Example: *Felis domesticus* is a member of the genus *Felix*—the cats—and the species *domesti-*

cus. (That, of course, is the common house cat.)

✦ If you recognize Linné's name, but have seen it spelled differently, it's because Linné wrote in Latin, as was the habit of scientists of the day, and signed his work "Carolus Linnaeus"—which is how he is commonly referred to today.

EMPIRICAL VS. ANECDOTAL

You've probably heard the phrase "empirical evidence" before. If you're like most people, you may need to brush up on the definition. "Empirical" is defined by *Merriam-Webster's Dictionary* as "originating in or based on observation or experience." The concept has its origin in a school of ancient Greek physicians who refused to accept what was the then-accepted theory about medicine, insisting instead on learning through experience. (The word itself goes back to the Greek *empeirikos*, meaning "experienced.")

✦ One of the foundations for the "scientific method" is that all evidence must be *empirical* evidence, that is, evidence that has been obtained through direct observation.

✦ *Anecdotal* evidence is the opposite—evidence not directly observed by the one using it, but based on hearsay or anecdote. (An anecdote is a short tale or story about a supposed actual experience.) An example of someone using anecdotal evidence: "I know for a fact that aliens exist—because my cousin knows a guy whose mother's sister was abducted by some."

ON GENIUS

"A man of genius makes no mistakes. His errors are the portals of discovery."

—James Joyce

CHAPTER 18

SPACE: THE KÁRMÁN LINE

Where does space begin? About 62 miles above the surface of
the Earth. Who decided? A Hungarian-American physicist and
engineer named Theodore von Kármán. In the 1950s, there was
no distinct scientific field of space travel; everything fell under
aeronautics—the study of flight. Kármán, already a revered
figure in the field, felt that space travel should be a study in
and of itself. The way to separate the two fields, Kármán and
his supporters decided: If thrust from an engine was needed to
maintain flight, it was *aero*nautics; if no thrust was needed, it
was *astro*nautics. (No engine power is needed to maintain flight
in space because of the lack of an atmosphere and, therefore,
friction.) After lengthy calculations, it was decided that that
change occurred at an altitude of approximately 100 kilometers
(62 miles). Von Kármán suggested they just use that, since it

was a nice round number. It's almost completely arbitrary—the atmosphere doesn't suddenly vanish at 100 kilometers, and weather conditions actually cause it to change constantly—but the "Kármán Line" is still internationally recognized as the boundary between Earth's atmosphere and space. The Department of Defense even uses it as the altitude above which a pilot is officially deemed an "astronaut."

NATURE'S WHEELS

The means by which animals move is known as *animal locomotion*. There are several types, including walking, running, hopping, crawling, slithering, swimming, flying, gliding, and inching (as inchworms do). And then there are these guys.

Golden Wheel Spiders. They live exclusively on sand dunes in the Namib Desert in Namibia, Africa, and look like small, pale tarantulas. Their main predator is the female *pompilid* wasp, which digs the spiders out of their burrows, injects them with a paralyzing toxin, lays eggs inside them (one in each spider caught), and then buries them in the sand. About a week later, the egg hatches and the larva feeds off the *still living* spider. To combat this, the spiders have developed a unique means of locomotion: If one gets the chance when attacked, it runs a short distance down a sand slope, then quickly forms semicircles with its legs, flips itself sideways, and rolls down the slope like a wheel. This allows it to move much faster than it can run—making up to 20 rotations and covering up to five feet per second. Once rolling, the spiders are rarely caught. Spider expert Dr. Joh Henschel wrote in 1990 that it was possibly the first conclusive evidence of the use of the wheel by a member of the animal kingdom (and the spiders were certainly using them long before humans "invented" the wheel around 3500 B.C.E.). Henschel, however, was wrong.

Mantis Shrimp. In 1979 marine biologist Roy Caldwell of the University of California at Berkeley discovered an unusual species of mantis shrimp. The shrimp has a long, flexible body along with weak legs unsuited for terrestrial movement. When the tide drops them on a beach, they can't walk or crawl back to the water. So they roll instead—a stranded shrimp lifts its tail up to its head and flips itself in a series of backward somersaults until it reaches the water. Caldwell witnessed one mantis shrimp that rolled continuously for about six feet.

Pangolins. Also called "scaly anteaters," these dog-sized creatures are found in tropical regions in Asia and Africa. They're covered in large, horny scales, and when threatened they curl into a ball, the scales protecting them like armor. They've been known to use that ability to move: When threatened on a hillside, a pangolin will run downhill (or at least try; they're quite slow), then curl into a ball and roll away from the danger.

The Mother-Of-Pearl Moth Caterpillar. When threatened, this small caterpillar clamps down with its rear legs on whatever surface it's on (usually a tree branch) and pushes itself up sharply with its front legs. This sends its head back to its tail, forming a circle shape with its body. At just the right moment, it lets its rear legs go and the momentum of the push-off sends it rolling away. A good push will get it five full revolutions.

SIMPLE GENIUS: THE MONEYMAKER

Appropriate Technologies for Enterprise Creation (ApproTEC) is a nonprofit in Nairobi, Kenya, that focuses on developing new technologies that can aid Africa's poor population in sustainable and affordable ways. In 1996 ApproTEC hit the proverbial jackpot when it designed a human-powered irrigation pump called the "MoneyMaker." It has been a huge success: Electricity is often nonexistent in poor, rural farming communities, and where it is available, it's often too expensive for poor farmers. And even if they can afford electricity, they often can't afford pumps. The MoneyMaker solved that: One person, by working levers with the feet (kind of like a stair-climber exercise machine) can pump water from deeper than 20 feet underground, send it through hoses to sprinkler units, and irrigate up to 1½ acres of crops in a single day. Using the device, farmers were able to increase their crop output by an average of *seven times* in a single year—all with no electricity, no gas, and no pollution. As of 2008, Appro-TEC estimates that 45,000 pumps are in use in Kenya and neighboring nations, bringing an average of $1,400 annually to people who previously earned less than $100 per year. On top of that, the device helped create more than 96,000 new jobs, and more than 50% of the pumps are managed by female entrepreneurs. Also:

✦ They're made from local materials (creating even more jobs).

✦ They're easily repaired without special tools.

✦ They're lightweight (25 pounds) for easy transport.

✦ And, most importantly, they're affordable, costing only $38 each.

SIX THINGS BEHIND *MONA LISA*

1. Two bodies of water (possibly connected)

2. Craggy mountain peaks

3. A winding road

4. The sky

5. A creek

6. A bridge over the creek

RHODES' WILL

When British-born South African diamond tycoon Cecil Rhodes died in 1902, he left much of his fortune to Oxford University to establish the Rhodes Scholarship, which has since become one of the most prestigious academic scholarships in the world. (Bill Clinton was a Rhodes Scholar in 1968.) Rhodes lived only to the age of 48, but it's lucky for us that he lasted as long as he did: In an earlier version of his will, he directed that his fortune go toward the creation of a secret society whose aim would be to reverse the American Revolution and restore the U.S. as an "integral part of the British Empire."

NEW COUNTRIES

Since 1990, 33 new countries have been created. The dissolution of the USSR and Yugoslavia in the early 1990s was responsible for most of them.

✦ In 1990 Namibia became independent of South Africa, North and South Yemen merged to form a unified Yemen, and East and West Germany merged to form a unified Germany after the fall of the Berlin Wall.

✦ Beginning in 1991, Yugoslavia dissolved into five independent states: Bosnia and Herzegovina, Croatia, the Former Yugoslav Republic of Macedonia (not to be confused with the Greek Macedonia), Serbia and Montenegro, and Slovenia.

✦ When the Soviet Union dissolved in 1991, 15 regions that had been under Russian and/or Soviet control for more some 200 years all declared independence. They are: Armenia, Azerbaijan, Belarus, Estonia, Georgia, Kazakhstan, Kyrgyzstan, Latvia, Lithuania, Moldova, Russia, Tajikistan, Turkmenistan, Ukraine, and Uzbekistan.

✦ In 1991 the Marshall Islands ceased being administered by United States and gained independence. Micronesia, previously known as the Caroline Islands, also became independent from the United States.

✦ In 1993 the Czech Republic and Slovakia became independent nations when Czechoslovakia dissolved.

✦ The remainder of the 33 new nations: Eritrea, once part of

Ethiopia (1993); the Pacific island nation of Palau (1994); East Timor, which broke ties with Indonesia in 2002; Montenegro and Serbia, which split into separate nations in 2006; and Kosovo, which declared independence from Serbia in 2008.

PLINY THE ODDER

Caius Plinius Secundus, better known as Pliny the Elder, was a Roman author who lived in the first century B.C.E. He wrote about everything, basically—art, astronomy, biology, geology, history, medicine, mineralogy, politics, warfare—in more than 100 volumes that he continuously updated for more than 40 years. How was he able to accumulate all that knowledge? By reading—all the time. Really. According to his nephew, Pliny the Younger:

> The only time he took from his work was for his bath, and by bath I mean his actual immersion, for while he was being rubbed down and dried he had a book read to him or dictated notes. When traveling he felt free from other responsibilities to give every minute to work; he kept a secretary at his side with book and notebook; and in winter saw that his hands were protected by long sleeves, so that even bitter weather should not rob him of a working hour. For the same reason, too, he used to be carried about Rome in a chair. I can remember how he scolded me for walking; according to him I need not have wasted those hours, for he thought any time wasted which was not devoted to work. It was this application which enabled him to finish all those volumes.

SUMPTUARY LAWS

In the 7th century B.C.E., the Greek politician Zaleucus wrote what is considered to be Greece's first written code of law. It included this passage: "No free woman should be allowed any more than one maid to follow her, unless she was drunk: nor was to stir out of the city by night, wear jewels of gold about her, or go in an embroidered robe, unless she was a professed and public prostitute."

✦ Zaleucus's codes are considered some of the earliest known *sumptuary laws*—laws ostensibly designed to restrict behavior deemed immoral, often in regards to clothing and food. More realistically, they were designed to keep poor people in their place, as they overwhelmingly restricted those in the lower social strata, rather than the aristocracy.

✦ In ancient Rome, sumptuary laws regulated such things as the number of stripes allowed on tunics, and how many people could be invited to a banquet.

✦ Sumptuary laws flourished again in the European Middle Ages. A curious one: In the 1500s, Holy Roman Emperor Charles V made the wearing of long-pointed shoes illegal.

✦ A law passed in the Massachusetts Colony in 1651 made it illegal for people of "mean condition" (poor people) to wear "gold or silver lace, or buttons, or points at their knees, or to walk in great boots."

✦ Sumptuary laws still exist in many places around the world today. Examples include laws in many Muslim nations that govern proper attire for women; laws in Israel severely restricting pig farming (pigs aren't kosher); and laws in some U.S. communities that make it illegal to wear underwear-revealing "low-rider" pants.

HOW TO MAKE TOFU

Tofu (also called bean curd) was first developed in China around 2,000 years ago. Today it comes in a variety of textures, from the delicate "silken" to soft, regular, firm, and extra-firm. It's a high-protein, low-cholesterol, low-sodium, and (usually) easy-to-digest food. Here's a brief description of how it's made.

✦ The basic ingredient is soy milk, a nondairy liquid made by soaking dry soybeans overnight, grinding the soaked beans with water, and then straining the resulting puree to extract the "milk."

✦ Next, a *coagulant* is added to curdle the soy milk and separate it into curds and "whey" (an amber liquid), much as cheese makers do with cow's milk. The coagaulant can be calcium sulfate, which occurs naturally in gypsum, or magnesium chloride, which is found in sea salt and commonly known by its Japanese name, *nigari*. The coagulant is gently stirred into the soy milk.

✦ When the semisolid curds float to the top of the liquid whey, they're skimmed off and placed in a cheesecloth-lined tofu form. A weighted lid is placed on the form to press down on the curds, allowing more of the liquid whey to drain out—a process that takes anywhere from 30 minutes to a few hours. The drained curds are the tofu, and the firmness of the tofu depends on how much liquid has been removed.

✦ The tofu is removed from the form, cut into convenient-to-use blocks, and soaked in cold water to further firm it up. The tofu can be used immediately or refrigerated for up to seven days.

BEEEEEACH

The longest beach in the world: Praia do Cassino (Casino Beach), a white sand beach in Brazil. It's more than 150 miles long.

THE TOP 10 COMPANIES TO WORK FOR IN 2008

(according to *Fortune* magazine)

1. Google

2. Quicken Loans (an online mortgage lender)

3. Wegmans Food Markets

4. Edward Jones

5. Genentech

6. Cisco Systems

7. Starbucks

8. Qualcomm

9. Goldman Sachs

10. Methodist Hospital System

JOURNEY THROUGH THE CENTER OF THE EARTH

What would happen if you dug a hole all the way through the Earth to the opposite side and then jumped in? Here's one theory: Considering the pressure, heat, solid iron core, etc., it would be virtually impossible to do so. But *if* you could, right after you took the plunge, you'd start accelerating as the gravity pulled you toward the center. By the time you reached it (about 20 minutes later), you'd be moving at roughly five miles per second. Even though there is no gravity at the exact center, you'd be moving so fast that your momentum would propel you right past it toward the opposite side. But as you traveled away from the center, gravity would begin to pull you back toward it, causing you to decelerate as you neared the other side. You'd *almost* make it, but just as you started to see daylight, you'd come to a stop and then start falling back toward the center. You'd slingshot past it once more and then *almost* return to your jump-off point, only to stop and start falling again. This yo-yo motion would continue forever...or until someone threw you a rope.

BIRTH OF THE BOSTON SYMPHONY

An investment banker named Henry L. Higginson was fed up with the amateurish state of symphonic music in Boston in the late 1870s. Performances suffered from a lack of quality musicians (and conductors) who often didn't show up for a performance if they got a higher-paying gig. Audiences some-times responded by throwing things at the players. Higginson yearned for the refined quality of European symphonies, so in 1881 he used his considerable wealth to sponsor a new orchestra in Boston. He advertised extensively, calling for only the best musicians and conductors. With that, the Boston Symphony was born.

But Higginson did something more with his symphony: He ran it as a CEO would run a corporation. His employees were bound to strict contracts that forbade them from playing for a higher bidder and also forced them to rehearse as a group far more often than most orchestras did. This business-minded approach worked: The musical quality of the Boston Symphony came to rival Europe's best, and Higginson's well-paid musicians considered it a badge of honor to play for a "respectable" sym-phony. The public responded by attending concerts in droves (and acting more refined themselves). Music-loving business-men in other cities saw Higginson's success and began forming their own corporate-run symphony orchestras. Today, nearly every major U.S. city has at least one symphony orchestra.

ERNST MACH'S SUPERSONIC PHOTOGRAPHS

You've heard of "Mach" numbers: When something is traveling at the speed of sound, it's said to be traveling at Mach 1. At twice the speed of sound, it's traveling at Mach 2. The term is named after 19th-century Austrian physicist Ernst Mach, who became famous for an experiment he performed in 1887.

Mach had theorized that objects traveling through the air faster than the speed of sound (761.2 mph) compressed the air in front of them into cone-shaped waves. And then he proved it. In a feat amazingly ahead of its time, Mach built a device that allowed him to fire a gun in such a way that as the bullet passed by a "shadow board," it broke two trip wires—one triggered an electric spark, the other activated the shutter of a high speed camera. The photographs captured the shadow of the passing bullet—and the shadows of the cone-shaped waves that Mach had predicted would be there. He had successfully proved the existence of what would later be known as "shock waves," a phenomenon that causes such things as the sonic booms from supersonic aircraft. In 1937, years after Mach died, scientists honored his achievement by naming the Mach number after him.

NÉE AND NÉ

✦ The maiden name of a married woman is often indicated by the word "née," usually in parenthesis. Eg., Laura Bush (*née* Welch).

✦ The word *née* is the feminine form of the French for "born."

✦ It can be spelled without the accent mark, eg., "nee."

✦ If used for a man who has taken his wife's last name (a practice that has become a fad of sorts in recent years), the word is "né" or "ne."

HOUSEHOLD GENIUS: RECYCLED CASSETTE TAPES

As the digital age rolls on, many people have old cassette tapes lying around, which (unless you still have a cassette player) are basically useless. So what can be done with them? Here are two ideas:

Make a business card holder. Remove the screws from the cassette tape, and remove the insides of the cassette (i.e., the tape). Use small pliers to break off the plastic pieces that protrude from the inside of the case so the business cards will fit inside. Wrap a rubber band around the two pieces to keep them together.

Knit with cassette tape. Among the items people have knitted with cassette tape: a protective sack for an MP3 player, baby booties, a messenger bag, and a Barbie doll dress. (Knitting tips: Cassette tape is not elastic, so knit loosely. To avoid tight stitches, begin with larger needles and then switch to smaller needles after the first row has been cast on.)

INTELLIGENCE VS. INFORMATION

During World War II, U.S. government and military officials knew they needed detailed and coordinated information on all foreign nations. At the time, there was a lot of overlap between agencies collecting "intelligence," so officials combined these efforts under one intelligence-gathering umbrella. After the war, operations were adapted to a peacetime world, and the Central Intelligence Agency (CIA) began operating on September 18, 1947. As defined by the CIA:

The Intelligence Cycle: the process by which information is acquired, converted into intelligence, and made available to policymakers

Information: raw data from any source that may be fragmentary, contradictory, unreliable, ambiguous, deceptive, or wrong

Intelligence: information that has been collected, integrated, evaluated, analyzed, and interpreted

Finished Intelligence: the final product of the Intelligence Cycle, ready to be delivered to policymakers. There are three types of finished intelligence:

✦ *Basic intelligence* provides the fundamental factual reference material on a country or issue. It is the foundation upon which the other two types of intelligence are constructed.

✦ *Current intelligence* reports on new developments and continually updates the inventory of knowledge.

✦ *Estimative intelligence* judges probable outcomes and revises overall interpretations for guidance of basic and current intelligence.

FOOD FOR THOUGHT. The CIA annually publishes *The World Factbook* with unclassified information on all countries, in the following categories: Land, Water, People, Government, Economy, Communications, and Defense Forces. The *Factbook* is available in print and online.

'ORD 'EARCH

As the English language grows, words sometimes get smaller—they're chopped, clipped, or taken out of phrases altogether. Sometimes this results in slang words ("tater" from "potato"), new words ("lone" from "alone"), contracted words ("don't" from "do not"), and poetic words ("ne'er" from "never"). Most shortened words are the result of a linguistic process called *elision*, the loss of unstressed sounds when words are spoken. But there are many ways to eliminate unwanted letters. Among them:

✦ **Aphaeresis.** Removing the first part of a word or phrase. One of the newest examples is "blog," shortened from "web log."

✦ **Aphesis.** A form of elision in which only the unstressed, first vowel is removed: "acute" becomes "cute," and "opossum" becomes "possum."

✦ **Apocope.** The loss of the final, often unstressed syllable or sound from a word. The word "sing" came from the Middle English *singen*, In informal usage, a word such as "darling" becomes "darlin'." (Sometimes two or more of these processes can work together to leave only the middle of a word, such as "influenza" shortened to "flu.")

✦ **Syncope.** When letters and/or sounds are deleted from the middle of a word: "lord" is derived from "loaf ward," and "spam" is short for "spiced ham." And one that's gained a lot of mileage in the first decade of the 21st century: from "double-u" to "dubya."

✦ **Clipping.** The reduction of a word to one of its parts: "photo[graph]," "pro[fessional]," "[ham]burger," "[alli]gator," and "sync[hronize]."

FOOD FOR THOUGHT. Who are some of the most prolific modern word choppers? Teenagers—kids from the 'burbs, who borrow cash from the 'rents and buy 'za or 'zines. (That's "suburbs," "parents," "pizza," and "magazines.")

APOSIOPESIS

This rhetorical device eliminates entire words from the ends of phrases, most often because they are implied. An example is the phrase "Early to bed, early to rise." (Rarely do we add the rest of the phrase, "makes a man healthy, wealthy, and wise.") Aposiopesis (A-po-SIGH-o-PEE-sis) can also be used for dramatic effect, as in "Give that back, or else!" or "Why, I oughta..."

THE BRACERO PROGRAM

On August 4, 1942, the U.S. and Mexican governments agreed on a program through which impoverished Mexicans could come to the U.S. to work as temporary laborers in the agricultural industry. Starting with just a few hundred workers in California to help with the diminished work force caused by World War II, the "Bracero" program, (from the Spanish for "strong arms"), spread rapidly. It continued after the war, with hundreds of thousands of Mexican workers crossing the border every year to work in the fields. More than four million would make the trip before it ended in 1964, and the *braceros*, as the workers were known, are credited with being an important part of America's post-war boom. The program was, however, rife with fraud and abuse— workers were given sub-standard housing, below poverty wages, little to no access to health care, and racism was rampant. And its demise saw the start of the modern era of illegal immigration: Before the Bracero program ended in 1964, the number of arrests for undocumented workers in the U.S. was under 100,000 per year. By 1976 it was nearly 900,000, most of them from Mexico, and most of them coming to work in low-paying jobs, especially in the agriculture business.

9 IMMIGRANTS WHO PASSED THROUGH ELLIS ISLAND

Isaac Asimov, Bob Hope, Bela Lugosi, Charles Atlas, Knute Rockne, Johnny Weissmuller, Irving Berlin, Frank Capra, and Max Factor.

OP ART

Op art (or optical art) was a kind of painting that was popular in the mid-1960s in America and Europe. Op art imagery was abstract, hard-edged, geometric, and made use of optical effects and patterns that gave the illusion of movement on the flat picture plane (i.e., spiral patterns that seem to be spinning). The point of op art was to fool the eye and make the surface of the canvas appear to jump, vibrate, bulge, compress, bend, flicker, swirl, or pulse. Many op art paintings were black and white, to achieve the maximum contrast and, thus maximum eye-popping effect. Though critics weren't particularly impressed by the work, the public took to it after 1965, when a major exhibit called "The Responsive Eye" was mounted at the Museum of Modern Art in New York City. Designers quickly began to use op art imagery in print media, advertising, fashion, and interior decoration, as well as on album covers and TV. Major op artists: Victor Vasarely, Bridget Riley, Richard Anusziewicz, Jesús Rafael Soto, Yaacov Agam, and Kenneth Noland.

THE OLDEST TOOLS IN YOUR HOUSE

Hammer. Perhaps the oldest of all human tools, the simplest form were rocks used to pound whatever needed pounding—bones, shells, other humans, etc. Fossil evidence from Africa reveals that they were being used more than 2.4 million years ago. Tools more akin to modern hammers—rocks tied to sticks with leather straps—were made at least 32,000 years ago. Hammers made from forged metals first appeared 6,000 years ago.

Needle. Cro-Magnon man in present-day France made bone sewing needles, complete with holes, at least 25,000 years ago. Needles made from iron dating to the 3rd century B.C.E. have been found in Germany, and around the same time iron needles and even thimbles were being used in China.

Spoon. Some archaeologists believe the earliest spoons—used for many thousands of years—were shells; the ancient Greek and Latin words for "spoon" were even derived from the name of a shellfish. Wooden spoons were used in northern Europe at least 2,000 years ago, and our word "spoon" probably stems from that: It comes from the Old High German *span*, meaning "splinter" or "chip."

Screw and screwdriver. Large, threaded wooden screws were common in the Mediterranean region 2,000 years ago (used, for example, on wine presses). Metal screws used as fasteners first appeared in the 1400s in Europe, and that century also produced the first screws with slots in their heads. The first screwdrivers—"turnscrews"—are then at least that old (the word "screwdriver" dates to 1779). The familiar Phillips-head screw and screwdriver, with their cross-shaped depression and point, were invented in 1936 by Henry F. Phillips. Their first use: in the 1936 Cadillac.

CHAPTER 19

HI, THERE!

Should you ever need to say hi to the following important
people, these are the correct formal greetings.

1. A member of the U.S. Cabinet (Secretary of State, Agriculture,
etc.): Mr. or Madam Secretary

2. A member of the U.S. Senate: Senator Smith.

3. A member of the House of Representatives: Mr. Smith

4. The Pope: Your Holiness

5. A Catholic Cardinal: Your Eminence

6. A Catholic Bishop: Your Excellency

7. An Episcopal Bishop: Bishop Smith

8. A King or Queen: Your Majesty (the rest of the Royal Family should be greeted with Your Royal Highness)

9. A Duke or Duchess (the nobleman or woman ranking just below royalty, at the very top of the nobility): Your Grace

10. Any of the Lesser Nobles (Marquess, Earl, Count, Viscount, Baron, Baronet, Knight, or their spouse): Lord or Lady Smith

BARNYARD TERMINOLOGY

✦ Male turkeys are *toms*, female turkeys are *hens*.

✦ A *Cornish game hen* is just a young, small chicken. They weigh less than two pounds and are about six weeks old.

✦ A *capon* is a castrated rooster.

✦ A female pig is a *sow*, an adult male pig is a *boar*, a pregnant female pig is a *farrow*, and a neutered male is a *barrow*.

✦ A *heifer* is a young female cow that has not yet birthed a calf.

✦ An *open heifer* is a young female cow that is ready for breeding.

✦ An adult male cow is a *bull*; a castrated male cow is called a *steer*.

EYES WIDE OPEN

Lots of people sleep with their eyes open, some even in the downright creepy *wide-open* variety. One cause: *lagophthalmos*, a physical inability to close the eyes. This can be caused by several factors, including neurological disorders, trauma, infection, and alcohol or drug intoxication. In any case, it can be very damaging because our eyes need the nourishment and moisturizing they receive during sleep. Prolonged eyes-open sleeping can, in the worst cases, lead to blindness.

✦ One way lagophthalmos is treated is by having small metal weights surgically implanted in the eyelids. The metal used is usually gold, since it is biologically inert and will not break down due to contact with human body fluids.

✦ The word *lagophthalmos* is derived from the Greek for "hares' eyes," and comes from the notion that hares sleep with their eyes open. (They don't.)

ANALOGY QUESTIONS

If you've ever taken intelligence tests (such as the SAT), you've probably seen what are called "analogy questions." A basic example: "Bark is to dog as moo is to ___." That's a very easy example. (Hopefully you answered "cow." If not, well…good thing you're reading this book!) These questions require you to determine the relationship between the given pair of words and, using that, find the missing word in the second pair. The ability to do so, especially with abstractly related concepts, can reveal an uncommonly sharp intellect.

✦ The short form of an analogy problem uses colons: "bark : dog :: moo : cow"

✦ On most tests, the questions are in a slightly more complicated form, with one analogy given as an example, then four or five choices from which to choose the analogy most like that example:

BARK : DOG ::
pasture : horse
eagle : mule
moo : cow
stones : beetles

✦ A key to solving such problems is finding a *relationship phrase* that most closely fits both the given pair and one of the multiple-choice pairs. From our example: "Bark *is the sound made by a* dog, and moo *is the sound made by a* cow." "Is the sound made by a" is the relationship phrase that best fits the example and the correct answer.

ANALOGY QUIZ

Want to try some yourself? Here are 10 questions taken from actual SAT tests.

1. MEDICINE : ILLNESS ::
law : anarchy
hunger : thirst
etiquette : discipline
love : treason
stimulant : sensitivity

2. LURK : WAIT ::
boost : elevate
deplete : drain
abscond : depart
bilk : cheat
topple : stabilize

3. STANZA : POEM ::
mimicry : pantomime
duet : chorus
act : opera
rhyme : verse
pirouette : ballet

4. EXHORT : SUGGEST ::
conspire : plan
tamper : adjust
crave : accept
goad : direct
instruct : teach

5. DOCTOR : HOSPITAL ::
sports fan : stadium
cow : farm
professor : college
criminal : jail
food : grocery store

6. SANDPAPER : ABRASIVE ::
gasoline : refined
gravity : irritant
polish : floors
acrylic : emulsion
oil : lubricant

7. CUB : BEAR ::
piano : orchestra
puppy : dog
cat : kitten
eagle : predator
fork : utensil

8. TENET : THEOLOGIAN ::
predecessor : heir
hypothesis : biologist
recluse : rivalry
arrogance : persecution
guitarist : rock band

9. MENDICANT : IMPECUNIOUS ::
hat : askew
liar : poor
complainer : petulant
critic : quizzical
philanthropist : prodigal

10. GARRULOUS : TALK ::
loquacious : joke
antagonist : retreat
ruthless : sympathize
enthusiastic : stimulate
extravagant : spend

1. law : anarchy; **2.** abscond : depart; **3.** rhyme : verse; **4.** instruct : teach; **5.** professor : college; **6.** oil : lubricant; **7.** puppy : dog; **8.** hypothesis : biologist; **9.** complainer : petulant; **10.** extravagant : spend.

COP, COP A PLEA, COP A FEEL

✦ The verb *cop*, as in "seize" or "grab," has its origin either in the Middle French word of the same meaning, *caper*, or from the similarly defined Dutch word, *kapen*. It first showed up in the English language in 1704.

✦ The noun *cop*, meaning "police officer," first appeared in 1859, and was shortened from *copper* with the above meaning attached—i.e., a copper seizes people. This usage has been around since at least 1846.

✦ The phrase *cop a plea*, meaning "to agree to a plea bargain in a court of law," first appeared in 1925; the phrase *cop a feel*, meaning "to fondle sexually," showed up shortly after that; the verb *cop out*, meaning "to back out or renege," first appeared in the 1940s.

THE DUTCH NATIONAL ACROSTIC

An *acrostic* is a type of poem in which the first letter of the first word on each line forms a new word or phrase, generally a special message or theme. (Example: a four-line poem about love in which the first letters of each line are L, O, V, and E.) The national anthem of the Netherlands, "Het Wilhelmus," ("The William") is an *acrostichon*—a song in which the first letter of the first line of each verse forms a word or phrase, in this case, the name "Willem Van Nassov." Van Nassov is better known as William the Silent, a 16th-century Dutch nobleman who led the nation's fight for independence.

HOW P2P WORKS

✦ Peer-to-peer file sharing, or simply P2P, refers to a specific type of Internet file-sharing network. It allows people with the appropriate programs to make their computers part of an entire file-sharing network, including its bandwidth (meaning how much data can be transferred) and storage capabilities. That means that as more people enter into a P2P network, they automatically increase the network's ability to handle more information.

✦ This stands against the more conventional client/server systems in which a finite number of servers—computers that "serve" many users in varying ways—can become slower as more and more people use them. (If you have an e-mail account with Yahoo! or Google, for example, you're the client, and you use their servers to send and receive e-mails.)

✦ The concept of a P2P system was actually part of how the early Internet first worked: In 1969 ARAPNET, the "Grandfather of the Internet," connected computers at UCLA, Stanford, U.C. Santa Barbara, and the University of Utah in what was basically a P2P system with which students could access the different schools' computers and files. Each computer was, therefore, both server and client.

HOW P2P TOOK OFF

✦ An important step leading to how P2P networks function today came in 1979 with the development of USENET, short for "user network," which allowed members to share messages directly with other members by transferring information to their computers over telephone lines. (USENET still exists today and has millions of members.)

✦ When the Internet expanded in the mid-1990s, regular people—not just computer geeks—wanted to send e-mail, view Web pages, shop, and so forth, and they weren't interested in the details of how the Internet worked. That changed the structure of the Internet enormously, leading to client/server being the dominant Internet paradigm.

✦ In 1999 Northeastern University (Boston) student Shawn Fanning developed what became the first famous P2P file-sharing service, Napster. It revolved around music, of course, allowing members to access each other's computers and download each other's songs onto their own computers. Napster went out of business after being sued for copyright violations by the music industry. (They were bought and remade as a music-for-pay service.) That, however, did not stop P2P.

✦ There are thousands of P2P networks today used by hundreds of millions of people to share music, news, videos, games, recipes, knitting patterns—just about anything. Some of the largest and must successful include Pando, Gnutella, Kazaa, and Bittorrent.

LATIN ABBREVIATIONS

Etc. The shortened form of the Latin *et cetera*. Its literal translation: "and the rest."

Ibid. Most commonly seen on a "works cited" page in a reference work, it's used to avoid repeatedly writing the name, author, and other information about a frequently cited source. *Ibid* is short for *ibidem*, which means "the same place."

Et al. Used to refer to "and all the rest," it's short for *et alia*, which means "and other things."

MARINE MAMMALS

Whales, dolphins, and porpoises are all descended from land mammals (see page 141). Here's a look at some of the other marine mammals:

✦ *Sirenians* comprise all the dugongs and manatees (aptly named "sea cows"), and they are the only marine mammal herbivores. Like the whales, they are believed to be descendants of hoofed land mammals and have small, remnant hind leg bones inside their bodies. Closest living relatives: elephants.

✦ *Pinnipeds* ("feather-" or "fin-feet")—all the seals, including eared seals and true seals, and walruses—are semi-aquatic and are believed to have evolved from bearlike creatures about 25 million years ago. There are about 35 existing species.

✦ *Lutrinae*—the marine otters—are another semi-aquatic former land mammal. Their evolutionary line is sketchy, but they're believed to have evolved from a small, carnivorous land mammal about five to seven million years ago. They're found all over the world, and though they're considered "semi-aquatic," some can actually spend their entire lives in the water. Closest relatives: Otters are in the family *Mustelidae* and are related to weasels, skunks, badgers, and wolverines.

✦ Some biologists classify polar bears as marine mammals, since they have undergone adaptations that allow them to spend long amounts of time—many hours—in extremely cold water (particularly their thick layers of fat, unseen in other bears).

FOOD FOR THOUGHT. Semi-aquatic freshwater mammals like the river otter, beaver, and muskrat are not considered marine mammals, although they have accumulated many adaptations for life in water, such as webbed feet.

THE AMAZING BRONTËS

The three literary Brontë sisters were born within four years of each other—Charlotte in 1816, Emily in 1818, and Anne in 1820—in West Yorkshire in northern England. They were all well-educated and regularly wrote poetry and narrative stories. In 1846, at ages 30, 28, and 26, the sisters published a book of poems titled *Poems by Currer, Ellis, and Acton Bell.* (They used male-sounding pseudonyms because female writers had little chance of success back then.)

✦ The book was a complete bust, but the following year, in 1847, the three young women changed English literature forever with three novels: Charlotte's *Jane Eyre*, Emily's *Wuthering Heights*, and Anne's *Agnes Grey*. The first two are considered masterpieces, and Charlotte and Emily are regarded among the best writers of any era. *Agnes Grey*, written by Anne, failed to receive the same acclaim of the other two novels, but is still considered great.

✦ Unfortunately, the Brontë sisters' writing skills were much stronger than their health. Emily died in 1848 before finishing another novel; Anne finished *The Tenant of Wildfell Hall* in 1848 and died a year later. Charlotte lived the longest of the three, to age 38, dying in 1855, and published two more novels, *Shirley* in 1849 and *Villette* in 1853. A fourth, *The Professor*, which she wrote before *Jane Eyre*, had been rejected by several publishing houses. It was published posthumously in 1857.

WHY PI?

Pi is the mathematical constant defined as the ratio of the circumference of a circle to its diameter, and is equal approximately to the number 3.14159. It has been known rudimentally by mathematicians for nearly 4,000 years. It wasn't, however, known by the Greek letter pi (π) until 1706. That's when self-taught Welsh mathematician William Jones gave it the designation, probably deriving it from the Greek word for circumference: *periphereia*. Over the next several decades, it became the accepted and universal symbol it is today.

THE OTHER JOHN KENNEDYS

In 1955 John Francis Kennedy, a stock clerk with the Gillette razor blade company, ran for Massachusetts state treasurer. His only qualification for office (other than his clerical skills) was that his name was similar to John *Fitzgerald* Kennedy, the state's popular freshman senator. John *Francis* Kennedy spent just $200 on his campaign, skipped the Democratic primary, and still won the race. When he ran for governor in 1960, not one but two John Kennedys ran to replace him as treasurer: John *Michael* Kennedy, a city manager, and another John *Michael* Kennedy, a commercial painter. That same year, a former construction worker named John *Philip* Kennedy ran for re-election to the state House of Representatives; John *Andrew* Kennedy, a tree warden, ran for another House seat; *I.* John Kennedy, manager of a cocktail lounge, ran for state senate; and John *Joseph* Kennedy, a bird repellent salesman, ran for county commissioner. In all there were 11 Kennedys on Massachusetts ballots in 1960, including seven Johns. (Nearly all of them lost.)

THE THINKING AWARDS

Thinking Food Award. In 1795 Napoléon Bonaparte's Society for the Encouragement of Industry offered a prize of 12,000 francs to anyone who could develop a food preservation method that would keep food edible long enough to be useful to soldiers on long campaigns. A 61-year-old confectioner by the name of Nicolas Appert decided to try. His process: Thick glass bottles were filled with food—meat, fish, vegetables, eggs—then corked and placed into boiling water for different amounts of time according to what food was used. It worked. Appert had invented the process known today as *canning* or *appertization*, and was awarded the prize in 1810.

Thinking Flight Award. In 1959 British industrialist Henry Kremer offered £50,000 (equal to about $1 million today) to anyone who could build a human-powered aircraft that could fly a mile-long, figure-eight course while more than 10 feet off the ground. In 1977 American aeronautical engineer Paul MacCready built the *Gossamer Condor*, a 70-pound, pedal-powered plane made out of plastic, mylar, and piano wire. He then got professional hang glider Bryan Allen to fly it—and won the prize. Kremer then offered a prize of £100,000 to the first person who built a human-powered aircraft that could cross the English Channel. Two years later, Allen made the 22-mile crossing in 2 hours and 49 minutes in another MacCready design, the *Gossamer Albatross*—and they won that prize, too.

Thinking Chess Award. In 1980 Edward Fredkin, a computer science professor at Carnegie Mellon University, offered $100,000 to whoever built the first computer program that could beat a reigning world chess champion. In 1996 a team of computer scientists at IBM built the supercomputer "Deep Blue," and got Russian chess master Garry Kasparov to play it. Kasparov won. The IBM team made improvements and challenged Kasparov again in 1997—and this time the computer won. IBM was so pleased with the publicity that they gave Deep Blue's designers an extra $700,000 (and even gave Kasparov $400,000).

Thinking Small Prize. The nonprofit Foresight Nanotech Institute, based in Palo Alto, California, and committed to increasing awareness about nanotechnology, offered a $250,000 prize in 1995 to anyone who could devise: 1) a motor; and 2) a machine capable of adding numbers. The twist: The motor had to be capable of moving atoms around—and could be no more than 100 nanometers wide in any direction. (A nanometer is a billionth of a meter.) And the counting machine could have sides no longer than 50 nanometers. That prize has not yet been won. (So get to work.)

6 COUNTRIES NAMED AFTER PEOPLE

Bermuda. Named after 16th-century Spanish navigator Juan de Bermúdez (died 1570), who happened upon the uninhabited islands sometime around 1503.

Cambodia. Called "Kampuchea" in the local Khmer language, the name is derived from the name of the ancient Khmer kingdom of Kambudja, itself named after the legendary Indian prince and conqueror Kambu Swayambhuva.

Bolivia. The northern South American nation was named after Símon Bolívar (1783–1830), one of the most important leaders of the independence movement against the Spanish. (Bolívar also aided in the independence of Venezuela, Colombia, Ecuador, Peru, and Panama.)

Gibraltar. Tariq ibn Ziyad (died 720 C.E.) was a Muslim general and a North African Berber tribesman who conquered the Iberian Peninsula (Spain, Portugal, Andorra, and Gibraltar) in the year 711. His name in Arabic: Jabal Tariq. The name of the tiny British territory at the southern tip of the peninsula, Gibraltar, is derived from that.

Colombia. Named after Christopher Columbus (1451–1506). His name was used for many geographic regions throughout the New World held by the Spanish (the Italian Columbus traveled under the Spanish flag), and was chosen as Colombia's name upon its founding in 1819.

Seychelles. These islands in the Indian Ocean were claimed by the French in 1756, and named after King Louis XV's minister of finance, Jean Moreau de Séchelles (1690–1761). In 1812 the British seized control of the islands, whose citizens did not gain independence until 1976, at which time they took the name Republic of Seychelles. (Séchelles, the finance minister, never set foot in Seychelles, the country.)

ODD ANIMAL PREGNANCIES

Delayed Implantation. This occurs in several species of carnivore. Bears, for example, have relatively long pregnancies—about eight months for the largest bear species—but they have remarkably tiny newborns. Polar bear and grizzly bear newborns weigh less than one pound at birth, and panda newborns weigh just three to four ounces. It's due to a biological safety mechanism called *delayed implantation*. In most mammals, including humans, the egg implants (attaches to the wall of the uterus) within days of fertilization. There, it is nourished via the placenta and grows for the entire duration of the pregnancy (from the time of fertilization until birth). Bears, however, mate in midsummer, and the egg isn't ready to implant until the mother begins her winter hibernation—about five months later. If she hasn't eaten enough in that period and is undernourished, the egg will be aborted. This ensures that no cubs will be born into an environment that can't sustain them. If there is enough food and the mother is good and fat, the egg implants in November or December and the cub (or cubs) will be born about two months later, during the hibernation. That short development time, regardless of the long gestation period, is why newborn bears are so tiny. The reason for it, biologists say, is because of the unpredictable nature of carnivores' diets. (Other species with delayed implantation include badgers, mink, weasels, river otters, and wolverines.)

Delayed Fertilization. Some species of hibernating bats, endemic to colder climate regions such as the northern U.S. and Canada, mate in fall—but the females don't immediately become pregnant. If they did, they'd give birth in early winter, and the pups wouldn't survive due to the lack of food. So the females store the sperm in their uterus—and produce no eggs (they don't *ovulate*)—throughout the winter hibernation. In late winter or early spring, the eggs are produced and then fertilized, and in the warm spring or summer months the bats give birth.

Pregnancy Block. This occurs in a few rodent species, including house mice and some lemmings. Using the mouse as an example: If a pregnant female comes across an unfamiliar male (or even just the scent of one), she may have a hormonal reaction that causes her to spontaneously abort her fetuses. This is believed to have developed because male mice often kill and eat the young of another male. It is therefore much more efficient for the mother to abort the fetuses and mate with the new male, rather than wasting the energy of completing the pregnancy just so the new guy can eat the kids.

Marsupial Delayed Implantation. Marsupials have remarkably short pregnancies, after which the tiny newborns are nourished in a pouch. Even the largest, the kangaroos, go only 29 to 38 days from mating to birth. They're also able to mate *immediately* after giving birth. Because kangaroo young spend up to one year suckling, a female can't keep having babies every 31 days and expect to feed them. So if a mother has a suckling *joey* (baby kangaroo) *and* becomes pregnant, the fertilized egg doesn't attach to the uterus but just floats around inside it. As soon as the joey has stopped suckling, hormonal changes in the mother will cause the egg to implant and the pregnancy to continue. This enables marsupials to reproduce almost continuously and quickly allows for a new baby should the one in the pouch die.

HOUSEHOLD GENIUS

To get the most juice out of fresh lemons or limes, roll them firmly under your palm on the kitchen counter before slicing.

TAROT CARDS

Tarot cards were invented as playing cards in 15th-century Italy, and are still commonly used in games in many parts of Europe. In the late 1800s, fortune-tellers began using them (and other types of playing cards) to advise their customers on questions of romance, health, and money. Fortune-telling with tarot cards exploded in popularity during the 20th century with the introduction of decks designed by two famous occultists: A. E. Waite's *Rider-Waite* deck in 1910, and Aleister Crowley's *Thoth* deck, published in the 1960s.

The decidedly unmystical-sounding U.S. Games Systems, Inc., is the largest publisher of tarot decks in the world today, with 110 different designs. Here are five of their best-selling decks, as described on their packages.

Gummy Bear Deck. "The bear creatures cast their magic spells, wield their wands, and delight in reaching out to people through their mischievous imagery in the cards."

Gentle Wisdom of the Faerie Realm Deck. "Sixty enchanting faeries reflecting the belief that each person has a unique Gentle Wisdom."

Russian Tarot of St. Petersburg Deck. "Russian folk tales and historical legends are framed within an oval, reminiscent of the Imperial Fabergé Easter Eggs."

Lord of the Rings **Deck.** "This deck unites two great traditions: the spiritual, mystical tradition of the tarot, and the world of folklore and fantasy which J. R. R. Tolkien brought to life in his timeless works. Every card is a glimpse into Middle-earth with scenes from *The Lord of the Rings* and *The Hobbit* books."

Tarot of the Cat People Deck. "A deck that combines science fiction and fantasy. A mystical rapport with cats is established in a distant place known as the 'Outer Regions.'"

10 MAJOR CATEGORIES OF THE DEWEY DECIMAL SYSTEM

The classification system used by most libraries today was developed by Melvil Dewey in the 1870s at Amherst College in Massachusetts. The system has gone through several revisions but still retains the basic guidelines that Dewey set up…while still a student and assistant librarian. Here's today's version.

000–099: General Works—encyclopedias, etc.—and Computer Science

100–199: Philosophy

200–299: Religion

300–399: Social Sciences

400–499: Language (includes dictionaries)

500–599: Pure Science

CAMEL EYE

Camels have specialized extra eyelids on each eye; they move from side to side and act as windshield wipers of sorts to clean sand out of their eyes. They're also translucent, and can be kept closed during sandstorms.

THE DIFFERENCE BETWEEN...

Infectious and Contagious. An *infectious* disease is one caused by microscopic germs; they can come from the air, water, an animal, or another human. If the culprit is another human, then the infectious disease is also considered *contagious*, the definition of which is any disease that travels from one person to another, either from direct contact—including touching, sneezing, and coughing—or from touching something that was touched by a person with the disease.

THE FIRST GOLD

In the year 776 B.C.E. Coroebus of Elis, a baker from the region of Eleia in southern Greece, won a *stadion* race (the word later became *stadium*). A footrace of about 190 meters (623.4 feet), it was the only event at the first Olympic Games in Olympia, Greece. Coroebus was awarded an olive branch for the win.

THE PULITZER PRIZE

Hungarian-born Joseph Pulitzer (1847–1911) was a major figure in American journalism: publisher of the *St. Louis Post-Dispatch* and the *New York World*, a crusader for public-spirited investigative reporting, and an advocate of professional training for journalists. In his will, he endowed annual awards for excellence in American journalism, letters, and music, and the first Pulitzer Prizes were given in 1917. Today the prize categories include many kinds of journalism (such as public service; investigative; local, national, and international; feature; and online) as well as music, photography, poetry, fiction, drama, history, biography, and general nonfiction. The yearlong selection process is managed by an advisory board comprised of prominent editors, news executives, and academics. The board appoints expert juries to review the work of hundreds of candidates, and chooses the winners from the finalists nominated by the juries. Each prize is $10,000 (and a certificate), except in public service journalism, which merits the Pulitzer Prize Gold Medal.

FOOD FOR THOUGHT. The only U.S. president to win a Pulitzer Prize was John F. Kennedy, in 1957, for *Profiles in Courage*.

KOSHER BASICS

The system of Jewish dietary laws is complex but is based on just a few guidelines from the Torah, or Old Testament. This list is *very* simplified, but here are the basic rules:

✦ Land-dwelling animals are *kosher* (Hebrew for "clean") if they both chew cud and have cloven hooves. Animals such as cows and goats are kosher; animals such as camels, pigs, and rabbits are not.

✦ Most fish is permitted, as long as it has both fins and scales (including tuna and salmon). This prohibits shellfish, such as shrimp, clams, and crab.

✦ Chicken, turkey, and duck are kosher, but birds of prey (such as falcons) and scavengers (such as vultures) are forbidden.

✦ Insects, rodents, reptiles, and amphibians are generally not permitted.

✦ Grapes and grape products, such as wine, are kosher, but only if they're specifically processed under Jewish law. This rule goes back to when many ancient religions (including Judaism) used wine in rituals. Because wine was used in pagan rites, it was important that the wine was prepared by Jewish people, for Jewish people.

✦ It's extremely important that the kosher eater doesn't consume any animal blood. Jewish tradition holds that the animal's soul lives in the blood, so it must not be used. A special kosher butchering process is used to get rid of the blood before eating. A *shochet*, a Jewish butcher, kills the animal with a single slash to the throat, which causes most of the blood to drain out quickly. The meat is then soaked, rinsed, and drained to remove as much additional blood as possible. This step must be done within 72 hours of slaughter, and before the meat is frozen or ground.

✦ Also forbidden: mixing meat with dairy. This stems from a verse that states "Do not boil a kid in its mother's milk." Meat cannot be served at the same meal as dairy—or even on the same set of dishes.

LOBSTER LOVE

✦ A female lobster interested in mating seeks out the male with the largest den or cave. She entices the male with her urine, which contains powerful pheromones. After a while he can't stand it and lets her in. They then have a "boxing match" with their claws, often ending with what has been called "cuddling," with the male stroking the female. She then sheds her shell, he turns her on her back, and they copulate. Then she leaves, and stores the sperm for many months.

✦ When she is ready, the female turns on her back, cups her tail, and pushes out up to 20,000 eggs from her ovaries and through the sperm receptacle. The eggs stick to the bottom of the female's tail, where they are carried for about a year until they hatch. When they do, she shakes off the tiny larvae (they look like bugs at this point) and they rise to the surface. Only about one in every thousand makes it; the rest are eaten by predators. They feed on tiny organisms for three to five weeks, and go through four molts, after which they're heavy enough to sink to the ocean floor.

DREAM GENIUS

Scottish author Robert Louis Stevenson wrote a chapter in his 1892 book *Across the Plains* (an account of a trip from New York to San Francisco) entitled "Chapter on Dreams." In it he revealed that he believed his imagination was fueled during dreams by what he called "Little People":

> Who are the Little People? They are near connections of the dreamer's, beyond doubt… they can tell him a story piece by piece, like a serial, and keep him all the while in ignorance of where they aim.

He goes on to explain how the "Little People" in his dreams were responsible for coming up with the idea of the split personality of the character in his 1886 novel *The Strange Case of Dr. Jekyll and Mr. Hyde*. Since then, the dream-inspired work has never been out of print.

TWEED

Tweed is a loosely woven woolen fabric known for its "unfinished" and soft, flexible texture and, sometimes, its mix of subdued colors. It originated in Scotland (fabric historians differ on whether it originated in the south or the Highlands), where it was originally known as *tweel*. That itself was a variant on *twidling*, which described a weave pattern often used in tweed, with its characteristic diagonal "ridged" lines. Several types of tweed exist today, including Donegal (from Ireland), and Harris Tweed, which can only be called genuine—by a 1993 act of Parliament—if it is "hand-woven by the islanders at their homes in the Outer Hebrides, finished in the islands of Harris, Lewis, Benbecula, Uist, and Barra and their several purtenances, and made from pure virgin wool dyed and spun in the Outer Hebrides."

HOW TO MAKE A HAMBURGER

1. A steer is ready for processing when it reaches two years old and 1,000 pounds, of which about 450 pounds will be edible meat.

2. Farmers send the live animal to a beef processor. The cow stays in a holding area for one day. It is not fed (to cut down on manure both inside the cow and in the holding area) but is given water to maintain its weight.

3. The cow is moved to the immobilization area, where it's incapacitated with a *bolt pistol*—a pneumatic tool that shoots a bolt against the cow's skull with enough force to render it unconscious.

4. The cow is placed in shackles and hoisted by its hindquarters onto a rail called a *dressing trolley*. The main arteries and veins are cut and the animal is bled to death, with the blood dripping into a floor drain. This is called *exsanguination*.

5. The cow, still overhead on the dressing trolley, is now placed in a cradle where the head and feet are removed by mechanized saws. The hide is removed from the carcass with electric rotating skinning knives.

6. Next, the organs are removed. The abdomen is opened from top to bottom, and the organs are loosened and removed. A worker with a handsaw then takes the carcass off the overhead carriage and saws it in half lengthwise, cutting through the center of the cow's backbone.

7. The product is now reduced to two large "sides" of beef. They are then washed of any remaining blood and bone dust before being placed in a chemical decontamination bath, which consists of water, acetic acid, lactic acid, chlorine, and hydrogen peroxide.

8. The sides are placed in cold storage, at 32°F, where they age for a week (to improve the taste).

9. The meat is cut into primal joints (wholesale cuts), and each is vacuum-packed. It's sold to butchers in this state.

10. Butchers separate the meat into its various parts. Less-tender and fattier cuts, which don't command as high a price as steak cuts, are used for hamburgers. The butcher grinds this meat into a sticky, pellet-like mass, where it's sold raw.

11. You take the raw ground beef home, form it into patties, and grill them (add onions, lettuce, tomatoes, and cheese, if desired).

SURVIVING A CAR CRASH INTO WATER

✦ If you lose control while driving and find yourself plunging into a body of water, try to roll down a window immediately. Although this will make the car sink faster, it will give you an escape route.

✦ If the car sinks to the bottom before you were able to open a window, then wait before you try the door. Opening it too soon will cause an onrush of water that could injure you. Let the car fill up with water until it's almost full; then the pressure outside will be roughly equal to the pressure inside and the door should open easily, allowing you to swim to safety.

✦ If neither the doors nor windows will open, try kicking the center of the windshield with your heel. Again, wait until most of the car fills up with water so the pressure on the windshield is reduced.

✦ If you can't escape, turn on all the lights to increase your chances of being spotted from the surface. Sometimes small air pockets will form and allow you to breathe.

ARKANSAW

The proper pronunciation of "Arkansas" has been argued since before it became a U.S. state in 1836. Neighboring tribes gave this name to the Quapaw people, who lived on what is now the Arkansas River. It was spelled many different ways by settlers, including "Akancea," "Acansea," "Acansa," and "Arkancas." When statehood came along, the spelling "Arkansas" was elected as the official name. Nearly 50 years later, in 1881, citizens of the state were still arguing about the proper pronunciation—including Arkansas' two U.S. senators—so a committee was appointed to find the correct version. Result: "arkansaw." That's the way it's been pronounced ever since.

RARE GENETIC DISEASES AND MEDICAL CONDITIONS

✦ **Lipodystrophy.** The body produces as much as six times the normal levels of food-burning hormones, which makes the victim unable to gain weight. In severe cases, they waste away.

✦ **Chiari Malformation.** The brain is squeezed against the spinal column, which stifles the brain stem, the part of the brain that controls vital functions such as sleep and blood circulation. In the case of chiari malformation, only sleep is affected, leaving the patient unable to sleep.

✦ **Aquagenic Urticaria.** It's an allergy to water. Showers, swimming, and even sweating cause the patient to break out in hives.

✦ **Cataplexy.** Anytime the sufferer feels a strong emotion—anger, fear, embarrassment, awe, or even joy—the muscles suddenly weaken, the body collapses, and the person goes to sleep.

✦ **Maple Syrup Urine Disease.** Medically known as *branched-chain ketoaciduria*, this is a rare but serious condition afflicting newborns that results in a buildup of amino acids and toxins in the blood. A common symptom is that the urine smells like maple syrup.

✦ **Kabuki Makeup Syndrome.** It's a birth defect that causes facial features to distort to the point where they resemble the over-pronounced, elongated made-up faces of Japanese Kabuki actors.

✦ **Hairy Tongue.** Also called *lingua villosa*, this is caused by tobacco use, overconsumption of coffee or mouthwash, or poor oral hygiene. The tiny hairs on the tongue grow abnormally long, and the tongue itself turns black, white, green, or pink.

✦ **Jumping Frenchmen of Maine Disorder.** A rare condition in which victims have an exaggerated reaction—jumping, screaming, or striking out—to sudden stimuli such as loud noises. It was first noted in French lumberjacks in Maine, and its cause is still undetermined.

ESCAPE FROM AMERICA: THE CONFEDERATES

When the Civil War ended in 1865, many former Confederate soldiers pulled up stakes and headed South of the Border.

✦ **Mexico.** As many as 2,500 Confederate families moved to Mexico. They did so with the encouragement of Mexico's Emperor Maximilian I, who set aside 500,000 acres' worth of 640-acre farms for people who could afford to pay $1.00 per acre; he also made additional, less desirable parcels of land available to those who could not. The resettlement plan ended in failure—most Confederates who could afford to buy the land preferred to tough it out in the United States, and those who were indigent made the free trip (courtesy of the Emperor) in greater numbers than there was free land set aside to give them. Most turned right around and returned to the U.S.; many settled in Texas. Nearly all those who didn't leave Mexico voluntarily were driven out in 1867, after Maximilian was overthrown and executed. The tiny handful of Confederate families that did stay were almost completely assimilated after two or three generations; there is virtually no trace of Confederate culture remaining in Mexico today.

✦ **Brazil.** The defeated Confederates who emigrated to Brazil fared much better. There is no accurate record of how many

Southerners went there, but historians have pegged the number at somewhere between 10,000 and 20,000 *Confederados*, many following the lead of William Hutchinson Norris, a former U.S. Senator from Alabama who was one of the earliest to arrive. So many Confederados settled in a spot about 80 miles north of Sao Paulo that Brazilians took to calling their community *Vila dos Americanos* (American Village); the city that grew up on the spot is still called Americana today. Fewer than 10% of the more than 200,000 people living in Americana now claim Confederate ancestry, and those who do have assimilated almost completely into Brazilian culture. Though a few old-timers still speak English as their first language—with a pronounced Southern drawl—the younger generations almost always grow up in homes where Portuguese is spoken. If they speak English at all, they do so with thick Brazilian accents. But that doesn't stop them from celebrating their Southern roots: Many descendants of the Confederados belong to an organization called the *Fraternidade Descendencia Americana* and still meet for picnics at the "Campo," the old Confederate cemetery and memorial, every January, April, July, and October.

(GRAND) AYATOLLAH

Ayatollah means "Sign of God" in Arabic and is a title given to high-ranking clerics in Shia Islam. There are no specific requirements to receive it. Most have attended seminaries in holy Shiite cities such as Najaf in Iraq or Qum in Iran, where the studies include theology, politics, law, philosophy, and science. From there, one must receive wide acclaim through his own writings and interpretations of the Koran before he can attain the title "Ayatollah," at which point he is able to teach at seminaries, be used as a reference for religious concepts, and judge aspects of Islamic law.

✦ Grand Ayatollah, or *Marja*, meaning "source to imitate," is a title given only to a few very high-ranking Ayatollahs and is usually bestowed by a group of high-ranking clerics. Marjas are considered the highest living sources of religious authority. Well known examples of Grand Ayatollahs include Ruhollah Khomeini, the leader of the Iranian revolution that overthrew the Shah of Iran in 1979; Ali Khamenei, the supreme leader of Iran since 1989; and Ali al-Sistani, the leader of all Iraqi Shiites since 1992. There are currently about 20 Grand Ayatollahs in the world, mostly in Iran, with the others scattered throughout the Middle East and India.

WHY FIVE DIGITS?

✦ Every animal with four limbs—the *tetrapods* ("four feet"), which include mammals, reptiles, amphibians, and birds—has five digits at the end of each limb, or is descended from animals that did. They includes all hooved animals, whose five digits were fused millions of years ago, becoming the hooves they have today; birds, whose fossil record shows five-digited ancestors; and even snakes, which are descendants of four-limbed, five-digited lizards.

✦ This trait is known as *pentadactyly*, from the Greek *pente* ("five"), and *dactyl* ("finger"). For many years biologists believed (and some still argue) that this arrangement prevailed because it offered some kind of advantage—for balance, grasping, tool manipulation, or some other ability. But most now believe that this is not the case. It's more likely that it was simply an accident of evolution. The evidence for this is that some of the earliest tetrapods didn't have five digits. For example, the *tulerpeton* was a large, lizardlike creature that lived about 355 million years ago and had six digits on each limb. *Icthyostega*, circa 360 million years ago, had *seven* toes on its hind limbs. And *acanthostega*, which lived around 365 million years ago and was one of the earliest land animals, had *eight* digits on each limb.

✦ So why is five the number today? Because none of those many-fingered creatures survived; they all went extinct relatively quickly. The tetrapods that *did* survive all had five digits.

FOOD FOR THOUGHT. Charles Darwin saw the fact that all tetrapods have five digits as powerful evidence for the theory of evolution. "What could be more curious than that the hand of man formed for grasping," he wrote, "that of a mole, for digging, the leg of a horse, the paddle of a porpoise, and the wing of a bat, should all be constructed on the same pattern and should include similar bones and in the same relative positions?"

WATER POISONING

Few people realize it, but drinking too much clean freshwater can actually kill you. Your kidneys are constantly working to keep the salt content of your blood at about 0.9% at all times. If you drink a lot of freshwater in a short amount of time, you can lower this level dangerously, resulting in a condition known as *hyponatremia*—low sodium—or water poisoning. In this condition, the opposite of dehydration occurs: the cells absorb water and bloat. They can even burst. Symptoms include light-headedness, nausea, severe headaches, vomiting, swelling of the brain, seizures, coma, and death. Common causes include water-drinking contests, in which large quantities are drunk in just minutes, and drinking substantial amounts of water after excessive exercise, when salt loss is already high due to sweating.

[(THE), HISTORY–OF: PUNC-TU-A-TION?!]

ANCIENTGREEKWRITINGCONTAINEDNOPUNCTUATION-ORSPACESBETWEENWORDS Why? Because reading alone to oneself was unheard of. Orators and actors, however, needed to know when to pause, and that marked the beginning of punc-tuation.

✦ **400 B.C.E.** Greek playwrights introduce the *paragraphos*, a horizontal line denoting the end of a spoken section. (That's the origin of the word "paragraph.")

✦ **195 B.C.E.** A librarian in Alexandria, Egypt, named Aristophanes (not the playwright of the same name) invents the *periodos*, the *kolon*, and the *komma*. They are points used to denote the length of pauses between spoken words. Although the terms will remain intact, their specific pause-length usage won't.

✦ **400 C.E.** Priests need to know when to pause while reading scripture to the illiterate masses, prompting Bible copyists to adopt the Greeks' use of points. They also add forward slashes, indentations, and upper- and lower-case letters. (Because points were the first punctuation marks, scribes were said to "point," from the Latin *punctus*, their texts—it is from this root that we get the words "puncture," "punctual," and "punctuation.")

✦ **700s.** With no set rules for "pointing" written texts, Alcuin of York, a scholar and adviser to Charlemagne, orders scribes to add more consistency to punctuation. Though few obey his wishes, the movement for consistent punctuation has begun. Also, the first question mark makes its appearance as the *punctus interrogativus*, basically a squiggly line turned upward. (This doesn't last long, however, and the question mark we know today will come much later.)

✦ **900s.** Spaces between written words become commonplace.

✦ **1400s.** A writer and bookseller named William Caxton introduces the first printing press in England and is among the first English writers to use punctuation consistently.

✦ **1500s.** As the printing press becomes more common, early publishing houses spread the use of punctuation by turning down manuscripts that lack the series of "little twigs" inserted to aid the speaker. In Italy, a printer named Aldus Manutius uses a single dot (period) to indicate a full stop and introduces the semicolon as well as italic type. Despite these early grammarians' best efforts, punctuation remains highly inconsistent over the next century, with most scholars still arguing that the symbols should primarily aid the speaker, not the reader.

✦ **1640.** A guide called *English Grammar* by English playwright Ben Jonson is released posthumously. He argues for *syntactical* punctuation—a significant step to solidifying the use of symbols for the primary purpose of reading comprehension. Parentheses make their widespread debut in this century (from the Greek *parentithenai*, meaning "put in beside").

✦ **1700s–present.** The practice is *really* catching on in English, so much so that now the problem becomes overpunctuation (such as, inserting commas, every few words). It is during this time that a slew of new symbols are introduced, including the question mark, dash, quotation marks, and two of the youngest: the apostrophe and the exclamation point.

WHAT'S AN ORCHID?

Orchids are flowering plants just like other flowering plants... except that they're not. More than 22,000 species of orchids exist, and they grow all over the world, except in the Arctic and Antarctic regions. They're made distinct from other flowering plants, such as roses, daisies, and petunias, by some very peculiar characteristics:

✦ Their *stamens* and *pistils* (male and female parts of a flowering plant) are fused together in a fingerlike structure known as a *column.*

✦ All orchids have three petals. Two of the petals are laterally (side to side) symmetrical, while the third (always lower) petal is shaped differently and is highly stylized. (The lower petal is called the *lip.*)

✦ They (usually) have three *sepals*, which can look like petals, but are actually the evolutionary remnants of flower bud coverings. They're always outside the petals.

Extra Orchid Facts: The orchid family contains more species than any other family of flowering plants.

✦ The plants can be very large, up to 20 feet high, and some flowers are 10 inches across. Other orchids are tiny, with flowers the size of a pinhead.

✦ They grow on the ground (terrestrials), on rocks (lithophytes), and on other plants, including high up in trees (epiphytes).

✦ The name comes from the Latin *orchis*—for "testicle"—after the shape of the bulbous root on terrestrial species.

✦ Vanilla beans are the fruit of the *Vanilla planifolia* orchid.

INSTANT SHAKESPEARE:
JULIUS CAESAR

Shakespeare primarily wrote three kinds of plays: comedies, tragedies, and histories. *Julius Caesar* (1599) is a history.

The plot: Two tribunes, Marullus and Flavius, scold the people of Rome for worshipping the emperor, Caesar, fearing he's growing too powerful. As Caesar leads a procession, a soothsayer warns him to "beware the ides of March," the day he will die; Caesar arrogantly ignores the warning. Cassius, an anti-Caesar revolutionary, successfully recruits Caesar's friend Brutus to help kill Caesar. Despite his reservations, Brutus joins the conspiracy, but argues against killing Caesar's top advisor, Mark Antony.

Caesar's wife Calphurnia tells her husband that she had a dream that foretold his death and begs him not to go to the senate the next day, the ides of March. Caesar agrees not to go, but Brutus convinces him to so as not to look weak to the senate. Caesar goes—and is stabbed to death by Brutus and several others.

At Caesar's funeral, Brutus and Cassius win support from Rome by explaining that they had to kill Caesar in order to stop him. Mark Antony gives a speech and turns the crowd against the conspirators; he plans to kill Brutus and Cassius. A war between the two sides' armies ensues at Philippi. Believing the enemy to be closing in, Cassius kills himself. Brutus kills himself, too, and Mark Antony becomes the new emperor.

Memorable line: "Friends, Romans, countrymen, lend me your ears; I come to bury Caesar, not to praise him." (Mark Antony, Act III, Scene 2)

SLINK

"To slink" is a farming term that means to give birth to an animal prematurely, usually used in regards to domestic animals such as cows and sheep. It is also used as an adjective for a premature newborn animal, i.e., a "slink calf." The noun "slink" is the name of such premature animals, and can also refer to their fur—slinks are known for being very soft, and are sold all over the world.

THE YEAR OF THE...

You may know that Chinese astrology designates certain animals as representatives of certain years—the "Year of the Dog," or tiger, or snake, and so on. The 12-year, 12-animal cycle is: Rat, Ox, Tiger, Rabbit, Dragon, Snake, Horse, Sheep, Monkey, Rooster, Dog, and Pig. How those animals were chosen is unknown—the calendar is more than 4,000 years old. But why they appear in that order is explained by a Chinese folk tale: The mythical Jade Emperor told all the animals that they had to race across a river; the order in which they finished would be the order in which they appeared on the calendar. The Rat finished first by making the trip on the back of the Ox—and jumping off just before the Ox made it to shore. (A side note to the legend: The Tiger was on the Ox's back with the Rat, but the Rat pushed him off halfway across the river. The Tiger never finished the race and swore that from then on he would be the Rat's mortal enemy.)

CHAPTER 21

THE DIFFERENCE BETWEEN...
"E.G." AND "I.E."

Both are Latin abbreviations: "e.g." stands for *exempli gratia*, which means "for the sake of example"; "i.e." stands for *id est*, which means "that is."

✦ Use e.g. when presenting examples or additional possibilities for the term in question. For example: "I like animals (e.g., dogs, cats, and wolverines)." A mnemonic device to help remember this: Associate e.g. with "example given."

✦ Use i.e. when explaining or rephrasing a sentence. Sample: "I like animals (i.e., I like them as friends.)"

✦ Always set off i.e. and e.g. with parentheses or a semicolon, and follow them with a comma.

PURR

Despite all of the geniuses that the human race has produced, we still don't know exactly how or why cats purr. What is known is that, although purring is commonly acknowledged to be a sign of contentment, cats also purr when they're in pain or trauma. (If it was just one or the other, it might be easier to figure out what biological advantage they obtain from purring.) It is no doubt also a form of communication, possibly signaling to another cat that it isn't an enemy, a willingness to mate, an "I'm alright" signal in times of danger, or simply a pleasurable release when being petted.

✦ Purring is believed to be caused by the rapid vibration of the *laryngeal* (voice box) muscles, which causes the *glottis*, the opening between the vocal cords, to open and close rapidly as the cat both inhales and exhales. It's controlled, experts say, by a unique "neural oscillator" area in cats' brains.

✦ Another theory is that purring involves the *hyoid apparatus*, a collection of small bones in the neck that support the tongue and tongue muscles. The cat's breathing can make one or more of these bones vibrate, thereby causing purring.

✦ As for which cats do it—even that's not clear. Many scientists believe that large cats like lions and tigers cannot purr—their ability to roar makes it impossible. Others claim that they can indeed purr, but only while exhaling. Still others contend that they can do it while inhaling and exhaling, but in a slightly different way than small cats.

THE POWER OF PURRING

In 2001 Dr. Elizabeth von Muggenthaler of the Fauna Communications Research Institute in North Carolina presented the findings of a study that examined whether a cat's purring has healing abilities. She found that when cats are injured, they purr. Purring takes lots of energy, so it doesn't make sense that they would do it in times of trauma unless it did them some good. And it does, says Von Muggenthaler: The frequency of purring stimulates bone, tendon, and muscle healing, and relieves pain. (Does holding a purring cat help injured humans? According to Muggenthaler, yes—it does.)

ROAR

We may not be sure which cats can purr, but we're very sure which ones can roar: those in the genus *Panthera*. These are the lions, tigers, leopards, and jaguars. Unlike the smaller cats, they have flexible hyoid apparatus bones in the neck. It is believed that this feature is what allows the big cats to produce their deep, booming roars.

✦ There is one exception: Snow leopards were once classified as members of *Panthera*, then were considered sufficiently unique to have their own genus, *Uncia*. One of the reasons: They can't roar...or maybe they just don't. But now most biologists are moving them back to *Panthera*; they recently discovered that snow leopards possess the flexible hyoid apparatus bones required for roaring. Why they can't—or don't—remains a mystery.

THE 10 LARGEST COUNTRIES IN THE WORLD (BY AREA)

Russia: 6,592,846 sq miles; population: 142,000,000; location: Europe/Asia

Canada: 3,602,707 sq miles; population: 34,000,000; location: North America

China: 3,600,947 sq miles; population: 1,326,000,000; location: Asia

United States: 3,539,242 sq miles; population: 305,000,000; location: North America

Brazil: 3,265,075 sq miles; population: 188,000,000;
location: South America

Australia: 2,941,283 sq miles; population: 21,000,000;
location: South Pacific Ocean

India: 1,147,949 sq miles; population: 1,130,000,000;
location: Asia

Argentina: 1,056,636 sq miles; population: 40,000,000;
location: South America

Kazakhstan: 1,049,150 sq miles; population: 15,000,000;
location: South Asia

Sudan: 917,374 sq miles; population: 39,000,000;
location: Africa

THE 10 SMALLEST COUNTRIES IN THE WORLD (BY AREA)

Vatican City: 0.17 sq miles; population: 824;
location: Rome, Italy

Monaco: 0.76 sq miles; population: 33,000;
location: Mediterranean Sea

Nauru: 8.1 sq miles; population: 13,700;
location: western Pacific Ocean

Tuvalu: 10 sq miles; population: 12,000;
location: South Pacific Ocean

San Marino: 24 sq miles; population: 30,000;
location: Adriatic coast

Liechtenstein: 62 sq miles; population: 35,000;
location: Rhine river

Marshall Islands: 70 sq miles; population: 62,000;
location: Pacific Ocean

St. Kitts and Nevis: 104 sq miles; population: 63,000;
location: Caribbean Sea

Maldives: 115 sq miles; population: 350,000;
location: Indian Ocean

Seychelles: 174 sq miles: population: 81,000; location: Indian Ocean

ROCK

There are three kinds of rock on Earth: *igneous*, *sedimentary*, and *metamorphic*.

✦ **Igneous** rocks are the products of cooled magma (molten rock). There are more than 700 types in two main groups: those that are made deep within Earth, and those made at the surface. *Intrusive* igneous rock forms at depths from 20 to 1,800 miles underground. There, it hardens very slowly—over thousands or even millions of years—and under immense pressure. Intrusive rocks are therefore very dense, and include granite and basalt. *Extrusive* igneous rocks are made at the surface from lava, which is magma that reaches the surface via volcanic activity. Lava cools relatively quickly and under little pressure, so extrusive rocks have a different makeup than those made deep underground. Examples include obsidian (a naturally made glass) and pumice, known for being very light—it contains air bubbles that were trapped while cooling. (Pumice actually floats on water.)

✦ **Sedimentary** rock is found only at the surface to a depth of several miles. As the name implies, it is made up of sediment that has been compacted into rock. It comes in three main categories based on the cause of sedimentation: *chemical* sedimentary rock is formed by chemical precipitation or evaporation, such as when water evaporates from a lake and leaves behind gypsum beds; *clastic* sedimentary rock is formed when weathering and erosion breaks down large rocks into fragments, which then adhere and harden back into rock; and *organic* sedimentary rock forms from material left behind by living things. Limestone and chalk, for example, are made from the remains of shellfish, and coal is made from biodegraded plant material.

✦ **Metamorphic** rock is any rock, including older metamorphic, igneous, or sedimentary rock, that has been physically and chemically changed by environmental forces, usually by the heat and/or pressure accompanying being buried. For example, if limestone is subjected to high enough pressure and temperature, it becomes marble.

THE GREAT TEA RACE

Explorers first brought tea leaves to England from China in the 1700s, and within a few decades, everyone from royals to street sweepers had developed a taste for tea. Eventually, India also became an important tea producer, and England's East India Tea Company established a monopoly on tea imports. But the long voyage from China or India to Europe by ship took a toll on the tea—the trip took so long (often more than a year) that some of the tea always spoiled. By the 19th century, the East India Company was looking for ways to protect its precious cargo and, in doing so, make more money. Competition to make the trip faster was fierce. Enter the clipper, a narrow, multi-masted, very fast ship developed in the mid-1800s that could cut travel time from the Far East to Europe by more than half.

In 1866, the East India Company unofficially sponsored a race to see which of nine clipper tea ships, each carrying more than one million pounds of tea, could make it from the China to England the fastest. The ships left on different days—all between May 29 and June 6—but that didn't make much of a difference in travel time. In fact, the ship that left the earliest, called the *Fiery Cross*, came in fourth. The Suez Canal through Egypt wouldn't be built until 1869, so the ships had to battle for nearly 14,000 nautical miles across the South China Sea and the Indian Ocean, around Africa's Cape of Good Hope, and then up the Atlantic to England.

Finally, on September 12, two ships turned into the English Channel and headed for London. The *Taeping* arrived first and won the top prize: an extra pound sterling for each ton of usable tea delivered and a percentage of the ship's earnings for the captain. Second place: the *Ariel*, which arrived just 26 minutes later. The two had made the trip in an incredible 99 days.

MODERN WEDDING ANNIVERSARIES

Most people are familiar with the traditional wedding anniversaries: the 25th is the "silver," and the 50th is the golden. That's thanks to famed etiquette writer Emily Post, who compiled and published the list of "traditional" anniversaries in 1922. What most people don't know is that she also compiled a "modern" list in 1957. Here are some examples:

1. Clocks	**17.** Furniture	**43.** Travel
4. Appliances	**26.** Photographs	**44.** Groceries
7. Desk sets	**27.** Sculpture	**46.** Original poetry
13. Furs	**41.** Land	**48.** Optical goods

MYSTERY WORDS

Slang. It first showed up in English in the mid-1700s, meaning a "secret language of thieves." Some etymologists theorize that it's a derivation of the Norse *slengja kjeften*, literally "to sling the jaw," or "to abuse with words," but its true origin is unknown.

Shenanigan. It first appeared around 1855 in *Town Talk*, a San Francisco newspaper, meaning something like "funny business." ("Are you quite sure? No shenanigan?" it read.) In the 1920s, it began to be used in the plural—"shenanigans"—with a lighter meaning—"tomfoolery." Some theories of its origin: It came from the Irish Gaelic *sionnachuighim* (pronounced something like "shenanigan"), meaning "I play tricks"; or from the Spanish *chanada*, a short form of *charranada*, meaning "trick" or "deceit"; or from a German slang word for "work"—*schinäglen*.

GOLD ALLOYS

Most of the gold you come across is actually gold mixed with other metals, which is how it gets its many colors. Some different gold alloys, with their makeups and colors:

Yellow Gold: gold, silver, and copper

Red Gold: gold and copper

Blue Gold: gold and iron

Purple Gold: gold and aluminum

White Gold: gold and platinum or palladium

OCCAM'S RAZOR

Occam's Razor is a philosophical principle of logic commonly attributed to 14th-century English philosopher and Franciscan monk William of Occam (often spelled "Ockham"). As he put it: "Plurality should not be posited without necessity." Translation: The simplest theory is the one that is most likely to be correct. (The "razor" shaves off all the unnecessary details.) The maxim is used in various applications—especially religion and science. A use of the phrase by a modern genius, Stephen Hawking, in *A Brief History of Time*:

"We could still imagine that there is a set of laws that determines events completely for some supernatural being, who could observe the present state of the universe without disturbing it. However, such models of the universe are not of much interest to us mortals. It seems better to employ the principle known as Occam's Razor and cut out all the features of the theory that cannot be observed."

FOOD FOR THOUGHT. A modern, if simplistic, example of a use of Occam's Razor: "If it looks like a duck, walks like a duck, and quacks like a duck—it's probably a duck."

NAME THAT EUROPEAN DISH

✦ **Tears of Christ.** According to an old Italian legend, when the Archangel Lucifer was cast out of heaven, he grabbed a piece of paradise—and fell in the area of Naples. When Jesus noticed the loss, he wept, and where his tears fell, grapevines grew. That's why this wine, made from the grapes around Naples, is still called *Lacryma Christi*, or "Tears of Christ."

✦ **Rotten Pot.** This is a Spanish stew made from different varieties of meat and vegetables. It's called *olla podrida*, which literally means "rotten pot." The name may come from the mutton it's often made with, which can emit a foul odor while cooking. Another theory says it's simply because *olla podridas* were often kept a long time and added to, like a "Mulligan stew," and naturally became stinky.

✦ **Devil's Fart.** The truth is that we don't (and probably never will) know for certain the exact origin of this word. Still, many etymologists list the following story as a possible origin, so we will, too: In New High German, *Nickel* was a shortened version of "Nicholas" and was a nickname of sorts for the devil or Satan; *pumpern* meant "to fart"—so *pumpernickel* means "devil's fart." This referred, apparently, to the reputed indigestibility of this dark, rich bread. (The word entered English in the 1750s.)

✦ **Prostitute Pasta.** This is an Italian pasta dish with a spicy tomato-based sauce made with simple ingredients found in most homes. Its Italian name is *pasta alla puttanesca*, meaning "pasta the way a whore would make it." It got the name in the 1950s, when tomato-based sauces were becoming popular among the Italian middle class, and arose from somewhere around the Bay of Naples—where brothels flourished. It's said to refer to the short preparation time of the dish, which the "working girls" could make between clients.

ON THINKING

"A thinker sees his own actions as experiments and questions—as attempts to find out something. Success and failure are for him answers above all."

—Friedrich Nietzsche

CANCELED AT WOODSTOCK

Jeff Beck Group: The band broke up in July, only weeks before the concert.

Iron Butterfly: The band claims that concert organizers were supposed to arrange for a helicopter to pick them up in New York City, but never sent it. Organizers say the band was pompously demanding a helicopter. (Both agree that organizers sent a telegram to the band, the contents of which we cannot reprint here.)

Joni Mitchell: She was supposed to play on Sunday, but her manager was worried that the massive traffic jams would make her miss her scheduled Monday TV appearance on *The Dick Cavett Show*. Crosby, Stills, Nash & Young, who did play on Sunday, made it to the Cavett show. And though she wasn't there, Mitchell wrote the song "Woodstock," which became a huge hit for CSNY.

Lighthouse: The Canadian band feared it would be a "bad scene."

BAMBI-EATING PIGS

Three things wild boars occasionally eat:
snakes, young lambs, and young deer.

XXX

The "triple-X" symbol can mean many different things:

XXX: the number 30 in Roman numerals

XXX: short for "XXXL," signifying plus-sized clothing

XXX: identifies especially explicit pornography

XXX: a "turkey," or three consecutive strikes in bowling

XXX: generic name for homemade "moonshine" whiskey

XXX: short for "Triple-X Syndrome," characterized by the presence of an extra X chromosome in human females

XXX: the name of a 1999 album by the rock group ZZ Top

XXX: the name of a Filipino investigative TV show (it's short for *XXX: Exklusibong, Explosibong, Exposé*)

XXX: used to signify the official flag of Amsterdam (which has three *X*'s on it)

XXX: "kisses" on a letter or in an e-mail

THE CONTINENTS

The Beginning. The concept of continents goes back to the Ancient Greeks, who designated the lands west and east of the Aegean Sea and the Black Sea as distinct and separate landmasses. They named these lands Europe (after the goddess Europa) and Asia (said to come from either Assyrian or Akkadian and referencing the rising of the sun). By about 600 B.C.E., they had added a third, Africa. This three-continent mindset lasted for nearly 2,000 years.

The New World. In 1501 Amerigo Vespucci sailed to South America, determining for the first time that it was not, as other explorers before him had thought, part of Asia. In 1507 German cartographer Martin Waldseemüller published the first world map showing four separate landmasses: Europe, Asia, Africa, and one he named America (after Vespucci).

Newer Worlds. Europeans landed on Australia for the first time in 1606, believing it was part of Asia. In the late 1700s, some mapmakers started regarding Australia, North America, and South America as separate landmasses. In 1838 Antarctica was first called a continent, although it wouldn't be included in most atlases as such for about another 100 years.

Today. The definition of "continent" remains arbitrary, generally being described as Earth's major landmasses, each separate and surrounded by water. Of course, that doesn't work for Europe and Asia (or South and North America) and arguments persist as to whether there are five or seven continents. But the most common count by geologists today is seven. From largest to smallest: Asia, Africa, North America, South America, Antarctica, Europe, Australia.

SEX CELLS

If you look at it in a certain way, you *could* say that you are as old as your mother, since the egg that developed into you was in inside her body since the day she was born.

✦ Female humans are born with all the sex cells, or eggs, they'll ever have—between one and two million of them, half in each ovary. Called *oocytes*, they are essentially "pre-eggs" that will, one at a time, once a month from puberty until menopause (except during pregnancy), develop into a *secondary oocyte*, and then into an *ovum*.

- ✦ One ovary or the other develops an ovum (they generally alternate from month to month) and, after about 14 days, releases it into the fallopian tube (there are two tubes, one for each ovary) in a biological process known as *ovulation*.

- ✦ Unlike women, men can produce sex cells, or sperm, continuously from puberty until old age.

- ✦ Sperm cells are produced in a man's testes, the male equivalent of ovaries. They develop there for about two weeks, growing heads and tails. They then travel up the *vas deferens* tubes (there are two, just like the fallopian tubes, one from each testicle), to two seminal vesicles, located behind the bladder. There they are combined with other fluids to form *semen*, which then goes to the nearby ejaculatory ducts. The entire process takes between 2 and 2½ months, at which point the sperm cells are ready to be propelled down the urethra and ejaculated during sexual intercourse.

- ✦ The semen is deposited near the cervix, the opening to the uterus. The sperm cells now have around 72 hours to find an ovum and fertilize it. Longer than that and they'll be dead. They swim—at about two millimeters per minute—through a thick mucus secreted by the female for a few days before ovulation occurs. This leads them through the cervix, through the uterus, and finally to the openings of the fallopian tubes.

- ✦ Depending on the woman's menstrual cycle, there may not be an ovum located in either tube. In that case, the sperm is trapped and stored until an egg is released. (It still has to happen within 72 hours.)

- ✦ If there is an egg inside one of the tubes, thousands of sperm cells swarm its surface (egg cells are thousands of times larger than sperm cells) and secrete enzymes that allow them to penetrate the ovum's outer surface. Only the strongest sperm cell can make it all the way through to the egg's watery inner cytoplasm. That sperm's tail then falls off.

- ✦ The egg is now biologically induced to secrete a fertilization membrane on its surface, preventing penetration by other sperm.

✦ The head of the successful sperm cell basically explodes inside the egg, where Dad's genetic material interacts with Mom's. The egg now goes through one division and is no longer an ovum but a *zygote*, with all the genetic material it will ever have, half from Mom and half from Dad.

✦ The zygote is propelled down the fallopian tube by *cilia* (hairlike structures) on the tube walls. As the zygote's cells continue to divide, it becomes what's called a *blastocyst*. The blastocyst then enters the uterus, and—in the case of a successful pregnancy—implants in the wall of the uterus after 10 to 14 days. At this stage it becomes an *embryo*. There a placenta develops to nourish the embryo as it continues to go through the process of division and growth.

✦ By about the ninth week, the embryonic stage is over and the embryo becomes a *fetus*, which it remains until birth, at which time it becomes an *infant*.

THE THREE TYPES OF HUMAN HAIR

Lanugo. Fine hair that covers nearly the entire body of fetuses

Vellus hair. Short, fine "peach fuzz" that grows during prepuberty in most places on the human body

Terminal hair. Fully developed hair, which is generally longer, coarser, thicker, and darker than vellus hair

MAKING HONEY

For thousands of years, people have been harvesting honey, often for medicinal use. It's anti-microbial, meaning it discourages the growth of bacteria, mold, and viruses, which makes it a great salve for wounds. (The ancient Egyptians even used honey as an embalming agent.) As a food it's very nutritious, and has the added bonus of lasting for a very long time—years, if it's kept in a sealed container.

Here's how honey is made: A bee collects nectar from flowers until its *crop*, or honey stomach, is full. (Bees have two stomachs: one for storing honey and one for regular digestion.) Once back at the hive, it regurgitates the nectar, passing it to other bees, who also regurgitate the nectar, who ingest and regurgitate it for about 20 minutes, until enzymes in their saliva partially digest it. Next, they store the substance in wax combs (the wax is made from a secretion emitted by young male worker bees) and fan it with their wings until most of the liquid has evaporated. (Nectar is about 75 percent water.) Finally, they seal the comb with wax to keep the honey fresh until they're ready to eat it (the honey is their only food source during the winter). In one year, a colony of 40,000 bees might produce and eat 150 pounds of honey. And to make one pound, bees have to visit about two million flowers.

9 SPIDERS WITH BODY PARTS IN THEIR NAMES

Cat-faced spiders

White-mustached portia spiders

Long-jawed orb weaver spiders

Star-bellied orb weaver spiders

Thorn-finger spiders

Red-back spiders

Six-eyed sand spiders

Baldlegged spiders

Aqua-lung spiders

CHAPTER 22

STAR BRIGHTNESS: ABSOLUTE

On page 233, *apparent* brightness was explained. *Absolute* brightness measures brightness based on how much actual light energy celestial bodies emit, making up for the obvious shortcoming of *apparent* magnitude: Very large, powerful stars located far away from Earth can seem very faint, while weak but close stars can appear very bright. Absolute brightness, therefore, determines how bright any given star would appear from a set, standard distance, that being 10 parsecs (1 parsec = 3.26 light years). And remember: The lower the number, the brighter the star.

✦ The 7th brightest star on the apparent brightness scale, for example, is Capella, at 0.08m. The 8th brightest is Rigel, with an apparent brightness of 0.12m—but it's about 1,400 light-years away from us, while Capella is just 41 light-years away.

✦ Rigel is an enormous star, and its absolute brightness is -8.1M (a big "M" is used for absolute measurements), whereas Capella, also a giant star, is at just 0.4M.

✦ Other examples: The Sun has an absolute brightness of +4.8M. Sirius, to us just a tiny star in the sky compared to the Sun, is in reality much bigger and brighter, and has an absolute brightness of +1.45M.

✦ LBV 1806-20 is a very distant star located in the constellation Sagittarius. It's invisible to the naked eye and was spotted by the Hubble Space Telescope in the 1990s. Its absolute brightness is estimated to be -14.2M . Astronomers believe it may be five million—and possibly as many as 40 million—times brighter than the Sun.

THE SENSE OF SMELL

Technically called *olfaction*, smell is the act of detecting molecules of chemicals in the air (*odorants*) via specialized olfactory receptors called *odorant-binding proteins* located in the roof of the two nasal cavities, just below and between the eyes. Recent studies suggest that the average human has about 50 million receptors of as many as 1,000 different kinds, each designed to react to just a few chemicals. When an odorant molecule contacts the receptor area, it contacts several different receptor types, all of which send signals to the brain, which combines them all into a particular odor or odors. Just how those chemicals do this is not yet known.

BEHIND THE IRON CURTAIN

The term "Iron Curtain" describes the physical and ideological barrier that split Europe in half after World War II.

✦ British Prime Minister Winston Churchill first used the term in a May 12, 1945, telegram to President Harry S. Truman, in which he said of Eastern Europe: "An iron curtain is drawn down upon their front. We do not know what is going on behind." The term became widely popular after Churchill used it in the "Sinews of Peace" speech he made on March 5, 1946, at Westminster College in Fulton, Missouri.

✦ Churchill may well have heard the phrase in a May 2, 1945, radio broadcast by German politician Count Lutz Schwerin von Krosigk, who ominously said, "In the East, the iron curtain behind which, unseen by the eyes of the world, the work of destruction goes on, is moving steadily forward."

✦ But Count von Krosigk most likely saw the term in *Das Reich*, the weekly newsletter of Nazi propagandist Joseph Goebbels. On February 25, 1945, Goebbels attempted to rally demoralized German forces by painting a picture of what Europe would be like if they surrendered to the Soviet Union: "An iron curtain would fall over this enormous territory controlled by the Soviet Union, behind which nations would be slaughtered."

✦ The Eastern Bloc Communist countries behind the Iron Curtain were: the Soviet Union, East Germany (including the eastern half of Berlin), Czechoslovakia, Poland, Hungary, Bulgaria, Romania, and Albania. Albania broke away from the Eastern Bloc and aligned itself with China in 1960. Yugoslavia also had a Communist government but maintained friendly relations with the West and was not considered to be behind the Iron Curtain.

FOOD FOR THOUGHT. In 1992 Mikhail Gorbachev, the last president of the Soviet Union, gave a speech at Westminster College in Fulton, Missouri, declaring the end of the Cold War.

TUG-OF-WAR GOLD MEDALISTS

Tug-of-war was an Olympic sport from 1900 until 1920. Teams consisted of six men in 1900, five men in 1904, and eight men in the remaining years.

1900: Gold went to Denmark and Sweden (they played as a mixed team); silver went to France; and there was no bronze, because they were the only two teams.

1904: The United States won gold, silver, and bronze.

1908: Great Britain won all three medals.

1912: Just two teams competed, Sweden winning gold and Great Britain winning silver.

1916: Due to World War I, no Olympic games were held.

1920: Gold went to Great Britain, silver to the Netherlands, and bronze to Belgium.

19TH-CENTURY "BASE BALL" TERMS

Aces: Runs (also called *counts*)

Hands: Outs

Behind: Catcher

Club Nine: Team

Cranks: Fans

Dew drop: Slow pitch

Hurler: Pitcher

Match: Game

Muff: Error

Striker: Batter

Tally: Score

FOOD FOR THOUGHT. Before rubber was first used in 1887, home plate was made out of wood, iron, or marble.

JFK ON TJ

At a dinner honoring several Nobel Prize winners in 1962: "I think this is the most extraordinary collection of talent, of human knowledge, that has ever been gathered together in the White House—with the possible exception of when Thomas Jefferson dined alone."

NUCLEAR POWER PLANTS

There are 439 operating nuclear power plants (as of 2008) in 31 countries worldwide. They provide roughly 17% of the world's electricity. Number of plants by country:

Argentina (2)	Germany (17)	Slovenia (1)
Armenia (1)	Hungary (4)	South Africa (2)
Belgium (7)	India (17)	South Korea (20)
Brazil (2)	Japan (55)	Spain (8)
Bulgaria (2)	Lithuania (1)	Sweden (10)
Canada (18)	Mexico (2)	Switzerland (5)
China (11)	Netherlands (1)	Taiwan (6)
Czech Republic (6)	Pakistan (2)	Ukraine (15)
Finland (4)	Romania (2)	United Kingdom (19)
France (59)	Russia (31)	United States (104)
	Slovak Republic (5)	

CATCH-18, *CATCH-11*, *CATCH-14*, AND *CATCH-22*

The first chapter of *Catch-22*, Joseph Heller's 1961 satirical World War II novel, was actually published six years before the novel's release, in 1955, in the magazine *New World Writing*. The title: *Catch-18*. That remained the working title until publication time, when Heller's agent told him it had to be changed, as it might be confused with the just released Leon Uris novel, *Mila 18*, about the Warsaw ghetto uprising during World War II (Mila 18 was a street address). Heller considered *Catch-11*, then *Catch-14*, and finally settled on *Catch-22*. "I was heartbroken," Heller said in a 1975 interview. "I thought 18 was the only number." The new title didn't do the book any damage: In 1998 the Modern Library Association named it #7 in the list of the top 100 novels of the 20th century.

OUR BIG CUE BALL

If Earth were shrunk down to the size of a billiard ball, it would actually be *smoother*. From the highest mountains to the lowest deserts, the difference between peaks and valleys is proportionately less than that of the miniscule bumps and cracks on an average billiard ball.

ABSOLUTE DATING TECHNIQUES

On page 67, we talked about the techniques used by archaeologists to date ancient artifacts. Those were *relative* techniques. Here is some information on more modern and more specific *absolute* dating techniques:

Radio-Carbon Dating. Also known as *carbon dating*, this was developed by a team headed by Willard Libby at the University of Chicago in 1949 and can date organic artifacts—from once-living plants and animals—between about 1,000 and 50,000 years old. It is one of the most widely used techniques and is believed to be the most accurate. It relies on a simple natural phenomenon:

✦ Plants absorb carbon dioxide—CO_2—from the atmosphere during photosynthesis.

✦ There are three different kinds ("isotopes") of carbon in the CO_2: Carbon-12; carbon-13; and carbon-14. (See page 253 for an explanation of isotopes and ions.)

✦ The most common kind by far is C-12, which makes up about

99% of the carbon in the atmosphere. C-13 makes up about 1%, and C-14 exists only in trace amounts. That ratio is the same in plants that absorb the carbon, and in animals that eat them.

✦ Carbon dating involves C-12 and C-14 only. C-14 is radioactive. When a plant or animal dies, it is no longer absorbing the carbons, and it begins losing C-14 due to that radioactivity. C12 is not radioactive, so the amount of C-12 remains the same.

✦ Since the rate at which C-14 decays is known, measuring the ratio of C-14 to C-12 can establish how long ago a living thing died.

✦ C-14 radiates away half its mass (whatever that mass is) every 5,730 years. Hence, 5,730 years is the *half-life* of C-14. If you have a flower found in an ancient tomb, for example, you know that, if it were alive, it would have a fixed amount of C-14 compared to C-12. But you find that it has half that amount, knowing that C-14 has a half-life of 5,730 years, you therefore know that the flower died about 5,730 years ago. If it has a quarter the amount living things have—then you know it died 11,460 years ago. And so on.

✦ Dendrochronology is used to date wooden structures. How it works: Every year a tree adds a new layer of wood to its trunk and branches, creating a new, viewable "growth ring." The width of the rings vary depending on the amount of rain that fell in a given year, making events such as long droughts easily notable in the rings. Studying the rings in very old, living trees (such as the bristlecone pine, which grows in the American Southwest and can live for more than 4,000 years), as well as the rings in very old and long-dead trees, a ring-pattern timeline can be developed. Find an old wooden structure, and the rings viewable in its wood can be compared to the timeline and dated. Such timelines based on local trees have now been established in locations all over the world. (One in Ireland stretches back more than 10,000 years.)

✦ Racemization was developed in the 1960s and is used to date organic materials between 5,000 and 100,000 years old. How it works: All living things have proteins; all proteins are made of amino acids; and all amino acids come in what biologists term either a "left-handed" or "right-handed" form (in regards to how they react to light). When something is alive, its amino acids are almost exclusively in the "left-handed" form (nobody knows why), and when something dies they begin to slowly change into the "right-handed" form. (That process is called *racemization*.) This happens at a measurable rate, so, like many other techniques, a measurement of the ratio of left- to right-handed amino acids is taken to determine how long ago the organism died. Racemization is a popular technique used to date mummies.

26 SHAPES OF SMOKING PIPES

Dublin	Woodstock/Zulu
Half Bent Dublin	Liverpool
Square-shank Apple	Calabash
Skater	Lumberman
Poker	Canadian
Prince	Rhodesian
Egg	Volcano
Billiard	Pickaxe
Saddle Billiard	Churchwarden
Large Half-bent Billiard	Ukulele
Full Bent Billiard	Blowfish
Author	Square Bulldog
Bulldog	Quarter Bent Squat Bulldog

HOW TO MILK A COW

1. Wash the cow's teats with warm, soapy water (you don't know where that cow's teats have been). The warm water also helps "loosen" her milk. Pat the teats dry with a towel. Then wash your hands (the cow doesn't know where your hands have been).

2. Rub a small amount of udder cream or Vaseline in the palms of your hands. This lessens friction in the milking, which irritates the cow.

3. Place a bucket underneath the cow's teats and sit on a stool or squat beside the cow. (If she gets hostile, you can get away fast from that position.)

4. Firmly grasp the base of the teat (the part of the teat closest to the udder) in the ring finger, pinkie, and thumb of your left hand.

5. Gently pull down on the udder and teat in one motion. Don't yank, but be firm.

6. Continue until the teat looks deflated. Repeat on the other teats.

A WALK IN THE ARTS

Part two of a timeline of the major movements of Modern Art can be found on page 265.

- ✦ **Photorealism (1960–70s).** This movement evolved from Pop Art (see page 129). In it, painters reproduced photographs of everyday things—kitchens, cars, people—with the intent of making the painting so exactly like the photograph that you couldn't tell the two apart. The most prominent names in the movement: Richard Estes, Chuck Close, Audrey Flack, Malcolm Marley, and Charles Bell.

- ✦ **Minimalism (1960s–80s).** Alongside photorealism grew this abstract school of painting that strove for extreme simplification. The artist, emotion, and expression were left out of the painting, and usually only a couple primary colors and basic geometric shapes were used. This was a disorganized movement and one that wasn't self-proclaimed. The term was first used to describe a painter in the 1920s and was reapplied to the new movement that flourished in the 1960s. Some of the biggest names: Frank Stella, Richard Allen, Mel Bochner, Sol LeWitt, Agnes Martin, and John McCracken.

15 ANIMAL HEART RATES

On the average, in beats per minute:

Human: 60	**Chicken:** 275	**Pig:** 70
Cat: 150	**Horse:** 40	**Rabbit:** 205
Small dog: 100	**Monkey:** 192	**Elephant:** 30
Large dog: 75	**Canary:** 1,000	**Giraffe:** 65
Hamster: 450	**Cow:** 65	**Blue whale:** 20

THE DIFFERENCE BETWEEN...

Optometrists, Ophthalmologists, and Opticians. If you need your eyes checked, an optometrist (an O.D., or Doctor of Optometry) can give you a routine examination and prescribe vision correcting lenses. For more specialized care, you see an ophthalmologist, an M.D. who can prescribe drugs and perform surgery. Opticians manufacture and dispense corrective lenses.

FOR POSTERIOR-ITY

Every year in late October, people of the Pacific island nation of Samoa keep watch for the moment when thousands of blue-and-pink worms appear at the ocean's surface and engage in a gooey mating frenzy. That will last for only a few hours. They're waiting for the *palolo* worm, a small marine worm about six inches long that makes its home in shallow coral reefs in the tropics, including those around the Samoan islands. Once the wiggling worms arrive, people scoop them up with their nets and begin preparing them for the annual Palolo Festival. All throughout the islands, the worms are cooked in a variety of traditional ways (they're said to taste like caviar).

The ritual goes back centuries, but it wasn't until the 1800s that a biologist noticed that palolo worms weren't really worms, at least not *complete* worms—they had no heads. The explanation: Every spawning season, the palolo's posterior section becomes swollen with either sperm or eggs. Then, at virtually the same moment for thousands and thousands of worms in a colony, the wriggling posteriors break off from the rest of the worms and "swim" to the surface. After about an hour, the sacs burst, allowing the sperm and eggs to intermingle and fertilization to occur.

FOOD FOR THOUGHT. The headless worm posteriors are equipped with light-sensing organs; they can "see" the surface, which is always lighter than the depths, even at night. And the posterior-less worms below? They grow new posteriors and will repeat the mating ritual the next year.

INSTANT SHAKESPEARE: *THE TEMPEST*

Apart from comedy, tragedy, and history, some scholars lump a few of Shakespeare's plays into a fourth genre: late romance, which combines elements of comedy and tragedy. Like a comedy, *The Tempest* (1610) ends with reunited lovers, but unlike a comedy, it's not bouncy or farcical. And while bad things happen to characters, nobody dies (especially not the hero), so it's not a tragedy. Whatever it is, *The Tempest* is one of Shakespeare's weirdest plays.

The plot. Prospero is a sorcerer as well as the exiled duke of Milan. He lives on an island with Miranda, his daughter. Twelve years earlier, Prospero's brother Antonio and Alonso, the king of Naples, conspired to take the throne, and sent Prospero and Miranda adrift at sea on a boat. They're now stuck on the island with Ariel, a magical spirit, and Caliban, the son of a witch, both of whom begrudgingly work as Prospero's servants.

After a vision tells Prospero that a ship with his enemies aboard is headed his way, he creates a storm to destroy it. Ferdinand, Alonso's son, washes up on the island, and he and Miranda fall in love. Antonio, Alonso, Sebastian, and Gonzalo land on the other side of the island and begin to search for Ferdinand. Two more shipwrecked sailors, Stephano and Trinculo, meet Caliban, who tries to get them to help kill Prospero so that he, Caliban, may rule the island, promising Miranda to Stephano as a reward.

Prospero continues to use magic to torment his old enemies, summoning a feast (actually a mirage) and sending Ariel as a ghost to torment them for their sins against him. At a masquerade to celebrate the engagement of Ferdinand and Miranda, Caliban's plot is revealed and thwarted. Prospero confronts Antonio and Alonso, demanding that his dukedom be restored. Antonio agrees, Alonso is reunited with his son Ferdinand, and Prospero releases Ariel and Caliban from service.

Memorable line. "We are such stuff as dreams are made on, rounded with a little sleep." (Prospero, Act IV, Scene 1)

WORD SEARCH: *CORRIGENDUM*

Corrigenda (single *corrigendum*) are errors found in a printed work after printing has taken place. They're printed on a separate page in a list of *errata* (Latin for "errors"). The word comes from the Latin *corrigere*, "to correct." (For an example, please see the next printing of this book.)

PRESIDENT KING

Who was the 38th president of the United States? Leslie Lynch King Jr. He was born in 1913 to Leslie Lynch King Sr., and Dorothy Ayer Gardner, both of Omaha, Nebraska. Dorothy left the alcoholic and abusive King shortly after their son's birth, moving him to Oak Park, Illinois, to live with her sister. In 1916 she remarried and started calling her son by her new husband's name. He was from then on known as "Gerald Ford Jr." (The name change wasn't made official until 1935, when Ford was 22 years old.) Ford became president in 1974, upon the resignation of President Richard Nixon.

OLIVES

The California Olive Industry created these standardized sizes for the olive industry.

Small: 128 to 140 olives per pound

Medium: 106 to 121 per pound

Large: 95 to 105 per pound

Extra Large: 65 to 88 per pound

Jumbo: 51 to 60 per pound

Colossal: 41 to 50 per pound

Super Colossal: 26 to 40 per pound

HANUKKAH

Here's the traditional story of how the Jewish holiday came to be. In the second century B.C.E., Syria (which included parts of what is now Israel) was under Greek control and Jewish peoples were a persecuted minority. Temples were desecrated, practicing the religion was against the law, and adherents were even killed. In

165 B.C.E., a Jewish uprising successfully overthrew the Greeks and deposed the local governor, Antiochus. Afterwards, Jewish leaders rededicated the Temple in Jerusalem. The ceremony required lighting the *N'er Tamid*, or "eternal light," but there was only enough oil to burn for one day. Somehow, the lamp burned for eight days, and the ceremony was completed. Today, those eight days are commemorated with the eight-day festival of *Hanukkah* (which comes from a Hebrew word meaning "to dedicate"). A candle is lit on the first day, then another each subsequent day, in a special candelabrum called a *menorah*, until all eight candles are lit to honor the "miracle of light."

PARTS OF A HARDCOVER BOOK

✦ **Front board:** The technical name for the front cover

✦ **Top edge:** The top edge of the front board (also called the *head*)

✦ **Tail:** The bottom of the book (the part that touches the table when standing upright)

✦ **Endsheet:** The piece of paper that is pasted to the inside of the front board and makes up what constitutes the "first page" of a book. (There's another endsheet found at the back of the book.)

✦ **Pastedown:** The pasted half of the endsheet

✦ **Flyleaf:** The free half of the endsheet

✦ **Hinge:** The joint between the board and the spine

✦ **Spine:** The hinged back of the book

✦ **Headband:** The visible top and bottom edges of the cloth (often striped) covering the spine

✦ **Headcap:** The top of the spine, boards, and block when the book is standing upright (the tailcap is on the bottom)

✦ **Back board:** The technical name for the back cover

✦ **Square:** The top edge of the back board

✦ **Fore edge:** The part opposite the spine

✦ **Book block:** The inside pages (also called the *text block*)

SEIZURES

Seizures are malfunctions of the brain's electrical system that result in a disruption of the brain's—and therefore the body's—normal functions. The location of the malfunction determines what parts of the body will be affected and what type of seizure will occur.

✦ Seizures can have many causes, including head injury, drug abuse, and brain tumors. They can also have no apparent cause. People who have such unprovoked seizures on a reoccurring basis are diagnosed as *epileptic.*

✦ There are many types of seizures, but they're generally divided into two main groups: *Primary generalized seizures* begin with a widespread electrical discharge involving both sides of the brain simultaneously; *partial seizures* begin with an electrical discharge in one area of one hemisphere of the brain.

✦ A*bsence* seizures are a type of primary seizure that result in episodes of "staring into space" for a few seconds. The ability to respond is lost, and the eyes may roll up into the head. These used to be known as *petit mal* ("small illness" in French) seizures.

✦ *Atonic*, or "drop," seizures are a type of primary seizure that results in sudden loss of muscle control and a drop to the floor. They're usually over in seconds and don't result in loss of consciousness.

✦ *Tonic-clonic* seizures are the most severe. These primary seizures start with a sudden stiffening of all the body's muscles; air is forced from the lungs, resulting in a sharp cry or moan.

The victim loses consciousness and falls to the floor; the arms stiffen and the legs begin to jerk arrhythmically. The jerking stops slowly after a few minutes, or sometimes a little longer, and consciousness slowly returns. The victim is usually sleepy and cranky afterwards.

✦ *Simple partial seizures* don't result in a loss of consciousness, but victims are unable to speak or control their bodies, even though they're fully aware of their surroundings. Different muscles may move uncontrollably as the electrical activity moves around the brain. Intense feelings of fear, rage, or joy often accompany the seizure.

✦ *Complex partial seizures* affect a larger area of the brain. Although victims may remain standing and even walking, they are unaware of their surroundings and will not remember the event. These seizures often start with a blank stare followed by lip-pursing or hand-twitching, and can progress to larger unorganized movements, sometimes including running and screaming. They usually last less than two minutes, though they may cause confusion for hours afterward.

✦ The first medical writing on the subject of seizures was by the Greek physician Hippocrates almost 2,400 years ago. In *On the Sacred Disease*—which is what epilepsy was called at the time, because it was thought to be a curse or a blessing from the gods—he wrote, "It is thus with regard to the disease called Sacred: it appears to me to be nowise more divine nor more sacred than other diseases, but has a natural cause like other affections."

TECHNICALLY SPEAKING...

The Queen of England owns all of the sturgeons, whales, and dolphins in the waters surrounding the United Kingdom. The law comes from a 1324 edict of King Edward II that still stands today.

CHAPTER 23

MOTHER AND CHILD UNION

Researchers have long known that cells from a developing embryo can enter a pregnant mother's bloodstream by traveling the "wrong way" up the umbilical cord. What wasn't known until the 1990s is that such cells can remain in the mother for decades. Further study completed in 2004 found that they may be stem cells—cells found in developing embryos that can become any type of cell in our bodies—and they may employ that ability in a therapeutic way in formerly pregnant women. One of the women studied had sustained liver damage after contracting hepatitis C. Her liver had repaired itself—with cells of male origin. This was easily determined by the presence of the Y chromosome only found (normally) in males. The woman had birthed a male baby years earlier—and the fetal cells from that baby, which had remained in her body, migrated to the injured liver. Then they divided and became liver cells. "A pregnancy lasts forever," geneticist Diana Bianchi of Tufts University in Massachusetts said, "because every woman who has been pregnant carries these little souvenirs of the pregnancy for the rest of her life."

SPEAK LIKE A GENIUS

Who or Whom? The quick rule: "Who" is used as a subject, as in "Who rang the bell?"; "whom" is used as an object—something is happening to the subject, as in "For whom the bell tolls."

✦ If you're still not sure, replace the "who/m" in question with either "he" or "him." "He" is the equivalent of "who" (the subject) and "him" is the equivalent of "whom" (the object). For example, "For whom the bell tolls" would still work as "For *him* the bell tolls," but not as "For *he* the bell tolls." (For plural, use "they/them.")

✦ "Whom" may be on its way out as English continues to lose much of its formality. Even though the correct sentence is "Whom are you calling?", most people would say, "Who are you calling?"

WHERE DO WHALES GO?

Biologists believe that there are three major, geographically isolated populations of humpback whales, one in the North Atlantic, one in the North Pacific, and one in the Southern Ocean (surrounding Antarctica). They all travel thousands of miles within those cold-water regions during their summer feeding migrations, and every winter to several different breeding grounds in warmer waters.

✦ The North Atlantic group spends the summer between Iceland and Norway, and in winter migrates to the Caribbean to mate. The largest known breeding grounds are off the island of Hispaniola (home to the nations of the Dominican Republic and Haiti).

✦ The North Pacific group spends the summers in waters off northern California up to Alaska and western Russia. In the winter, three groups within this larger group travel to their own breeding grounds: off the coast of Baja California, both on the ocean side and in the Sea of Cortez; around the Hawaiian Islands from Kauai to Hawaii; and around Japan's southern islands and Taiwan.

✦ The Southern Ocean group spends summers around Antarctica. In winter, different groups migrate to different breeding grounds, including locations around Australia, and up both sides of the African and South American continents.

FOOD FOR THOUGHT. A fourth and unique population of humpbacks inhabits the Arabian Sea, primarily off the coast of Oman. They don't migrate, and are the only humpbacks known to both feed and breed in tropical waters.

TYPES OF SAUSAGE

There are more than 1,000 different types of sausage. (You can read a lot more about sausage on page 25). Ten standouts:

Andouillette. A mildly spiced, French smoked sausage, made with mustard, vinegar, onions, and pig tripe (stomach and colon). The words "not for everyone" are often associated with andouillette, as the aroma is said to resemble pig feces. Served hot or cold.

Banger. A British-cooked, mildly spiced pork (usually pork butt) sausage. Fried or boiled, commonly served in British pubs with mashed potatoes as "bangers and mash."

Blood sausage. Pig or cow blood is mixed with filler (breadcrumbs or oatmeal), onions, and spices, cooked until it congeals, and stuffed into casings. Nearly black in color, usually sautéed.

Boudin blanc, white boudin. French fresh white sausage made from pork and chicken—and fresh milk and cognac. Cooked and served hot. (The Cajun version mixes pork, chicken, onions, rice instead of milk, and brandy—and is much spicier.)

Chorizo. Spanish and Portuguese smoked, very spicy pork sausage seasoned with garlic, chiles, and paprika, and often containing other pig parts—such as cheeks, salivary glands, and lymph nodes. Though it's often served cold, it's sometimes used in soups and casseroles. (The Mexican version uses fresh pork and is popular in the U.S. mixed with eggs as a breakfast dish.)

Goetta. Originated with German immigrants near Cincinnati, Ohio, and made as a means to stretch out food supplies (as many sausages are), these are cooked, mild sausages made from pork (sometimes mixed with beef) and steel-cut oats. It's often called "Cincinnati Caviar."

Loukanika. Greek fresh sausage made with lamb, pork, wine, spices (especially fennel seeds), and grated orange rind. Usually sliced and sautéed.

Saucisse de Sanglier. French game sausage made with wild boar and pork and flavored with red wine, apples, and cranberries.

Toulouse. Thick, long, fresh French sausage made with coarsely ground pork, sometimes with smoked bacon, wine, and pepper.

Weisswurst (white sausage). Mild, fresh, white sausage originally made in Munich, Germany. Made from lean calf meat, bacon, lemon, and parsley, as well as other spices. An Oktoberfest staple, usually eaten with potato salad (and beer).

ODD ANIMAL FACT

Virginia opossums, the only marsupials (mammals with pouches, such as kangaroos) found in North America, are one of the few mammals in the world that have an odd number of nipples. They are located on the female's belly, inside the pouch, and are arranged in a circle of 12 with one extra in the middle.

MOHS HARDNESS SCALE

In 1812 German mineralogist Friedrich Mohs developed a scale to measure the hardness of different materials. He based it on ten commonly used minerals. Here they are, from softest to hardest:

1. Talc: used in talcum powder

2. Gypsum: used in plaster of Paris

3. Calcite: found in limestone

4. Fluorite: used in the manufacture of steel and glass

5. Apatite: found in tooth enamel and most types of rock

6. Feldspar: found in granite

7. Quartz: quartz crystals

8. Topaz: gemstone

9. Corundum: found in sapphires and used in abrasives

10. Diamond

The scale works by determining the hardest material on the list that another material can scratch. For example, a human fingernail can scratch gypsum (#2) but can't scratch calcite (#3). Human fingernails therefore have a hardness of 2.5 on the Mohs scale. Window glass can scratch apatite (#5) but not feldspar (#6)—and has a hardness of 5.5. Because the relative hardnesses of the minerals are not mathematically proportional, the Mohs scale is very simplistic. Gypsum is twice as hard as talc, but diamond in nearly four times as hard as corundum. The scale is, however, still used today as a relative hardness measurement.

ART AND MUDSLIDES

✦ Several major archaeological finds have been made possible by mudslides. They include the discovery of one of the most famous statues from ancient Greece: the 2,500-year-old life-size bronze known as "The Charioteer of Delphi." (Most other bronze statues of the era were melted down long ago.) It was erected in around 470 B.C.E. in the Greek city of Delphi, and was once part of a group of statues that included the chari-oteer's horses. It was buried in a mudslide at some point in its history and lay protected until archaeologists uncovered it in 1896.

✦ In 2003 an ancient *necropolis*—literally "city of the dead"— was discovered under the Vatican. It contains the tombs of more than 250 Romans, rich and poor, from the first through fourth centuries C.E., and is lined with mosaics, frescoes, tombstones, inscriptions, and sculptures. It was deluged by a mudslide sometime after the 4th century and was dis-covered during the construction of a parking lot. It is now a museum.

TOURETTE'S SYNDROME FACTS

✦ Tourette's Syndrome (TS) is a neurological syndrome char-acterized by multiple, repeated, involuntary movements and vocalizations known as *tics*.

✦ TS tics are not simple "twitches," such as those of an eyelid, but involve movements of more than one muscle, such as an entire arm. They can be fast or slow, quick or *tonic* (held). The most extreme tend to be complex patterns of large motions: hopping, twisting, grimacing, or a combination of these movements. Vocally, they can be anything from throat-clearing to complete words or sentences.

✦ There is no test for TS. The syndrome is diagnosed if a patient has multiple, changing patterns of tics for at least 12 months; if the onset of symptoms began before age 18; and if the symptoms cause social impairment or distress.

✦ Fewer than 15% of people with TS exhibit *coprolalia*, an involuntary compulsion to use socially unacceptable words, or *coprolaxia*, a compulsion for obscene gestures, such as grabbing one's crotch.

✦ Tics usually peak between ages 10 and 12, and the syndrome often improves in the late teens and early 20s. Male TS patients outnumber female patients three to one.

✦ Symptoms may wane or disappear for months at a time, after which new tics may appear.

✦ Although TS is considered a genetic disorder, the genes associated with it have not yet been identified.

✦ Many people with TS show signs of other syndromes, such as Attention Deficit Hyperactivity Disorder and Obsessive Compulsive Disorder.

✦ The condition was named for French physician Georges Gilles de la Tourette (1859–1904) by one of his students.

THE DIFFERENCE BETWEEN...

Centipedes and millipedes. It has nothing to do with the number of legs they have. Centipede means "100 feet" in Latin—and different centipede species have from 28 to 358 legs. Millipede means "1,000 feet"—and they have from 22 to 750 legs. The real differences: centipedes have one pair of legs per body segment; millipedes have two. Centipedes are venomous and are almost exclusively carnivores, eating insects; millipedes are almost exclusively *detritivores*, meaning they eat detritus—decomposed organic matter. In addition, centipedes can and do bite humans (and the venom from many species can cause substantial pain), whereas millipedes lack structures to bite and are harmless to humans.

Alligators and crocodiles. The most noticeable difference is jaw shape: Alligators have wide, U-shaped snouts, and crocodiles tend to have more pointed, V-shaped snouts. And alligators' upper jaws are wider than their lower jaws, so when their mouths are closed, the teeth in the upper jaws are visible, while the teeth in the lower jaws are not. Crocodiles' upper and lower jaws, on the other hand, are about the same width and when the mouth is closed, several lower teeth overlap the upper jaws and are visible. Also: there are just two existing alligator species, the American alligator, native to the southeastern United States; and the extremely endangered Chinese alligator, native only to the Yangtzee River. There are 23 existing species of crocodile, and they're found in tropical waters in Africa, Asia, the Americas, and Australia.

WHY WE VOTE FOR SENATORS

The right of U.S. citizens to vote for senators is so taken for granted that many people find it hard to believe that this wasn't always the case. But in fact, for more than the first 120 years of the United States' existence, regular citizens did not choose their senators—politicians did.

✦ This was part of the "Great Compromise" forged at the Constitutional Convention in 1787. One of the most difficult issues to get delegates to agree on was how to ensure that the federal government would not infringe on the power of the states. All of the 13 states already had their *own* constitutions. In a way, they were all little nations of their own, and they had just won their independence from the oppression of England's powerful central government.

✦ The compromise stipulated that the elected legislators from each state, rather than the people of each state, would elect their two senators. (This is known as an *indirect election*.) This gave the states, as entities, direct representation in Washington. Senators were basically their states' ambassadors to the federal government. Members of the House of Representatives, on the other hand, would be directly elected by the people, and would, therefore, represent the peoples' interests.

✦ There were problems with this system, however, a major one being "deadlock." If members of a state legislature couldn't agree on their senatorial choices, they simply didn't get senators. And it happened: New York didn't have senate representation in the very first Congress for three months, and deadlock became increasingly common in the late 19th century.

✦ Another problem: The U.S. was designed to be a government "of, for, and by the people." So why were politicians, not the people, choosing representatives?

✦ Resentment toward indirect elections built up in the early 1900s and led to the passing of the 17th Amendment to the Constitution in 1913, making direct election the means by which senators are chosen. It is, of course, still the way it is done today.

THREE LAWS OF ROBOTICS

Devised by science fiction author Isaac Asimov and first presented in his 1942 short story, "Runaround," these are the unofficial "rules" by which humans (if science ever gets around to making advanced robots) should program their robots and robots should, accordingly, behave.

First Law: A robot may not injure a human being or, through inaction, allow a human being to come to harm.

Second Law: A robot must obey the orders given to it by human beings except where such orders would conflict with the First Law.

Third Law: A robot must protect its own existence as long as such protection does not conflict with the First or Second Law.

MIND YOUR MANNERS (1948)

In 1948, *Vogue* magazine published an etiquette book that included this list of rules that children should learn by the time they turned 10. Here they are:

1. Say "How do you do?" and "Goodbye"; and, even more important, look at the one they are shaking hands with.

2. Bow (for boys) and curtsey (for girls), whenever they say, "How do you do?" or "Good-bye" to adults.

3. Say "Yes, thank you" and "No, Mummy" and "Yes, Mrs. Smith," not just "Yes" and "No."

4. Say "Thank you for a very nice afternoon" or, "Thank you, I had a lovely time" when they say good-bye to their hostess.

5. Do not interrupt older people.

6. Wait at doorways until older people have gone through. Boys should also learn to let girls precede them.

7. Take hats off in the house or when talking to older people; this, of course, for boys.

8. Answer when they are spoken to.

9. Eat neatly, without dawdling and without argument.

10. Be scrupulously polite to nurses, maids, waiters—to anyone who receives wages in return for service. The kind of rudeness which should never be tolerated is that which refers to the fact that these people are employed.

ONE BILLION YEARS AGO...

Earth completed one rotation in just 18 hours. The Moon was much closer and completed its orbit in just 20 days, making a month about a third shorter than it is now. One billion years later—in other words, today—the Moon is still spiraling away from us…at a rate of about 1.6 inches per year.

THE RISE AND FALL OF MERCURY

✦ Mercury is one of the 94 naturally occurring chemical elements. In its pure form, it's a silver-white, shiny, odorless liquid and is the only metal that is liquid at room temperature. In nature, it is rarely found in its free form; it commonly combines with other elements, such as chlorine and sulfur, to form minerals.

✦ As long as 4,000 years ago, humans discovered that heating a red rock we know today as *cinnabar* or *mercury sulfide* resulted in the extraction of a shiny liquid. Ancient peoples were transfixed by the substance. The ancient Chinese, Hindus, Egyptians, and Greeks, among many others, believed it had medicinal powers and used it both topically and internally.

✦ The name "mercury" is derived from the ancient Roman God Mercury, known for his speed. Romans also called it *hydrargyrum*, which meant "liquid silver" (this is the source of its chemical symbol, Hg). It was also called *quicksilver*, which dates to the 11th century and meant "living silver" in Middle English.

✦ In 1643 mercury was used in the world's first barometer; in 1714 it was used in the first thermometer. Why mercury? Because it's very sensitive to changes in atmospheric pressure and temperature, both of which cause it to expand or contract. Also, it doesn't freeze in normal temperature ranges.

✦ In the 1800s, many people in Europe and the U.S., including Abraham Lincoln, took "Blue Mass" pills—sugar, licorice root, glycerin, and mercury—as a laxative. Some historians have speculated that the toxin was the cause of Lincoln's well-known depression.

✦ After 1900, mercury began to be used in lightbulbs, explosives, batteries, medicines, pesticides, and was used in paper, glass, and plastic manufacturing, among many other things.

✦ By the 1980s, increasing awareness of mercury's toxicity slowed its use dramatically. The largest mercury mine in the world, in Almaden, Spain, went out of business in 2000 due to falling demand.

✦ A mercury poem:

> Little Willy from his mirror
> Licked the mercury right off,
> Thinking in his childish error
> It would cure the whooping cough.
> At his funeral his mother
> Brightly said to Mrs. Brown:
> "Twas a chilly day for Willy
> When the mercury went down."

(Harry Graham, *Ruthless Rhymes for Heartless Homes*, 1899)

THE DIFFERENCE BETWEEN...

Revolve and rotate. The two words are often used interchangeably—and incorrectly. Scientifically speaking, *revolution* is the movement of a body around a point outside that body, an example being that Earth revolves around the Sun. *Rotation* is the movement of a body around a point within that body, such as Earth rotating on its axis. Some examples: A spinning top rotates; two dancers revolve around each other; a merry-go-round rotates—but the people riding on it revolve around the center.

FOOD FOR THOUGHT. The cylinder on the handgun known as a "revolver" doesn't revolve; it rotates around a shaft that has its own axis. The gun is known as a revolver because the bullets that are loaded into the cylinder revolve around the shaft.

MORE FOOD FOR THOUGHT. According to biographer Barry

Miles, author of *Paul McCartney: Many Years From Now*, alternate names proposed for the 1966 Beatles' album *Revolver* included *Magic Circles, Abracadabra, Pendulums, Beatles on Safari*, and *Fat Man and Bobby*. *Revolver* was finally chosen, he wrote, and "did not mean a gun, but something that revolves, like a record." (Records, however, don't revolve—they rotate.)

MEDICAL PREFIXES AND SUFFIXES

There are literally thousands of Greek- and Latin-based prefixes and suffixes used in medical terminology. Here are just a few, with their meanings (and examples):

-algia: "pain" (myalgia, or muscle pain, and nostalgia, from the Greek for "pain of returning home")

an-: "without" (anemia, insufficient blood or red blood cells in the body)

brachy-: "short" (brachydactyly, or abnormally short fingers and toes)

-crine: "to secrete" (endocrine glands secrete hormones)

-emia: "in the blood" (leukemia, anemia)

endo-: "inside" (endocrine glands secrete inside the body; *exo-*crine glands, such as sweat glands, secrete out of the body)

hema/hemo-: "blood" (hematoma, or a bruise filled with blood)

leuk-: "white" (leukemia, a disease of the white blood cells)

myo-: "muscle" (myopathy, any disease of the muscle tissue)

-oma: "tumor" or "swelling" (melanoma)

-rrhage: "burst forth" (hemorrhage, bleeding)

-rrhea: "flowing," "discharge" (diarrhea, gonorrhea)

xanth-: "yellow" (xanthoma, a fat-cell tumor that causes yellow nodules in the skin)

WATER ON THE...

...lungs is the common name for a condition known as *pleural effusion*, characterized by overproduction of pleural fluid, which is found in sacs around the lungs.

...knee is the name used to describe a buildup of fluid in or around the knee joint, resulting in swelling and sometimes a large bump in the knee area. Different kinds of fluid can be involved, depending on the condition causing it. Related conditions: arthritis, gout, cancer, simple injury, and bursitis. In the case of bursitis, the fluid is an oily substance that comes from the *bursa sacs*, small fluid-filled sacs found especially near joints that allow muscles and tendons to slide over bone smoothly.

...elbow is basically the same as water on the knee.

...brain is the common name for *hydrocephalus*, an excessive buildup of cerebrospinal fluid in the brain. It is often caused by premature birth and can result in severe enlargement of the head, seizures, and brain damage. It can also be caused later in life by disease or injury.

4 BIG WORDS

✦ **Calumny** is a false charge meant to harm another's reputation, or the act of uttering such a false charge. It dates to the 15th century and has its origin in the Latin *calumnia*, from *calvi*, for "to deceive."

✦ **Progenitor** means "direct ancestor," and can be used in reference to biology or popular culture. For example, "Edgar Allan Poe's *Murders in the Rue Morgue* is considered the progenitor of the modern detective novel."

✦ **Juggernaut** entered the English language in the 1630s as a term used to describe enormous decorated wagons—more than 40 feet tall—built by Hindus in rituals worshipping the god Krishna. It was a corruption of the Sanskrit name for Krishna: Jagannatha. "Juggernaut" evolved to become the name of any large truck, then to anything likened to an unstoppable force that crushes everything in its way.

✦ **Salubrious.** If you just took a large gulp of salubrious air… good for you. *Salubrious* means "healthful" or "wholesome." It comes from the Latin *salubris*, similar to *salvus*, meaning "safe" and "healthy," and it appeared in English in the mid-1500s. Other uses: taking a salubrious walk in the woods; going to a salubrious health spa; and remembering, with a mix of regret and nostalgia, a rather *in*salubrious era of your youth.

GODWIN'S LAW

In 1990 Mike Godwin, a lawyer and frequent user of Usenet, an early Internet discussion forum, made this observation about the often inflammatory comments people made: "As a Usenet discussion grows longer, the probability of a comparison involving Nazis or Hitler approaches one." That became known as "Godwin's Law" and it's still frequently cited today—especially during inflammatory discussions on the Internet.

Extra: Another early Usenet user named Richard Sexton is said to have written in 1989—a year earlier than Godwin's statement—"You can tell a Usenet discussion is getting old when one of the participants drags out Hitler and the Nazis." This led many to claim that Godwin stole the idea from Sexton…and that, in turn, led to heated Internet discussions on the issue, during which several people were compared to Hitler and the Nazis.

CHAPTER 24

EINSTEIN'S BRAIN

In 1955 pathologist Thomas Stoltz Harvey of Princeton Hospital in New Jersey performed an autopsy on the recently deceased Albert Einstein. It wasn't an ordinary autopsy: Harvey removed Einstein's brain, weighed it, measured it, photographed it, cut most of it into slices, and preserved it. Whether or not Einstein had requested this remains disputed, though his family maintained they knew nothing about it. In any case, Harvey was fired—but he took the brain with him when he left. Harvey disappeared from the public eye for more than two decades.

✦ In 1978 a young magazine writer in New Jersey named Steven Levy was given a strange assignment: Find Einstein's brain. He tracked down Dr. Harvey to Wichita, Kansas, and visited him. Levy wrote: "At first he didn't want to tell me anything, but after a while he finally admitted that he had the brain. After a longer while, he sheepishly told me it was in the very office we were sitting in. He walked to a box labeled 'Costa Cider' and pulled out two big Mason jars. In those were the remains of the brain that changed the world." (Levy is now an acclaimed author and former editor of *Newsweek*.) The huge media storm caused by the story attracted numerous biologists who wanted a chance to study the brain. A handful have gotten the chance.

✦ In 1985 Dr. Marian Diamond of the University of California at Berkeley compared it to other brains that she had on hand and found only one unusual aspect: "an above-average number of *glial* cells (which nourish neurons) in those areas of the left hemisphere thought to control mathematical and linguistic skills." This led some to believe that the neurons in this area of Einstein's brain were "super-nourished," though biologists disagree on whether that would actually have any effect on intelligence.

✦ In 1996 Harvey gave the brain back to Princeton Hospital, and in 1999 scientists at McMaster University in Ontario, Canada, were allowed to study it. They also compared the brain to others, and reported that Einstein's lacked a particular wrinkle, known as the *parietal operculum*, common to most brains. The missing wrinkle allowed the areas on either side of it, the *inferior parietal lobes*, to grow larger than normal, making the brain about 15% wider than average. That, the researchers said, may have allowed for easier transmission of neural activity between the two lobes, regions known to be related to mathematical and spatial reasoning.

✦ Those studies, and the few others done since, found nothing conclusive about the brain that would explain Einstein's genius. The brain is still at Princeton Hospital, so maybe we'll find out more someday.

HIGHLIGHTS OF WOMEN'S SUFFRAGE

✦ In 1755 the Mediterranean island of Corsica declared its independence from the Republic of Genoa in Italy and henceforth became the first nation to grant universal voting rights to women. Corsica was taken over by France in 1769, however, and that right was taken away.

✦ In 1776 the independent colony of New Jersey granted women the right to vote, as long as they owned property. (It also granted voting rights to property-owning blacks.) Both were rescinded in 1807.

✦ In 1893 New Zealand became the first major independent nation to grant universal suffrage to all citizens over 18 years of age (although women could not hold office until 1919).

✦ In 1920 women received the right to vote in the United States.

✦ In 1990 women in the Canton of Appenzell Innerrhoden received the right to vote in local elections, making universal suffrage, for the first time, a reality in all of Switzerland.

✦ In July 2008, women gained full suffrage rights in Bhutan.

✦ There are five countries in the world today where women's right to vote is restricted: In Lebanon women must provide proof of elementary education (not required of men); in Saudi Arabia, women are banned from voting; in Vatican City, the only elections held are by the cardinals when electing a new pope (women are not allowed to be cardinals); the United Arab Emirates and Brunei (located on the island of Borneo) are monarchies, and while elections are held for an "advisory council" in the UAE, neither men nor women in either country are allowed to vote for their leaders.

HOUSEHOLD GENIUS

Use old tissue boxes to store plastic grocery bags and then "pop" one out whenever you need it. To make an even larger plastic bag dispenser: Take a large plastic bottle and cut a small, rectangular hole in the bottle's side. Reinforce the edges of the hole with packing tape to prevent snagging. Put bags in through the top, and pull them out through the rectangular hole as they're needed.

PLASTIC FANTASTIC GENIUS

✦ In May 2008, Daniel Burd, a 16-year-old from Waterloo, Ontario, decided he wanted to do something about the problem created by plastic bags: Nearly half a billion are produced every year, and most end up in landfills, where they can take up to 1,000 years to *biodegrade*—break down by being consumed by microorganisms. (Many also end up in the ocean. See page 16 for that.)

✦ Burd had a simple and ingenious idea: Maybe there was a way to speed up the process. To find out, he had to figure out a way to isolate the microorganisms that break down plastic and then find a way to produce them in a concentrated form.

✦ He ground several plastic bags into powder and mixed the powder with different amounts of household chemicals and yeast (to encourage microbe growth), carefully measuring the rate at which the plastic degraded. After three months, he finally had a culture with a high concentration of plastic-eating microbes.

✦ Burd put equal amounts of the culture into three small containers along with carefully weighed pieces of plastic bag. He also put pieces of plastic into three containers *without* the culture.

✦ In six weeks, the plastic in the culture weighed an average of 17% less than the strips without it—meaning that the microbes were eating the plastic, and quickly. Further experiments with specific bacteria strains and temperature alterations upped it to 46%.

✦ In May 2008, Burd took his experiment to the Canada-Wide
Science Fair in Ottawa, Quebec—and won the $10,000 first
prize and a $20,000 scholarship. He hopes to use the money
to continue his experiments, and that one day plastic-eating
industrial plants will be devouring plastic bags—not in a
millennium, but in as little as three months. (Let's hope he's
right.)

THE FIVE MAJOR EXTINCTIONS

The National Wildlife Federation estimates that nearly 30,000
species per year—about three per hour—go extinct, many from
manmade causes such as pollution and habitat destruction.
Many biologists believe this could be the "sixth extinction," the
latest in a series of mass disappearances of species and ecosystems. There have been five mass extinctions in Earth's past,
caused by major natural disasters that altered normal climatic
or geologic patterns. The five major extinctions were:

1. The Ordovician-Silurian Extinction, which took place about
440 million years ago, was a result of climate change caused by
sudden global cooling, particularly in the tropical oceans. There
was little or no life on land at the time, but nearly 25% of marine
families disappeared (a family contains anywhere from a few to
thousands of species).

2. The Late Devonian Extinction occurred about 370 million years
ago. Possible reasons: asteroid collisions that triggered volcanic lava floods, or environmental changes due to tectonic plate
movements in the early formation of the continents. Another
theory: the "Devonian Plant Hypothesis," which claims that
the expansion of plant life on land caused the death of 22% of
animal life in the oceans.

3. The Permian-Triassic Extinction, about 250 million years ago,
was the deadliest mass extinction. Paleontologists once believed
that this "Great Dying" took millions of years to occur, but many

now think it took between 8,000 and 100,000 years, barely a blip on the geological timetable. The impact and explosion of a *bolide* (a large meteor) the size of Mount Everest might have accelerated the climate change that was already taking place as a result of greenhouse gases released by volcanic lava floods and tectonic plate shifts. In all, 95% of existing species, including 53% of marine families and 70% of land species (plants, insects and early vertebrate animals), were wiped out.

4. The End Triassic Extinction happened 200 to 215 million years ago, soon after dinosaurs and mammals first evolved, and is the most mysterious of the five mass extinctions. In addition to the 22% of marine families that were lost, an unknown number of vertebrate land-animal species also went extinct. Causes similar to the previous Permian-Triassic Extinction are suspected, including volcanic lava floods, shifting continents, and bolide explosions.

5. The Cretaceous-Tertiary Extinction, the most recent and best-known of the five mass extinctions, occurred about 65 million years ago. One or several bolide collisions are probably to blame, which caused lava floods that so completely disrupted Earth's ecosystems that many terrestrial and marine species rapidly went extinct. The extinction killed 16% of marine families and 18% of vertebrate families on land, including—most famously—the dinosaurs.

10 CLOSEST STARS TO EARTH

1. The Sun (0.000016 light-years)

2. Proxima Centauri (4.2 light-years)

3. Alpha Centauri A (4.3 light-years)

4. Alpha Centauri B (4.3 light-years)

5. Barnard's Star (5.96 light-years)

6. Wolf 359 (7.6 light-years)

7. Lalande (8.11 light-years)

8. Alpha Sirius (8.7 light-years)

9. Beta Sirius (8.7 light-years)

10. A Luyten (8.93 light-years)

CANCER BASICS, PART II

On page 169, we learned that cancer is a genetic disease, a defining characteristic being gene mutations. A gene that is mutated is one whose biochemical structure has been altered. One of the molecules that comprises it is in the wrong location, is missing altogether, or has been duplicated, or the like. There are many ways mutations can happen—many more than are known. Some that are known:

Inheritance. The nucleus of a human egg cell contains 23 chromosomes—long, chainlike molecules of DNA. When fertilized, those 23 chromosomes chemically bond and "pair up" with 23 chromosomes located in the nucleus of the sperm cell. As we grow, that collection of DNA is duplicated and passed into every single cell in our bodies. If your parents had any mutated genes, you will have that exact same mutation on that exact same gene in every cell of your body. If they are the right (or wrong) genes, it could lead to the development of a cancer. This is also how other genetic diseases occur. Most of them, like Huntington's disease and sickle cell anemia, can occur *only* through inheritance. Cancer, on the other hand, most often arises from mutations that occur later in life.

Ultraviolet (UV) radiation. All light travels as photons, ultra-small packets of energy. Visible light travels as photons that are the wrong "size" to enter skin cells. UV light, which we can't see, has photons that are just the right size and can penetrate skin cells and even enter their nuclei. (That's why the sun feels warm, and why our skin tans and burns.) Inside the nuclei, UV photons can directly affect molecules that make up a gene, altering their molecular structure. Enough damage on the wrong genes, and this can lead to skin cancer.

Smoking. Tobacco smoke contains at least 43 carcinogenic agents that biochemically interact with DNA molecules and alter their structure. Smoking is linked to more than 10 different cancers, including lung, stomach, and colon cancer.

Asbestos. *Mesothelioma* is cancer that affects the body's mesothelium, the cells that line most organs. Asbestos can cause this, most commonly within the lining of the lungs. Exactly how this happens is not known, but it is believed that asbestos fibers are so small that they can enter cell nuclei and actually cause physical damage to genes, resulting in mutations.

Viruses. Viruses are also small enough to enter nuclei and interact with genes (it's how all viruses, even the ones that cause the common cold, work). Some viruses are known to cause mutations that can lead to cancer.

GREEN DIAMONDS

✦ In 1904 British scientist Sir William Crookes buried several small diamonds in radioactive radium bromide salts. They turned green. The color change affected only the surface and took months to occur. And the diamonds were unsafe for wearing—they were radioactive.

✦ In 1942 researchers at a particle accelerator in Michigan tried again. This time they were able to irradiate and change the color of diamonds in just days, and their radioactivity was gone within a few hours. These diamonds were also green, but by the 1960s, irradiation and processes involving extreme heating allowed for the sale of green, blue, yellow, brown, red, and black diamonds. And diamonds of all these colors can be found in nature, too, as a result of being naturally irradiated or heated.

SURVIVING A POISONOUS SNAKEBITE

What not to do:

✦ Don't try to suck the venom out with your mouth—it can enter the bloodstream through your digestive system and poison you.

✦ Don't put ice on the wound—it will make it more difficult to remove the venom.

✦ Don't cut around the wound—it may cause infection.

✦ Don't try to catch the snake so a doctor can identify it—you could easily get bitten again.

What to do:

✦ A snake can't poison what it can't get its fangs through, so if you're hiking anywhere that venomous snakes are known to inhabit, wear long pants and high-top hiking boots, not shorts and sandals. Although few snakes will attack unprovoked, simply stepping over a bush could be enough to startle an unseen viper and cause it to strike.

✦ Carry a snakebite kit in your first-aid kit whenever you're out hiking, or keep one at home if poisonous snakes live in your area. The kit comes with a suction device and detailed instructions.

✦ If you do get bitten, assume the snake is poisonous unless you are 100% certain that it isn't. One general rule: Most (but not all) poisonous snakes have triangular heads that resemble a shovel.

✦ Wash the affected area with water (and soap if possible).

✦ If you don't have a snakebite kit, the most important thing to do is stay calm. The faster your heart beats, the more quickly the poison will spread through your bloodstream, so take long, deep breaths.

✦ Immobilize the bite, and keep it below the heart to decrease blood flow. To minimize the flow of venom to the rest of the body, wrap a bandage or cloth between the heart and the bite, no more than four inches away from the bite. Be careful not to tie it too tight—cutting off the blood flow completely could damage an artery or limb. You should be able to fit one finger between skin and bandage. Loosen the bandage for about 30 seconds every five minutes.

✦ Get to a hospital as soon as possible. The longer you wait, the more the venom may spread through your body, increasing the chances of a severe reaction.

WORD SEARCH: *PARCHMENT*

In the third and second centuries B.C.E., the Greek city of Pergamon (in modern-day Turkey) housed one of the era's greatest libraries, home to more than 200,000 books. That was too many, according to the jealous keepers of the other great library of the time, in Alexandria, Egypt. So in about 190 B.C.E. the Egyptians put an embargo on Egyptian papyrus, the most popular writing medium of the time. That forced the Greeks in Pergamon to use the ancient technique of writing on prepared animal hides. They started referring to the material as *pergamenon*, meaning "of Pergamon." The Romans later took that word to Latin as *pergamenum*; in Old French it became *perchemin*; and sometime in the 1300s it came to English as *parchment*. It still refers to the skin of an animal (usually a sheep or goat) that's used to write on, but has evolved to also refer to any thick paper meant to resemble animal hide. And it's not the same as leather because parchment isn't tanned—it's simply stretched and scraped and allowed to dry, making it very thin and usually translucent.

THE WIZARD OF OZ AND POLITICS

In speaking about his book *The Old Man and the Sea,* Ernest Hemingway said that "there isn't any symbolism. The sea is the sea. The old man is the old man. What goes beyond is what *you* see." He meant that writers just write the books and anything deeper is subject to individual interpretation. In 1964 *American Quarterly* published Henry M. Littlefield's "*The Wizard of Oz*: Parable on Populism," which described hidden meanings in the book as it related to the politics of turn-of-the-century America, when L. Frank Baum wrote the book. Among Littlefield's concoctions:

✦ **The Wicked Witch of the East** represented barons of industry and the banks.

✦ **Munchkins,** oppressed by the Witch, represented the working class.

✦ **The Scarecrow** was a stand-in for naive farmers.

✦ **The Tin Man** represented overworked industrial laborers.

✦ **The Cowardly Lion** was a thinly veiled attack on William Jennings Bryan, the 1896 Populist presidential candidate.

✦ **Dorothy's ruby slippers** were silver slippers in the books. (The producers of the movie made them ruby red so they'd be more photogenic and colorful.) The silver slippers were a reference to the Populist Party's solution for the economic woes: unlimited production of silver-based coinage.

Over the years, Littlefield's interpretations were reprinted in economic and literature textbooks without crediting Littlefield, leading many people to believe that the symbolism was actually the work of—and the intent of—L. Frank Baum. Whether or not Baum intended that symbolism is a mystery; he never publicly admitted to it.

WHY YOUR TEA WASN'T PERFECT

It may just be a cup of tea to you, but to the British, it's a science.

Reason #1. You didn't use fresh water: The most important thing about tea water is the "O" in the "H_2O." Oxygen is what "roughs up" the tea leaves and causes them to release their flavor. Using water that was previously boiled, or hot water from the tap that has been sitting in a hot-water tank and losing oxygen, or water that's been boiled too long all result in flat tea. Use fresh, cold water.

Reason #2. You didn't "take the teapot to the kettle." You want the water to be boiling the moment it hits the tea, so take the teapot to the stove and pour the water into it straight from the kettle.

Reason #3. You didn't warm your teapot. While you're preparing the tea, fill the teapot with hot water and pour it out just before you're ready to brew the tea. This prevents a cold teapot from cooling the water too quickly and shortening the brewing time.

Reason #4. You overbrewed or underbrewed the tea. Steep the leaves too long and bitter-tasting tannins are released. Steep them too quickly and the desired flavors aren't given enough time to be released. Optimum brewing time: three to five minutes in a kettle; one to two minutes in a cup.

Reason #5. You used tea bags. Loose tea is able to circulate in the pot and the flavor is more easily extracted.

Reason #6. You poured milk into the teacup after you poured the tea. This is a disputed point among tea drinkers, especially the British. Many say you should pour milk into the cup first. That way, the hot tea combines with the milk slowly, preventing the milk from being scalded.

Reason #7. You poured milk into the teacup before the tea. Most Britons say it's the other way around, and no less an authority than acclaimed British author George Orwell (*Nineteen Eighty-Four*) wrote about it: "This is one of the most controversial points of all; indeed in every family in Britain there are probably two schools of thought on the subject. The milk-first school can bring forward some fairly strong arguments, but I maintain that my own argument is unanswerable. This is that, by putting the tea in first and stirring as one pours, one can exactly regulate the amount of milk, whereas one is liable to put in too much milk if one does it the other way round."

Reason #8. You added sugar. That's Orwell again, though he admitted to being in a very small minority on this point.

FOOD FOR THOUGHT. Self-described experts also say that tea tastes better when drunk from a cup made of fine bone china.

GIVE THEM A HAND

Human hands are comprised of 27 bones. There are eight in the *carpus* (wrist), five in the main body of the hand, and 14 in the digits (fingers).

WHAT IS THE DEFINITION OF LIFE?

"Living beings are systems that have three simultaneous features: They are self-supported, they reproduce themselves, and they evolve through interaction with the environment."

—**Haboku Nakamura (Biology Institute, Konan University, Kobe, Japan)**

"Life is a chemical system able to replicate itself through autocatalysis and to make mistakes that gradually increase the efficiency of the autocatalysis."

—**André Brack (Centre for Molecular Biophysics of CNRS, France)**

"Living beings are protein-made bodies formed by one or more cells that communicate with the environment through information transfer carried out by electric impulses or chemical substances, and capable of morphological evolution and metabolism, growth and reproduction."

—**Sidney Fox (South Alabama University)**

ERNEST HEMINGWAY'S
4 RULES FOR MANHOOD

"Plant a tree, fight a bull, write a book, have a son."

THE LAST...

...year that Olympic gold medals were made entirely of gold: 1912.

...wild grizzly bear spotting in California took place in 1924. (The animal is still depicted on the state's flag.)

...major studio album released on 8-track: *Fleetwood Mac's Greatest Hits*, released by Warner Bros. in 1988.

...woman to be awarded the "Miss Canada" pageant title was Nicole Dunsdon, in 1991. (Low ratings and shifting attitudes toward women's rights put an end to the contest shortly thereafter.)

...bare-knuckle boxing title match was fought in Mississippi in 1889. It took 75 rounds for John L. Sullivan to knock out Jake Kilrain.

...state to issue driver's licenses without photos: New York (1983).

...witchcraft trial in England took place in 1712—it was determined that Jane Wenham was not a witch.

...*official* words from the Moon were spoken by Apollo 17 astronaut Eugene Cernan on December 14, 1972: "We leave as we came, and God willing, as we shall return, with peace and hope for all mankind." (Last *unofficial* words spoken from the Moon, also by Cernan: "Let's get this mother out of here.")

INDEX

"Information is not knowledge, knowledge is not wisdom, and wisdom is not foresight. Each grows out of the other, and we need them all."

—**Arthur C. Clarke**